D1216823

WELSH CASTLES

A Guide by Counties

WELSH CASTLES

A Guide by Counties

Adrian Pettifer

THE BOYDELL PRESS

© Adrian Pettifer 2000

All Rights Reserved. Except as permitted under current legislation
no part of this work may be photocopied, stored in a retrieval system,
published, performed in public, adapted, broadcast,
transmitted, recorded, or reproduced in any form or by any means,
without the prior permission of the copyright owner

First published 2000
The Boydell Press, Woodbridge

ISBN 0 85115 778 5

The Boydell Press is an imprint of Boydell & Brewer Ltd
PO Box 9, Woodbridge, Suffolk IP12 3DF, UK
and of Boydell & Brewer Inc.
PO Box 41026, Rochester, NY 14604–4126, USA
website: http://www.boydell.co.uk

A catalogue record for this book is available
from the British Library

Library of Congress Cataloging-in-Publication Data
Pettifer, Adrian, 1959–
    Welsh castles : a guide by counties / Adrian Pettifer.
    p. cm.
    Includes bibliographical references and index.
    ISBN 0–85115–778–5 (hbk. : alk. paper)
    1. Castles – Wales – Guidebooks.   2. Wales – Guidebooks.
I. Title.
DA737.P48 2000
914.2904'86 – dc21   00–026130

This publication is printed on acid-free paper

Printed in Great Britain by
St Edmundsbury Press Ltd, Bury St Edmunds, Suffolk

CONTENTS

ILLUSTRATIONS

Copyright material is reproduced by permission, as listed under Acknowledgements.

ACKNOWLEDGEMENTS

The castle plans are closely based on copyright material which has only been modified as much as has seemed necessary for relatively small-scale reproduction in this volume. Permission to reproduce the plans is gratefully acknowledged, as follows:

Beaumaris, Caernarfon, Caerphilly, Carreg Cennen, Castell-y-Bere, Chepstow, Cilgerran, Conwy Castle and Town Wall, Criccieth, Denbigh, Dinefwr, Flint, Harlech, Kidwelly, Llansteffan, Raglan, Rhuddlan, Skenfrith, Tretower, White Castle: by kind permission of Cadw: Welsh Historic Monuments. Crown Copyright.

Cardiff: by kind permission of Cardiff County Council.

Carew: plan by R. F. Walker from *Archaeologia Cambrensis* 105. By kind permission of the editor.

Manorbier: plan by D. J. Cathcart King from *Archaeologia Cambrensis* 119. By kind permission of the editor.

Pembroke: reproduced by kind permission of the Pembroke Castle Trust.

Tenby: plan of Tenby Town Wall by R. F. Walker from *Archaeologia Cambrensis* 142. By kind permission of the editor.

Permission to reproduce the plates is gratefully acknowledged, as follows:

Beaumaris, Caernarfon, Caerphilly, Carreg Cennen, Chepstow, Conwy, Criccieth, Harlech, Kidwelly, Raglan, Rhuddlan: by kind permission of Cadw: Welsh Historic Monuments. Crown Copyright.

Cardiff: by kind permission of Cardiff County Council.

Carew: copyright Pembrokeshire Coast National Park Authority.

Chirk: copyright National Trust Photographic Library/Matthew Antrobus.

Pembroke: copyright Pembroke Castle Trust.

Powis: copyright National Trust Photographic Library/Michael Allwood-Coppin.

FOREWORD

This book is intended as a companion to my *English Castles* (Boydell, 1995). It serves the same purpose: to provide a brief account of every Welsh castle worth visiting. Although most Welsh castles were built by Anglo-Norman invaders, there are some striking contrasts with England. In a country with relatively few great churches and abbeys, and even fewer unfortified manor houses, the castles of Wales form the most imposing group of monuments left from the Middle Ages. In terms of grandeur they are second only to the dramatic landscape.

English masonry castles cover every period from Norman to Tudor times. However, Wales has only Chepstow to compare with the great Norman keeps of England, while Raglan is the sole Welsh example of the castle-palaces of the late Middle Ages. The vast majority of Welsh stone castles were built in the thirteenth century, a dramatic period when Wales was nearly united under native rule but then succumbed to Edward I's conquest. This struggle coincided with the zenith of the European castle. It was the age of the round flanking tower, the twin-towered gatehouse and the concentric outer wall.

Because of this, Wales has one of the most formidable groups of castles in Europe. Or rather two groups, because the great castles are mainly located on the coastal plains and river valleys of the north and south. The Edwardian strongholds of North Wales – Caernarfon, Conwy, Harlech and Beaumaris – are justly famous and are now designated as World Heritage sites. However, they are matched in South Wales by the great baronial castles of Pembroke, Kidwelly, Caerphilly and Chepstow. In both north and south some fascinating castles of the native princes should not be overlooked, such as Criccieth, Powis and Dinefwr. Most of the castles of mid-Wales are quite fragmentary. This is a consequence of the poor local mortar, but their panoramic locations (as at Cefnllys, Castell Dinas and Castell Dinas Bran) amply compensate for the meagre remains.

The visitor will find that the vast majority of Welsh castles are ruined, or at least empty shells. Many became redundant once the English conquest of Wales was complete, and Civil War slightings increased the desolation. Inhabited castles are rare in comparison with England. Chirk and Powis are stately home castles of the north, while Cardiff, St Donat's and Picton are exceptions in the south.

Thankfully the vast majority of Welsh masonry castles can be visited. Many of the greats are maintained by Cadw ('Guardian'), the Welsh historic monuments organisation. Cadw continues to uncover and consolidate some of Wales' more ruinous castles, particularly in recent decades those of the native princes. Hence a number of erstwhile fragmentary and overgrown sites have become interesting again. Many Cadw castles – even some major ones – are now freely accessible at any time. Most of their staffed monuments are open daily, though some now close during the winter months. English Heritage and Historic Scotland members can use their passes to obtain admission. The National Trust (NT in the text) owns a few of the habitable castles, while some others are in the care of local authorities (LA). A number of privately-owned castles can also be visited, at least at certain times. Access details are given at the end of each entry, but specific opening times have been avoided because they are apt to change. Several annual publications provide up-to-date details, and tourist information offices can be consulted. It is advisable to confirm opening times in advance if you are travelling any distance.

Many earthworks and some of the lesser ruins lie on private land, which may or may not tolerate visitors. These sites have not usually been cleared and consolidated, so you should proceed with caution. If there is no obvious right of entry, permission to visit should be sought at the nearest house. I have indicated where such castles appear to be accessible, but this may depend on the whims of changing owners, so my advice in the text should not be taken to override conditions on the day. Some of the hilltop castles involve a stiff ascent which should only be tackled by the moderately fit wearing adequate footwear.

This book contains an entry for each masonry castle except the most fragmentary. It includes the excellent town walls of Wales, which were built in conjunction with the castles, but is more selective with the many Norman earthworks. Although motte-and-bailey castles can be fascinating, the majority will only appeal to the specialist. Hence only the more impressive and historically important ones are included as main entries. The remaining earthworks and masonry fragments are covered in an 'other sites' section at the end of each county.

The gazetteer is divided into counties for greater convenience to the traveller. Since 1974 Wales has seen two local government reorganisations, and the current administrative divisions are a confusing jumble. Consequently, as with *English Castles*, I have had little option but to use the traditional counties. They lasted long enough to be regarded as the natural divisions of Wales.

Finding the great castles will not be a problem, but some of the lesser ruins are hidden in the hills and woods. This is even the case with one or two Cadw sites where signposting is inadequate. There is insufficient space for detailed directions, but Ordnance Survey references are given in the index. I have used the place names which are most familiar, whether English or Welsh (common equivalents are shown in the index). Some castles – not necessarily the native ones – have always been known by their Welsh names.

INTRODUCTION

Origins

Wales has historically followed a different course to the more fertile England, even though complete independence from its powerful neighbour has seldom been possible. The mountainous terrain posed difficulties for the Roman legions which had so swiftly overrun lowland Britain. Although it was brought into the empire in a series of campaigns, the Roman occupation was purely a military one, with a network of forts connected by roads to the legionary fortresses at Chester and Caerleon. Unlike their compatriots in lowland Britain, the Britons of the peninsula did not embrace Roman ways. Towns were few, and many of the inhabitants kept to their old hill-forts. For them the Roman evacuation at the beginning of the fifth century cannot have made much difference.

Up to this time the Celts had shared a common kinship throughout Britain. The Germanic and Scottish invasions changed all that. Despite a long struggle forever associated with the mythical Arthur, Celtic Britain was gradually reduced to Wales, Cornwall and Strathclyde. Powerful kingdoms were emerging among the Anglo-Saxons, but geography prevented the Welsh from being swallowed up. King Offa of Mercia (757–796), inspired by Hadrian's Wall, acknowledged the limits of his sovereignty by digging his great dyke along the 167-mile frontier between Prestatyn and Chepstow. Not that the Welsh posed a serious threat, even if they were capable of some devastating raids. Isolated and impoverished, they suffered from political fragmentation. The equal division of property between sons, egalitarian as it seems, was already the cause of innumerable petty feuds. Nevertheless the Welsh retained a sense of nationhood, and in the ninth century Rhodri Mawr demonstrated that they could unite to repel a common enemy – at that time, the Vikings. Waves of unity under strong leaders, followed by strife between successors, would form the basic pattern of native Welsh history.

Given Welsh geography it is not surprising that a unified Wales would be difficult to maintain. In the Dark Ages four main kingdoms emerged: Gwynedd in the north-west, Deheubarth in the south-west, Morgannwg in the south-east, and Powys in the borders. They fought each other incessantly, sometimes in alliance with the English. Their rulers acknowledged the nominal overlordship of the English kings, but English invasions of Wales achieved little.

It should be emphasised that no castles existed in Dark Age Wales, even if Welsh kings held court in strong sites such as Deganwy and Dinefwr, which would later become castles. The private fortress known as the castle emerged in northern Europe out of the break-up of the Carolingian empire, when royal authority collapsed and feudal lords had to defend their territory. This trend had yet to cross the English Channel. In England the strong rule of the House of Wessex postponed the development of feudalism and the appearance of the castle. Wales, though suffering from divisions akin to those in Europe, was largely cut off by England. Furthermore, European castles were a feature of settled communities, amassing wealth through agriculture and trade. Wales was a pastoral land with no towns and few villages.

In the mid-eleventh century Wales enjoyed one of its brief periods of unity under Gruffudd ap Llywelyn. He raided the English borders with impunity, even sacking Hereford, until he was killed in battle by Harold Godwinson in 1063. Not for the last time, a great Welsh leader would be thwarted by an equally competent Englishman who could command greater resources. Harold, of course, went on to become king of England before being struck down by the Normans at Hastings in 1066.

The Norman Invasion

Like the Roman invasion before it, the Norman conquest of England was swift. William the Conqueror did not lead his followers into Wales, but after the recent threat from Gruffudd ap Llywelyn he regarded Wales as a potential danger. For this reason the Welsh borderlands became a buffer zone awarded to three semi-independent, 'palatine' earls: William Fitz Osbern of Hereford, Roger de Montgomery of Shrewsbury, and Hugh d'Avranches of Chester. All three were charged with the defence of the realm. They regarded this as an opportunity to colonise, but they had much more limited resources at their disposal. Thus the Norman invasion of Wales began and continued as a piecemeal operation. The most immediate gains were made by William Fitz Osbern. He crossed the River Wye and overran much of Gwent (now Monmouthshire) before his death in 1071. In the 1070s Hugh d'Avranches extended Norman control along the north coast as far as the Conwy estuary, while Roger de Montgomery pushed more slowly up the Severn valley. Except for Chester the palatine earldoms did not last long, but they set the precedent that Wales would be a zone of private conquest for Norman adventurers.

Under William II the conquest of Wales gained new impetus, though the first initiative proved to be short-lived. Around 1088 Hugh d'Avranches overran Gwynedd, but he was soon driven back to the Conwy by Gruffudd ap Cynan. Even royal intervention did not reverse the situation. Gruffudd founded a dynasty of princes who would keep this corner of Wales under native rule for the next two centuries. However, in the south the Normans made spectacular gains. From 1091 Robert Fitz Hamon seized the coastal strip of Morgannwg, founding the lordship of Glamorgan. Then, in 1093, the Normans defeated and killed Rhys ap Tewdwr, the king of Deheubarth. In the wake of the Welsh collapse Bernard de Newmarch overran Brycheiniog and became lord of Brecon, while Roger de Montgomery's son Arnulf swept across central Wales to establish the lordship of Pembroke.

The arrival of the Normans led to the belated introduction of castles in both England and Wales. In England, William the Conqueror's firm rule ensured that all the castles raised to subdue the defeated populace were either in his own hands or held by trusted deputies. Although there would be subsequent spells of civil strife, when baronial castle building got out of hand, England usually remained in the grip of a strong monarchy which imposed tight controls. The whole land was administered from a network of royal castles. Barons had to obtain permission to build castles of their own, and unlicensed castles were destroyed. Not so in the Welsh Marches, as the conquered lands became known. The 'Marcher' barons and their sub-tenants erected castles to control their conquests as they saw fit, with little royal interference.

Norman castle-building in Wales begins promisingly with William Fitz Osbern's hall-keep on the cliff at Chepstow – the first stone castle in Britain. Apart from this splendid exception, the Welsh castles of the Norman invaders were all of earth and timber. The standard type was a mound of earth called a motte, with a wooden tower on top. There would usually be one or more enclosures (baileys) beyond, surrounded by a stockaded rampart and a ditch. Some fine examples survive from the first wave of Norman conquest, such as Tomen-y-Mur, Hen Domen, Builth and Cardiff. Sometimes, especially in Glamorgan, there was just an embanked enclosure (called a ringwork) with no accompanying motte. Earthwork castles are common in Wales, reflecting the parcelling out of land to feudal sub-tenants and the shifting frontier with the Welsh.

Welsh Resistance

With Henry I encouraging Norman and Flemish colonisation in the south-west, and Roger de Clare invading Ceredigion from 1110, the Normans appeared to be the masters of all but Gwynedd. However, their settlements in South Wales were largely confined to the coastal strip, where they could be provisioned by sea. In central Wales the Norman penetration was only valley-deep. The uncultivated uplands held little attraction for colonists, and here native life continued. Nevertheless the Welsh princes were not content to be pushed into the hills, and here the heavy Norman cavalry lost its superiority. As the Welsh became more familiar with their adversary, they were able to resist more effectively.

Their opportunity came during the Anarchy, when the Norman barons were preoccupied with the inconclusive struggle between Stephen and Matilda. The Welsh of Gwynedd were quick to take advantage. In 1136 Owain Gwynedd advanced south into Ceredigion, defeating the Normans at Crug Mawr. He later recovered the disputed territory of the Four Cantrefs (north-east Wales) from the earl of Chester. Next Rhys ap Gruffudd – the Lord Rhys – turned Deheubarth into a force to be reckoned with, raiding the Norman settlements of the south-west. Henry II reasserted his overlordship, but his invasion of 1165 temporarily united the Welsh princes. It should be admitted that his army was defeated as much by the torrential rain as by the harrying Welsh, but this disaster persuaded Henry to turn his attention to other parts of his vast Angevin empire.

Wales was saved, but the Welsh princes quickly resumed their internal struggles for dominance. Owain Gwynedd's advances had brought him into conflict with Powys and Deheubarth, the Lord Rhys regaining Ceredigion from the northerners. Owain and Rhys then united against their weaker neighbour, the prince of Powys, who was only able to survive with English support. After Owain's death in 1170, Gwynedd was torn by feuds between his sons. The Lord Rhys thus became the leading Welsh prince, enjoying two decades of peaceful co-existence with the

Normans. Only during Richard I's absence on crusade did he take the opportunity to threaten the Marcher lordships again. However, Rhys also bequeathed a divided principality on his death in 1197. Deheubarth was permanently crippled, but Gwynedd was about to enjoy a renaissance under Llywelyn the Great.

By this time the Welsh were no longer an alien and backward culture. There was much intermarriage with the Normans, and the native princes benefited from direct contact with European developments after centuries of isolation. As a result of the Norman invasions, the Welsh began building earthwork castles of their own. The native mottes of Tomen-y-Rhodwydd and Tomen-y-Faerdre, and the ringwork of Caer Penrhos, are as good as their Norman counterparts. In disputed areas it is often impossible to tell whether an earthwork was raised by the Normans or the Welsh.

Stone castles became common in twelfth-century England, but this was not the case in Wales. Here most castles continued to be motte-and-bailey earthworks. This was a consequence of the Marcher barons' insecurity. Settled conditions were needed to invest in the expensive and time-consuming business of building castles in stone. Hence Norman masonry castles are confined to the south. Here lay the de Clare lordships of Pembroke and Chepstow, the earl of Gloucester's lordship of Glamorgan, and the de Braose lordship of Brecon. Even in these comparatively secure Marcher territories, only the keeps at Ogmore and Penllyn date from the early twelfth century. They are followed (perhaps a generation later) by Monmouth's hall-keep and the shell keep on the motte at Cardiff.

Masonry castles do not begin to appear more frequently until the last quarter of the century. Typically they consisted of a walled courtyard, with a single square tower commanding the entrance. Although towers such as Coity, Hay and Usk may be described as keeps, they are dwarfed by the great tower keeps of England. A few shell keeps (notably Tretower) and another hall-keep at Manorbier complete the picture. Architecturally these castles are quite perfunctory, with the exception of the earl of Gloucester's elaborate gateway at Newcastle (Glamorgan). Owain Gwynedd's sons responded with some rude drystone efforts of their own. Before the year 1200, despite the exaggerated praise of the travelling scholar Giraldus Cambrensis, stone castles in Wales were quite modest by the standards of the time.

Gwynedd Triumphant

All this was to change in the thirteenth century, as the princes of Gwynedd extended their sway over much of Wales. From 1194 Owain Gwynedd's grandson Llywelyn ab Iorwerth united Gwynedd once again. He is remembered as Llywelyn Fawr – Llywelyn the Great. Llywelyn had been brought up in England as a ward of the king. He even married King John's daughter, but John became suspicious of his son-in-law's ambitions. In 1212 he launched an invasion which might have subdued Gwynedd half-a-century earlier had it been pushed to its conclusion. However, John's mounting troubles compelled him to return to England. Llywelyn joined the English barons who forced John to sign the Magna Carta (1215). In the civil war which followed, Llywelyn overran feud-ridden Deheubarth. With the formidable William

Marshal defending England against a French invasion, Llywelyn even chipped away at his earldom of Pembroke.

Although William Marshal the Younger reconquered the Marcher lordships of the south-west in 1223, Llywelyn was soon expanding his dominions once again. In 1232 the king's justiciar, Hubert de Burgh, was stripped of his offices for failing to bring Llywelyn to heel. Despite his growing power Llywelyn remained on good terms with some of the Marcher barons. He even enjoyed the military assistance of the rebellious earl of Pembroke, Richard Marshal. Furthermore, Llywelyn still acknowledged Henry III as his overlord. He made no claim to rule all Wales, and was content to be addressed as 'prince of Aberffraw and lord of Snowdon'. Remarkably for a medieval ruler, Llywelyn retired to become a monk in the abbey of Aberconwy (1240).

Llywelyn bequeathed Gwynedd to his son Dafydd, overriding the claim of his illegitimate son, Gruffudd. In 1241 Henry III took advantage of the resulting turmoil to invade, driving the Welsh back to the River Conwy. Gruffudd later fell to his death while attempting to escape from the Tower of London. His sons, Owain and Llywelyn, jointly succeeded Dafydd but were forced to acknowledge Gwynedd's weakened position at the Treaty of Woodstock (1247).

Gwynedd's paralysis came to an end in 1255 when Llywelyn ap Gruffudd overthrew his brother and became sole ruler. He reoccupied the Four Cantrefs. Like his grandfather before him, Llywelyn 'the Last' was assisted by unrest in England. He forged an alliance with Simon de Montfort, the leader of the baronial opposition. During the civil wars of the 1260s Llywelyn took the opportunity to occupy all of central Wales, destroying Builth Castle and even overrunning the solidly English lordship of Brecon. Despite Simon de Montfort's defeat and death, the ageing Henry III was forced to come to terms. In 1267 the Treaty of Montgomery ratified Llywelyn's conquests and recognised him as the first prince of Wales. With all but the Marcher lordships of the south coast under his control, Llywelyn appeared to be achieving the impossible dream of a Wales united under native rule.

Despite the growing power of Gwynedd, the Marcher lordships of the south actually expanded somewhat at the expense of weakened Deheubarth and Morgannwg. It was in these territories that the first ambitious Welsh castles appeared – castles at the forefront of the military innovations which characterised the period. Much of the inspiration came from the fortifications of the Holy Land, many knights of the Welsh Marches having been on the Third Crusade. Instead of the static oblong keeps and simple 'curtain' walls typical of Norman England, a more formidable system of defence was emerging. Stronger curtains were flanked by mural towers designed to rake the adjacent sections of wall with arrow fire. These towers were circular, or at least rounded towards the outside world, so that there were no corners to undermine. The vulnerable entrance – previously just a gateway through the curtain or a modest tower – evolved into a long gate passage defended by several obstacles, its outer facade flanked by a pair of round-fronted towers.

William Marshal, earl of Pembroke and the most capable of the Marcher barons, was the first to build castles in the new idiom. His impressive circular keep at Pembroke and his towered cross-wall at Chepstow were erected in the early years of the thirteenth century. Both castles were expanded by William Marshal's five sons (1219–45) into extensive, multi-towered complexes. The Marshals raised other towered curtains at Cilgerran and Usk, while Hubert de Burgh followed their lead at Grosmont and Skenfrith. Caldicot, Manorbier and Laugharne are other examples. Pembroke's circular keep inspired a number of smaller versions, such as Caldicot, Skenfrith, Bronllys and Tretower. The feuding Welsh princes of Deheubarth raised round keeps of their own at Dinefwr and Dryslwyn.

Henry III took over Cardigan and Carmarthen castles to bolster the tottering Marcher lordships of the south-west. His new castle at Montgomery, begun in 1223 to contain the power of Gwynedd, had the first twin-towered gatehouse in Britain. After the invasion of 1241, Henry raised castles at Dyserth and Deganwy to consolidate his occupation of the Four Cantrefs – an area which had previously been quite devoid of stone castles. They foreshadowed the chain of castles which his son would build to overawe Gwynedd, but they were destroyed when Llywelyn the Last recovered this territory in 1263.

Both Llywelyns destroyed English castles rather than attempt to garrison them, but they did build stone castles of their own. If they are not quite as formidable as the best of the English work, they are magnificently situated in the mountainous terrain of North Wales. Llywelyn the Great followed English developments closely. Thus we see an oblong keep at Dolwyddelan, a circular keep at Dolbadarn, a towered curtain at Castell-y-Bere, and a twin-towered gatehouse (inspired by Montgomery) at Criccieth. Llywelyn the Last strengthened some of his grandfather's castles. He also erected the U-shaped keep of Ewloe close to the English border. Meanwhile his ally, the lord of Ial, erected Castell Dinas Bran – the first native stone castle of Powys.

The Edwardian Conquest

As a result of Llywelyn the Last's conquests, even the Marcher lords of the southern coastal plain felt threatened. In 1266 Gilbert de Clare, earl of Gloucester and lord of Glamorgan, took the initiative by invading Senghenydd (as the truncated principality of Morgannwg was called). The powerful Castell Morgraig, which the prince of Senghenydd had been building, was left abandoned. In its place Gilbert began Caerphilly Castle, which so perturbed Llywelyn that he attacked the building site twice. Nevertheless the castle was nearly complete by the time Henry III arranged a truce between Llywelyn and Gilbert in 1271. With its parallel curtains this was the first major concentric castle in Britain, and the gatehouse broke new ground in being large and strong enough to serve as the keep. Caerphilly set a new standard for military architecture, inspiring the castles which Edward I would erect in North Wales. Gilbert went further than anyone in surrounding his castle with an artificial lake, held in place by a massive dam.

Henry III's son, Prince Edward, had suffered much at Llywelyn's hands during the wars of the 1260s. His castle-building career probably began in those years with the strengthening of White Castle. He returned from crusade as Edward I in 1274 to find Llywelyn invading Powys. Gruffudd ap Gwenwynwyn, the prince of Powys, had joined a plot to seize control of Gwynedd, hatched by Llywelyn's own brother Dafydd. Both had fled to England and were launching raids from Shrewsbury. Llywelyn refused to do homage to the new king while the conspirators were enjoying his protection. Edward insisted on homage first, and after rejecting several summonses Llywelyn was declared a rebel. Another source of contention was Dolforwyn Castle, which Llywelyn was building provocatively close to the royal castle of Montgomery.

Emboldened by his earlier successes, Llywelyn hoped that Edward would prove as ineffectual as his father. However, he was in for a rude awakening. After intensive preparations, in 1277 Edward launched a three-pronged invasion which drove Llywelyn back into his Gwynedd heartland. No doubt Llywelyn anticipated this. The Welsh had never been able to stand their ground against the full force of a royal campaign. Llywelyn probably calculated that Edward, like his predecessors in 1212 and 1241, would be forced to withdraw once he had failed to come to grips with the Welsh in the mountains of Snowdonia. However, Edward employed a small fleet provided by the Cinque Ports to blockade the Menai Strait, and invaded Anglesey to deny the Welsh their grain supply. Llywelyn's army melted away, and he was forced to come to terms.

Despite Edward's victory, the Welsh war of 1277 did not result in the English conquest of Wales. Edward was surprisingly lenient in his settlement, the Treaty of Conwy allowing Llywelyn to retain Gwynedd but none of his conquests beyond. The princes of Powys and Deheubarth, who were only too eager to see Gwynedd broken, supported Edward and retained their lands. Llywelyn's brother Dafydd actually received much of the Four Cantrefs as a reward for his support, and built the last of the native Welsh castles at Caergwrle.

The second war was not of Llywelyn's choosing. It is likely that he would have learned from his miscalculation and waited for fresh opportunities to arise. However, the dissatisfied Dafydd precipitated a new conflict by storming Hawarden Castle in 1282. Llywelyn was reluctantly obliged to go to his aid. Attempting to rally his allies in central Wales, Llywelyn was ignominiously cut down in a skirmish with some English soldiers near Builth. Dafydd then assumed command of Gwynedd, but Edward's invasion of 1283 was a repeat of his successful strategy six years before. Again the Menai Strait was blockaded, and the Welsh castles surrendered one by one. Dafydd himself was captured and taken to Shrewsbury, where he was hanged, drawn and quartered as a traitor.

This time Edward had resolved to annex Gwynedd, and a formidable group of new castles rose with astonishing speed. A decade of English rule, with its alien system of justice, sparked a rebellion under Madoc ap Llywelyn. Edward was forced to invade Gwynedd for the third time in 1295. Although he was cut off from his army and besieged at Conwy for a while, Madog's forces were routed at the battle of Maes Moydog. Meanwhile, the English conquest had been extended to Deheubarth. In 1287 Rhys ap Maredudd, alarmed because his castles were still in royal custody, rebelled and was swiftly crushed. The campaign involved a prolonged siege of Dryslwyn Castle. Of the Welsh principalities only a truncated Powys remained, but its Anglicised princes soon became indistinguishable from their Marcher baron neighbours. By 1296 the Edwardian conquest was complete, and Edward was able to turn his armies northwards to invade Scotland.

The castles which Edward built to consolidate his conquest of Gwynedd are justly celebrated. They were an integral part of his strategy, hence the army of ditchers and quarriers which accompanied the invasion force. Builth, the first of the group, was rebuilt on the older motte-and-bailey earthworks. It was Edward's only inland castle, and is the only one to have disappeared. All the others were situated on or near the coast of North Wales, to facilitate supply by sea like the Norman castles of the south. During the campaign of 1277 Edward commenced castles at Flint, Rhuddlan and Aberystwyth. They were positioned to contain Gwynedd and form a barrier against any renewed expansion. Flint is curious for its massive round keep, while Rhuddlan and Aberystwyth adopted the concentric layout so magnificently introduced at Caerphilly. These castles were largely complete in time to resist Dafydd ap Gruffudd.

They are eclipsed by the second group of castles built in Gwynedd itself after Dafydd's fall. Of the three begun in 1283, Caernarfon stands out by reason of its sheer bulk and its polygonal towers. Conwy presents a noble array of towers on its narrow rock, while Harlech is a classic concentric castle with a keep-gatehouse of the Caerphilly type. These castles proved their strength during Madog ap Llywelyn's revolt, only unfinished Caernarfon succumbing to the rebels. The rebellion prompted Edward to add another castle to the chain. Both concentric planning and the keep-gatehouse theme were perfected at Beaumaris on Anglesey. James of St George, Master of the King's Works in Wales, designed the 'big four' of Gwynedd. Edward also repaired and garrisoned the native castles of Gwynedd, but only coastal Criccieth proved to be tenable during Madog's revolt. The royal accounts known as the Pipe Rolls show that Edward spent over £81,000 on his Welsh building programme – an enormous sum for the time. His treasury was too exhausted for anything similar to be attempted during his invasion of Scotland.

Edward created a royal principality out of conquered Gwynedd and Deheubarth, divided into English-style counties. However, Dafydd's lands in north-eastern Wales were shared between some of Edward's military commanders, so Marcher territory also increased as a result of the conquest. The new lords built castles to emulate their king's, and James of St George may have designed them. Hence the polygonal towers of Caernarfon are reflected in Henry de Lacy's castle at Denbigh. Unfinished Chirk was modelled on Beaumaris, while Hawarden has a circular keep inspired by Flint. Powis Castle, built by the prince of Powys, is dominated by an Edwardian gatehouse.

The old Marcher baronies of the south remained outside Edward's conquests. William de Valence of Pembroke, Gilbert de Clare of Glamorgan, Roger Bigod of Chepstow and Humphrey de Bohun of Brecon all proudly maintained their independence. Edward attempted to control them, intervening in the baronial feud which erupted when Gilbert de Clare built Morlais Castle on territory claimed by Humphrey de Bohun. Gilbert's earlier castle at Caerphilly inspired the Marcher barons to build some powerful new castles of their own, although their work is poorly documented in comparison with the royal castles. The earl of Lancaster transformed Kidwelly into a concentric fortress, and the Stradlings did likewise at St

Donat's. Keep-gatehouses dominate Kidwelly and Llansteffan. Many Edwardian towers in South Wales rise from square bases, which sink back into the body of the tower as pyramid spurs. They were designed to be proof against undermining. Picton is a unique fortified hall-house with projecting towers. One royal effort in South Wales was Queen Eleanor's castle of Haverfordwest.

Although the castles of Edwardian Wales were strong fortresses, they were also lordly residences, and the accommodation within them was becoming more luxurious. Hence fine halls and other apartments can be found within the stout walls of Conwy, Chepstow, Oystermouth and Carew. This was also the age of town walls. Towns – an alien phenomenon to the native Welsh – had been founded in conjunction with castles from Norman times. The Edwardian castles of North Wales all had boroughs of English settlers attached to them. Edward provided Conwy and Caernarfon with stone walls regularly flanked by semi-circular bastions. Other town walls were built under baronial patronage at Denbigh, Chepstow and Tenby, while Monmouth preserves its fortified bridge. In the Edwardian age even the monks of Ewenny Priory built themselves a fortified precinct wall.

A Conquered Land

As well as being instruments of conquest, Edward I's castles were designed as royal palaces capable of housing a large retinue. According to tradition, in 1284 Edward presented his baby son to the Welsh as their new prince – one born in Wales who could speak no English! If there is any truth in this story, then Edward had already decided to perpetuate the title by keeping it in the family. Prince Edward, born in Caernarfon, was formally invested in 1301. However, with Wales already becoming a forgotten province by that time, the ideal of a resident prince was never realised. Even when there was an adult heir bearing the title, he seldom visited Wales. Under Edward II building continued at Caernarfon and Beaumaris, but ground to a halt – with the castles still unfinished – on his deposition in 1327. The royal castles of the principality became little more than garrison outposts, their lead and timber parts slowly rotting in the notoriously wet weather. A survey commissioned for the Black Prince in 1343 describes the decay, but little was done except for some new roofs at Conwy.

Although the Scots regained their independence on the battlefield at Bannockburn, the conquered Welsh were unable to take advantage. The last native revolt of the Edwardian period took place in Glamorgan. Having suffered as the result of a paranoid English initiative to dismiss Welsh officials, Llywelyn Bren sacked several castles in 1316. He even had the temerity to attack Caerphilly before his capture and execution. Five years later the castles of Glamorgan were burning again, but this time it was due to baronial unrest. The Marcher lords rebelled against the growing power of Edward II's favourite, Hugh le Despenser the Younger, who had been made lord of Glamorgan. Edward intervened to reinstate his friend, but Glamorgan was the scene of their downfall and capture in 1326. This was an ironic fate for the first English prince of Wales. Effective power temporarily passed to his queen's lover, the Marcher baron Roger Mortimer.

Edward II's reign saw the tail-end of the Edwardian castle-building boom. Construction of some of the baronial castles, such as Denbigh and Kidwelly, continued well into the fourteenth century. Others, like Chirk, were left incomplete as conditions became more secure. The last of the de Clares built castles with Edwardian keep-gatehouses at Llangybi and St Quintin's, before his death at Bannockburn. Hugh le Despenser contributed another gatehouse at Neath, but most of his additions were of a domestic nature, as at Caerphilly and Dinefwr. Newport (Monmouthshire) was the last new castle to be built in the Edwardian tradition.

Afterwards castle building declines to a trickle, with nothing whatsoever in the north. Some of the existing castles were already surplus to requirements. Furthermore the Marcher barons, like the prince, were becoming absentees. The Welsh lordships were concentrating in the hands of great magnates like the dukes of Lancaster, who held large estates elsewhere. Occupied in the wars with France and Scotland, they regarded their Welsh estates as little more than a source of income. With the Welsh apparently subdued and their English lords seldom in residence, many castles continued to function merely as administrative centres and prisons.

By contrast, England witnessed a revival of castle building in the fourteenth century, financed to a large extent by booty from the Hundred Years War. Though inspired by the Edwardian castles of Wales, these new castles were rarely as formidable, with considerable concessions made to domestic comfort. Weobley is the only Welsh example of such fortified manor houses. The bishops of St David's were confident enough to erect undefended palaces at Lamphey and St David's, though they did build a semi-fortified close wall around their cathedral.

A revival in the south-west was due to the reversal of fortune in the Hundred Years War. In the 1370s there was a possibility that the victorious French would launch a counter-invasion. Owain Lawgoch, the Welsh rebel leader in exile, exhorted them to land in Wales until he was assassinated by an English agent. Hence castles which had been built near the coast for supply by sea became involved in coastal defence. Edward III ordered the repair of a number of castles, adding a tower at Cilgerran. Coity was rebuilt, while the bishop of St David's fortified his palace at Llawhaden. The planned invasion did not take place, and the only significant work elsewhere in the late fourteenth century is the earl of Gloucester's new gatehouse at Caldicot. Unrest in South Wales may be reflected in a handful of tower houses – miniature keeps which formed the defensive homes of local gentry. Scethrog, Candleston and the prior's tower at Caldy are examples, though the numbers are small compared with the pele towers of the Scottish border. At the end of the fourteenth century most Welsh castles were unprepared for the storm which lay ahead.

The Last Revolt

In 1399 Wales was the scene of the downfall of another English king – Richard II. Having seized the throne, Henry IV was vulnerable to similar attempts by others, and the sudden destabilisation of the English monarchy forms the background behind the last Welsh bid for freedom. It began as a private feud between the lord of Ruthin and his Welsh neighbour, Owain ap Gruffudd. Better known as Owain

Glyndwr, he was a descendant of the princes of Powys and Deheubarth. Owain's attack on Ruthin in 1400 sparked uprisings throughout Wales. Although they were initially suppressed, Owain organised a mounting resistance aimed at achieving an independent Wales with him as prince. Once again, a Welsh leader was able to exploit discord in England. Henry IV was preoccupied with the earl of Northumberland's revolt, although the younger Henry Percy's attempt to link up with Glyndwr met with disaster at the battle of Shrewsbury. From 1403 Owain was master of North and Central Wales, and no corner remained untouched by his raids. The French landed an expedition force to assist him in 1405. It ravaged much of South Wales and, according to tradition, was only turned back near Worcester.

However, by 1407 the revolt was on the wane. Henry IV, having overcome his enemies and arranged a truce with France, was able to force Owain onto the defensive. Owain had relied upon surprise attacks, his guerilla forces being ill-equipped to meet the English in the open field. Prince Henry assumed command of the reconquest and energetically set about reclaiming his principality. The future victor of Agincourt won his spurs in Wales, and by 1409 English rule had been restored. Owain vanished, shunning the magnanimous offer of a pardon.

Although Owain Glyndwr controlled the uplands and sacked a number of towns, most of the Welsh castles proved to be beyond his reach. Garrisons of archers deterred attacks on some strategically important castles, while Owain's raids into South Wales were seldom equipped for siege warfare. Here, only Carmarthen Castle was held for any length of time, and sustained attempts to capture Cardiff and Coity met with stern resistance. Those castles which did fall, such as Carreg Cennen, were dismantled as part of a scorched earth policy. Owain enjoyed some successes in Gwynedd, which became his main power base. Conwy was temporarily captured by a ruse. Harlech and Aberystwyth fell after long sieges in 1404, when a French fleet prevented supplies reaching them by sea. They became Owain's chief strongholds until succumbing to Prince Henry, who brought with him a new element in warfare – cannon. In Gwynedd, Caernarfon alone managed to hold out for the duration of the rebellion.

After the revolt the royal castles of Wales were kept in a better state of repair for a while. They had become more numerous owing to the amalgamation of the duchy of Lancaster with the Crown on Henry IV's usurpation. In the south-west, Carmarthen's gatehouse was rebuilt, Kidwelly was completed after a century of neglect and Carreg Cennen was restored from ruin. These works were prompted by fears of another French landing after Henry V spectacularly renewed the Hundred Years War. However, the Marcher barons contributed little under the Lancastrian kings. Newport (Monmouthshire) was remodelled, while Coity and Powis castles received new gate towers. Even new domestic buildings are rare, though the earl of Warwick added a new hall at Cardiff. Already at Tretower the older castle had been abandoned for a new manor house with only token defences.

The showy castles raised in England by a new generation of war lords are absent in Wales with one magnificent exception. Raglan Castle, with its moated, hexagonal keep and its machicolated towers, is the noblest example of late castellated architecture in Britain. Although castles of the fifteenth century were no longer designed to be impregnable instruments of warfare, Raglan was strong by the standards of its day. Except for a tower on Tenby's town wall, it is the only Welsh fortification to show any provision for the primitive firearms of the period.

Raglan is largely the work of William Herbert, who rose to prominence in the Wars of the Roses. No new Glyndwr rose to exploit this latest round of English dynastic strife. On the whole the Welsh showed a surprising loyalty to the dethroned Henry VI. A few castles stubbornly resisted the Yorkist usurper, Edward IV. Carreg Cennen was again slighted, while Harlech endured another long siege in 1468. The conflict ended with a note of optimism in Wales. In 1485 Henry Tudor landed in Milford Haven. Reinforced by Welsh volunteers, he marched on to defeat Richard III at Bosworth. A Welsh lord had become king of England.

Decay and Destruction

Despite the new Tudor dynasty, the Welsh had to wait until 1536 before long-overdue reforms came. The Act of Union abolished the prerogatives of the Marcher lords, their territories being divided into counties like those of the royal principality. It was a formal annexation, but it did remove the apartheid laws which had reduced the Welsh to the status of second-class citizens in their own land. There was comparative order and prosperity, so Wales did not become like Scotland or Ireland, where innumerable tower houses attest the general anarchy of those times.

As in England, additions to existing castles in the Tudor period are purely domestic in character. Henry VII's supporter Sir Rhys ap Thomas improved the accommodation at several of his castles in south-west Wales, and a new mansion was built within the walls of St Donat's. In Elizabethan times Sir John Perrot erected grand new wings at Carew and Laugharne, while the Herberts modernised Raglan and Powis castles. These additions are in harmony with the existing buildings, but the castle as a fortification was a thing of the past. Far more numerous were those castles which had been abandoned for up-to-date mansions, often in England. The antiquary John Leland, who visited Wales in the 1530s, found many castles already in ruins.

There was to be a dramatic postscript in the Civil War. Lacking the Puritan movement which drove the great rebellion in England, the Welsh gentry largely supported Charles I when war broke out in 1642. Consequently the Civil War in Wales is largely the story of its slow conquest by the forces of parliament. A number of Welsh castles were dragged into the conflict as ready-made strongpoints. They had been built in a pre-artillery age and were not designed to withstand bombardment by cannon, but this limitation was equalised by the inadequate artillery of many Roundhead besiegers. Only the curtains of Pembroke and Chepstow were massively thickened to resist the new weapon, and that was done by Roundhead garrisons.

South Wales was gradually conquered in 1644–45. Here Major-General Laugharne captured a number of castles, though Raglan – which the marquis of Worcester re-inforced with artillery-proof earthworks – held out until the war ended in the summer of 1646. Most of the Edwardian castles in the north also remained in Royalist hands until the final months. Some of them put up a long resistance to the parliamentary commander, Major-General Mytton. Harlech, espousing a lost cause to the bitter end as usual, held out into the following year. As in England, there followed a policy of dismantling or 'slighting' potentially danger-ous strongholds. Fortunately the great castles of Gwynedd escaped significant damage, but Pembroke and Caerphilly did not.

Wales saw more fighting in the Royalist uprising of 1648. General Laugharne went over to the Royalist camp after becoming disillusioned with the new order, but he was routed at the battle of St Fagan's. This time it was the turn of Pembroke and Tenby to be pounded with Roundhead cannon, directed by Oliver Cromwell himself. Chirk Castle suffered the last siege of the Civil Wars in 1659, after its owner (another disillusioned Roundhead) prematurely declared for Charles II.

Recent Times

By no means all of the ruined castles of Wales can be blamed on the Civil War. Abandoned castles and redundant town walls provided a convenient source of build-ing stone. Fortunately, diligent ownership and local pride prevented random destruction in many places. The Civil War did take its toll of those castles which had remained inhabited. As a result, very few Welsh castles continued as stately homes. In the borders, Chirk and Powis are exceptions. They display the many alterations wrought by changing taste over the centuries, while retaining their Edwardian pro-files. In the south, Fonmon and Picton have been Georgianised.

Ruins were deliberately retained as eye-catchers in the landscaped parks of the eighteenth century, as at Dinefwr and Hawarden. Towards 1800 painters such as Turner found many subjects among the ruins of Wales, and these became familiar to a growing number of visitors who came in search of the picturesque. The Gothic revival of the early nineteenth century produced some new mansions in a castellated style, financed by the profits of the rapidly expanding coal and slate industries. Bryn Bras, Gwrych and Cyfartha are good examples, though the most extravagant of the group is the magnificent neo-Norman castle of Penrhyn. In Victorian times, the marquess of Bute commissioned William Burges to Gothicise the state apartments of Cardiff Castle. They also rebuilt Castell Coch (Glamorgan) as the Victorian ideal of a medieval castle.

St Donat's was the last inhabited castle to undergo sweeping alterations. In the 1920s the American press baron, William Randolph Hearst, aggrandised it with plunder taken from other old buildings. Meanwhile, major restorations were being undertaken at Caerphilly and Pembroke to undo the devastation of the Civil War. Since then the principle of careful conservation has taken root. Excavations have exposed a number of castles which had virtually disappeared beneath an accumula-tion of rubble, and Cadw is continuing this work.

THE COUNTIES OF WALES

The Gazetteer

Anglesey

Anglesey (Mon in Welsh) formed part of the ancient principality of Gwynedd. The motte of Castell Aberlleiniog probably dates from a brief Norman occupation under the earl of Chester around 1088. That episode apart, the island remained securely Welsh until the Edwardian conquest. Perhaps that is why it has no native castles – not even at Aberffraw, the traditional 'capital' of the princes. This is all the more surprising considering that the fertile plains of the island – such a contrast to Snowdonia – formed the granary of Gwynedd. Edward I's fleet, controlling the Menai Strait, effectively starved out the mainland Welsh during his invasions. The castle which Edward built at Beaumaris after the Welsh uprising of 1294 compensates for the dearth elsewhere. It is a formidable stronghold and the finest example in Britain of concentric fortification.

BEAUMARIS CASTLE is one of the four great Edwardian castles of Gwynedd. Owing to its low-lying site close to the Menai Strait – the name means 'Beautiful Marsh' – the castle does not dominate as much as its sisters. It would have done so had it ever been completed but this, the last of Edward I's castles, was left unfinished and rather lower than intended. It thus has a squat profile, accentuated by the square layout and the double line of walls. This latter feature is the castle's greatest claim to fame, because Beaumaris is the perfect concentric castle of the Middle Ages.

It is possible that Edward intended a castle here, complementing Caernarfon on the mainland, after his conquest of Gwynedd in 1283. However, the building of Caernarfon, Conwy and Harlech drained the exchequer, and the apparent pacification of Wales then made the enterprise seem unnecessary. The revolt of Madog ap Llywelyn in 1294 made Edward despatch his veteran castle builder James of St George to the site. As Master of the King's Works in Wales, James had designed the earlier Edwardian castles of Gwynedd. Work began in April 1295 and progressed at a prodigious rate. According to the royal accounts known as the Pipe Rolls £10,687 was spent here in the next two years – the most concentrated burst of expenditure in Edward I's entire Welsh building programme. About 2600 diggers, quarriers and masons were employed. The initial works on a castle were always disproportionately expensive, with materials to be quarried and transported to the site, a moat to be dug and foundations laid. Nevertheless the bulk of the castle must have been standing by the end of 1296, since this large sum represents nearly three-quarters of the eventual total spent. Work then virtually ground to a halt, leaving the castle incomplete and certainly indefensible. A long section of the outer curtain had not yet been started, and even the portcullises were not in place.

The stoppage was due to Edward's invasion of Scotland. Building only resumed in 1306 owing to fears of a Scottish landing (a band of Scots actually raided Beaumaris later in the century). Work continued throughout Edward II's reign, as at

Caernarfon, at least £3,055 being spent here. Nicholas de Dernford was now in charge of building operations. Even when work petered out in 1330 much remained to be done. A survey of the Welsh royal castles, conducted for the young Black Prince in 1343, describes the inadequacies in some detail. The truth was that Gwynedd had indeed been conquered, and this remote castle did not need to be fully completed. Thankfully time has been kind, and although the castle is now an empty shell it has lost little more than its battlements.

One of the enjoyable features of the castle is the wet moat, a rarity in Wales. Unfortunately the moat is now incomplete, but on the two-and-a-half sides where it remains the outer curtain is reflected in its water. This concentric curtain formed part of the original plan, though only the lower half dates from 1295–96 and the northern stretches were not even begun at that time.

The outer curtain was important enough to be finished to the original design after 1306. It is the most sophisticated concentric fortification in Britain. Built in eight straight sections, it forms a flattened octagon which could face attack from any direction. A concentric outer curtain was not meant to be very high – the inner curtain should overlook it to allow arrow fire from several levels simultaneously. Nevertheless the outer curtain of Beaumaris was capable of independent defence. It represents an advance on the concentric walls at Rhuddlan and Harlech, which merely screened the main curtain from direct attack. The curtain is copiously pierced by arrow slits, and so are the merlons of the battlements where they survive. Further arrow slits peep out of the twelve round towers which comprehensively flank the curtain – a luxury which even Edward I's outer wall around the Tower of London does not possess. These towers are not large, though the two at the northern angles are bigger than the others.

In addition to the mural towers there are two small gatehouses along the outer curtain. They are not quite in line with the main gatehouses behind them in order to frustrate a direct assault – an unusual refinement. The Sea Gate on the south side, with pointed flanking towers, has an early row of machicolations above the gateway. Beside it, a thick spur wall (containing a mural passage) guards the dock where ships would have berthed with supplies. The northern gatehouse – Llanfaes Gate – appears to consist of deep buttresses and connecting vaults. This is because the rounded flanking towers were never completed. As usual in a concentric castle, the outer ward is just a narrow space between the two lines of walls.

The inner curtain – fifteen feet thick – is much more massive than the outer. Circular towers project boldly from the four corners, while there are U-shaped towers midway along the east and west walls and massive gatehouses placed centrally on the north and south. An archers' gallery festooned with arrow slits runs through the exceptional thickness of the curtain. The wall-walk, which is well provided with latrines, is unbroken except at the gatehouses, so defenders could have rushed to any point under attack. Despite its formidable appearance, it was the inner curtain which suffered most as a result of the fourteenth-century cuts. All the flanking towers were meant to be three storeys high, but they were left without their top floors. Instead they were finished off with a parapet barely higher than the connecting lengths of curtain, and the watch turrets which should have crowned them were never built.

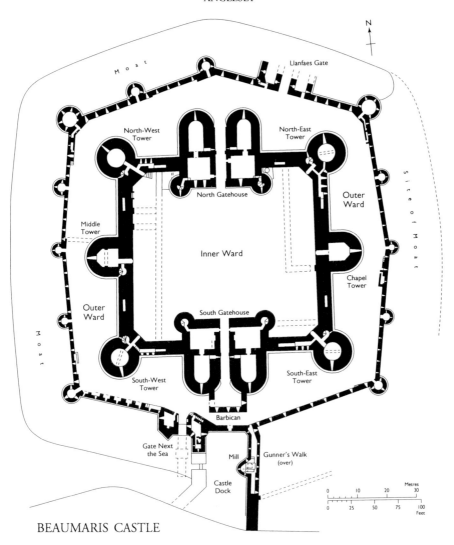

BEAUMARIS CASTLE

Both gatehouses were also left at two storeys, except for the outer front of the North Gatehouse which was carried to its full height. They are fully developed Edwardian gatehouses, like the smaller but more complete example at Harlech. U-shaped towers flank the outer gateway, while large inner portions project into the courtyard. The North Gatehouse had three portcullises, two pairs of gates, and several murder hole slots in the long gate passage. Its first floor formed a handsome residence for the constable, with chambers in the twin flanking towers and a hall filling the large courtyard projection. By analogy with Harlech, these arrangements would have been duplicated on the top floor had it ever been built. The courtyard facade of the gatehouse, with stair turrets at either end, is imposing. However, the row of five large windows lighting the constable's hall detracts from security, even if

5

they were once protected by iron grilles. So although the gatehouse may be described as a keep-gatehouse – a self-contained residence capable of independent resistance – it could only have held out temporarily if the inner ward fell into enemy hands.

Originally the South Gatehouse was intended to be its twin. One wonders why Beaumaris should have required two gatehouses on such a grand scale. Perhaps James of St George was more interested in architectural symmetry than a pragmatic design – he had already provided two matching gatehouses at Rhuddlan. Once economies were made it became clear that two keep-gatehouses would be an unnecessary extravagance. The inner part of the South Gatehouse stands just a few feet up and the 1343 survey shows that it has never stood any higher. As a result its gate passage is only half as long as that of the North Gatehouse, and a small square barbican was added between the flanking towers by way of compensation. The Gothic window between the towers of the South Gatehouse lit a chapel. Had both gatehouses been completed to the original plan they would have contained four large halls, which would surely have been excessive.

It was logical for the constable of an Edwardian castle to occupy the gatehouse and control the portcullises, but the castle accommodation was intended to be much more extensive. Fireplaces and windows (some later blocked) in the upper floors of the flanking towers show that they were meant to be lived in. However, some of the towers were never roofed, despite the stone arches which are still waiting to support the floors of the upper chambers. The eastern mid-wall tower had a special purpose, as the narrow lancet windows suggest. It is the Chapel Tower, containing an apsidal chapel of surprising beauty, with wall arcading and a ribbed vault (the only significant vaulting in any of the Edwardian castles). The location of this chapel suggests that a suite of royal apartments was intended against the east curtain, but the thin foundations show that only a modest timber-framed wing was actually built.

In fact the royal household never came here, and the subsequent history of the castle is one of sorry neglect. Consequently this distinguished stronghold has a mediocre military record. The castle fell to Owain Glyndwr in 1403, despite the naval force which had been dispatched for its relief. It was recaptured when the English fleet recovered Anglesey two years later. During the Civil War the castle was garrisoned as a strongpoint guarding the king's vital supply route to Ireland. It surrendered without a fight to Major-General Mytton in June 1646, and again after a brief resistance during the Royalist uprising of 1648.

Edward I accompanied his castle with a borough of English settlers. The attractive town of Beaumaris lies south-west of the castle, but the only other relic of the Edwardian period is St Mary's Church. Unlike Conwy and Caernarfon, stone defences were only built after 1405 to prevent the town falling to any future Glyndwr. Unfortunately the town wall has disappeared except for two short pieces. One hides behind some houses to the south of the church, while the other forms a boundary wall off Church Street.

Access: Open daily (Cadw).
Reference: Guidebook by A. J. Taylor. *HKW* (I).

Relations: Edward I's castles of Caernarfon, Conwy and Harlech. Harlech is concentric, along with Edward's earlier castles at Aberystwyth and Rhuddlan. Caerphilly is the other great concentric castle of Wales.

CASTELL ABERLLEINIOG   is the predecessor of Beaumaris. It lies two miles to the north, off the road to Llangoed. The impressive Norman motte was probably one of those raised by Hugh d'Avranches, earl of Chester, when he overran Gwynedd around 1088. It is surrounded by a ditch, and there is a bailey platform below. The castle overlooks the Menai Strait opposite Hugh's castle mound at Abergwyngregyn on the mainland, showing that coastal communications were important to the Norman invaders as well as Edward I. In 1094 Hugh was driven out by Gruffudd ap Cynan, who returned from Ireland to liberate Gwynedd. Anglesey remained under native rule until Edward's conquest, and we do not know if the castle was occupied by the Welsh princes. On top is the stump of a square tower with rounded angle turrets. It appears to be a later medieval tower house, but historically it is quite obscure. The interior is curiously backed by an earth rampart. Apparently the tower was converted into an artillery redoubt by the Royalists in the Civil War, to guard the approach to Beaumaris.

Access: On private land.
Reference: RCAHMW *Anglesey.*
Relations: Hugh d'Avranches raised the mottes of Abergwygregyn and Tomen-y-Mur. Compare the Civil War defences of Chepstow, Newcastle Emlyn and Pembroke.

OTHER SITES   There is only one. *Castell Trefadog*, overlooking the sea near Llanfaethlu, has a rampart which may be native Welsh, though the enclosure was later occupied by a manor house.

Breconshire

Bernard de Newmarch invaded Brycheiniog in 1093 and established the lordship of Brecon. Although castles are quite numerous here, few are well preserved. There is the usual group of Norman mottes, notably Brecon, Crickhowell and Trecastle. Builth's fine motte-and-bailey earthworks formed the centre of a separate lordship. Stone castles only appeared in the late twelfth century, Tretower's shell keep being the best preserved. The other castles of this period are attributed to the formidable William de Braose, lord of Brecon, before his flight into exile in 1207. Brecon retains part of another shell keep, while Hay preserves its small tower keep. Castell Dinas and Castell Blaen Llynfi were extensive fortifications in elevated positions, but both are now fragmentary.

The Bohuns rebuilt the chief castle of the lordship at Brecon in the thirteenth century, though only part of their hall survives. Brecon also retains a stretch of its town wall. Bronllys and Tretower admirably illustrate the contemporary fashion for round keeps, though others at Camlais and Castell Coch have been destroyed to their foundations. Fragmentary Castell Du is native Welsh. It recalls the dominance of Llywelyn the Last, who even gained control over this solidly English lordship in the 1260s. Edward I's stone castle on the Norman earthworks of Builth has vanished, but some Edwardian masonry survives at Crickhowell. Rare examples of later medieval tower houses can be seen at Talgarth and Scethrog, while Llanddew had its fortified bishop's palace. Tretower Court was built by the Vaughans to replace the older castle during the Wars of the Roses. Though primarily a mansion, and notable for its two halls, it has an embattled curtain closing off the courtyard.

BRECON CASTLE AND TOWN WALL Bernard de Newmarch founded the castle when he established his lordship of Brecon in 1093. The lordship soon passed to the powerful de Braose dynasty. King John seized the castle in 1207 after driving William de Braose into rebellion, but it was recaptured by his son Reginald during the Magna Carta war. In 1241 Brecon and its lordship were inherited by the Bohun earls of Hereford. The castle resisted three attacks by Llywelyn the Great, but Llywelyn the Last managed to capture Brecon while allied to Simon de Montfort in 1264. After the Bohuns died out in 1372 the castle and lordship passed to another powerful family, the Stafford dukes of Buckingham. Owain Glyndwr was repulsed in 1404. A final siege took place in 1645, when Brecon surrendered to the parliamentary commander Rowland Laugharne.

The castle occupies high ground overlooking the confluence of the rivers Usk and Honddu. As a result of Civil War slighting and later stone-robbing there remain only two isolated portions – the motte and one side of the hall – now separated by a road. The prominent motte is reached by an earth causeway, a curious later addition designed to ease the ascent. On the summit part of a Norman shell keep survives – just three sides of a polygonal enclosure wall with a projecting turret. This keep may have been the work of William de Braose in the late twelfth century. A circular keep was later added inside the shell wall, as at Tretower, but that has vanished.

A towered curtain once surrounded the bailey. Everything has gone except for the outer wall of the hall, which survives intact in the grounds of the Castle Hotel. This wall doubled up as the curtain and preserves its battlements. The thin lancet windows which lit the hall signify a thirteenth-century date, probably after Humphrey de Bohun acquired the lordship in 1241. Projecting at one end is the narrow, semi-octagonal Ely Tower which contained a suite of latrines. This tower, a fourteenth-century addition, takes its name from the bishop of Ely. He was imprisoned in the castle in 1483 until he persuaded his captor, the duke of Buckingham, to launch a premature revolt against Richard III (see Hay Castle). The Ely Tower masks an earlier corner tower, circular but rather shallow to command this vulnerable angle. The stretch of embattled wall beyond is a folly.

Brecon town, which grew up on the opposite bank of the Honddu, was important enough to be surrounded by a stone wall in the Bohun period. It had four gatehouses and ten semi-circular bastions in the Edwardian manner. However, the town wall was another victim of Civil War destruction. A patched-up stretch from the south-eastern part of the circuit survives, with one bastion, along Captain's Walk (behind Danygaer Street). The medieval town's prosperity is still evident in its religious houses. Bernard de Newmarch founded a priory at the same time as the castle. Its early Gothic church is now Brecon Cathedral, while the buildings of a friary are preserved across the Usk in Christ College.

> *Access:* The Castle Hotel is open to non-residents. The motte and town wall are visible.
> *Reference: Castles* by C. Oman. BOW *Powys.* GAHW *Clwyd and Powys* for the town wall.
> *Relations:* Castell Dinas, Hay, Abergavenny and Oystermouth all contain work by William de Braose. Compare the Bohun castle of Caldicot, and the shell keeps at Tretower and Cardiff.

BRONLLYS CASTLE, overlooking the Afon Llynfi, guarded the route between Hay and Brecon. It was founded after Bernard de Newmarch's invasion by his vassal Richard Fitz Pons, who founded the Clifford family. They were infamous Marcher lords, although the best known member of the family is Rosamund Clifford, Henry II's mistress. The motte-and-bailey earthworks are typically Norman, but the castle has the distinction of a round keep on top of the motte. Circular keeps were popular in South Wales in the thirteenth century, and this is a smaller version of the classic keep at Pembroke which set the trend. The keep was probably built by Walter de Clifford, the last of the Clifford lords (d.1263). Although a shell, it is almost complete and a good example of its kind.

The keep is a plain cylinder rising from a tall plinth. Its first-floor entrance is reached by a wooden stair – a modern replacement of the original. Within is a hall lit by two lancet windows. It has no fireplace so would not have been a very hospitable chamber. Steps from one of the window embrasures descend to the vaulted basement. This must have been used as a prison, because there is a long drop to the floor from the end of the stair.

On the entrance floor the other window embrasure leads to a stair curving upwards in the thickness of the wall. It ends at the second floor, again with two windows and this time a fireplace as well. This was the solar – at first the only habitable room in a rather spartan keep, because the next curved flight of steps originally led to the parapet. The third floor was added early in the fourteenth century and formed a more comfortable chamber. It had three windows, another fireplace and its own latrine (a feature surprisingly lacking elsewhere in the keep). Unfortunately this top storey is now quite ruinous. The heightening of the keep is attributed to Rhys ap Hywel, a Welsh knight who acquired Bronllys as a reward for his military service to Edward I.

By that time the keep probably served as ancillary accommodation, inhabited by the lord only during emergencies. The main residence was a more spacious hall in the bailey. Its masonry is embedded in the stables of a Georgian successor house. There is no trace of any stone curtain around the bailey. The later history of Bronllys is one of absentee landlords, and the castle was a ruin by 1521.

Access: The keep is always open (Cadw).
Reference: Guidebook by J. B. Smith and J. K. Knight.
Relations: Pembroke and other round keeps such as Tretower, Skenfrith, Caldicot and Dinefwr. Walter de Clifford also built nearby Clifford Castle (Herefordshire).

BUILTH CASTLE was the first of Edward I's great Welsh castles, but it differs from the others in several respects. It was not a new castle but stood on the earthworks of an older motte-and-bailey. Nor was it a coastal fortress directly intended to subjugate Gwynedd, although the threat from Llywelyn the Last prompted Edward to commence building in May 1277. Most obvious today, Builth is the only one of Edward's castles to have vanished. The Norman earthworks are still formidable but, owing to stone-robbing, not a scrap of masonry can be seen.

The little town of Builth Wells has grown up around the castle. Philip de Braose probably laid out the earthworks about 1095. It is one of the strongest motte-and-bailey castles of the Welsh Marches, comprising a ditched motte and two baileys, the whole surrounded by an outer rampart. The castle changed hands several times in the struggles between the Braose lords and their Welsh neighbours. Controlling the route to Brecon and the south, Builth became the most hotly contested of the Marcher castles. King John strengthened the castle after he had seized it from William de Braose. Llywelyn the Great, who had failed to take it by siege, acquired the castle in a marriage settlement. From 1242 the Mortimers were building in stone here after recapturing Builth for the English. Llywelyn the Last destroyed the castle in 1260, and it is not known how much survived when Edward I began the reconstruction. Llywelyn returned in 1282 and attempted to persuade the constable to surrender the newly-rebuilt castle, before riding off to be struck down in the infamous skirmish at nearby Cilmeri.

With Llywelyn's death and the invasion of Gwynedd royal expenditure came to a halt, the castle being left unfinished despite another attack during the Welsh uprising of 1294. The cost recorded over those years is £1,666. This is a modest sum compared with Edward's other castles, since the earthworks and perhaps some of the masonry already existed. Little is known of the stone castle and no excavations have been undertaken. The buried footings are still waiting to be uncovered. A round keep crowned the motte, surrounded by a concentric wall with flanking towers. It has been suggested that the keep was a survivor from the earlier stone castle, though Edward I built another round keep at Flint. A curtain with six towers and a gatehouse surrounded the main bailey. We do not know the architect. Edward's master mason, James of St George, was fully occupied in North Wales and there is no evidence to connect him with Builth. The castle was garrisoned against Owain Glyndwr but its abandonment soon followed.

Access: Freely accessible.
Reference: HKW (I). *Brycheiniog* (XVIII). GAHW *Clwyd and Powys.*
Relations: Philip de Braose also raised New Radnor Castle. Compare Edward I's other castles of 1277 at Aberystwyth, Flint and Rhuddlan.

CAMLAIS CASTLE rises high up on the edge of the Brecon Beacons, three miles south-east of Sennybridge. The conical Norman motte is surrounded by a ditch, but unusually there is no sign of any bailey. On top of the motte is the buried base of a circular keep, its rubble core visible to a depth of several feet internally. The castle (otherwise known as Blaen Camlais or Cwm Camlais) was held by the lords of Brecon. It may have been built by the last William de Braose, or by Humphrey de Bohun who inherited the lordship in 1241.

Access: On private land.
Reference: Brycheiniog (XI).
Relations: The well-preserved round keeps of Bronllys and Tretower.

CASTELL BLAEN LLYNFI occupies a spur overlooking the village of Bwlch, three miles west of Tretower. This once-extensive castle is now reduced to some overgrown fragments concealed in the woods. Clearly the mortar was of poor quality, a factor which has destroyed a number of the elevated castles of Central Wales. A deep ditch surrounds the large bailey, which is oblong with two canted corners. The long south side is marked by the collapsed rubble of a curtain, with some footings of a hall against it. At the end of this stretch is the base of an oblong tower positioned diagonally at the corner. Beyond, a short chunk of the east curtain still rises high. A masonry castle with only one square flanking tower suggests the late Norman period. William de Braose may have been the builder before his exile in 1207. It is reminiscent of William's castle at Hay, though here the position of the entrance is unclear. During the Magna Carta war Reginald de Braose recovered the castle, but he soon lost it when King John invaded. Blaen-Llynfi was one of the castles captured by Richard Marshal during his short-lived rebellion of 1233. Excavations have shown that at least two round towers were later added to the curtain. It was forfeited by the Mortimers in 1322 and has been crumbling ever since.

Access: On private land.
Reference: Mediaeval Military Architecture by G. T. Clark.
Relations: William de Braose's castles of Brecon, Hay and Castell Dinas.

CASTELL COCH, a mile north-east of Ystradfellte, occupies a promontory overlooking the confluence of the rivers Llia and Dringarth. A strong rampart and ditch cut off the more level approach from the north. Beyond the outer enclosure is a small inner bailey at the apex of the promontory. This was walled in stone, with a circular keep at the rear. The poorly-mortared masonry has crumbled away, though the foundations lie buried in the turf. The 'Red Castle' is first mentioned in 1239, when it was held by the last William de Braose. It was probably built by him, though an oblong platform within the bailey may represent an earlier Norman keep.

Access: Visible from the road.
Reference: Brycheiniog (XIII).
Relations: Compare the other *castelli* Coch in Glamorgan and Pembrokeshire.

CASTELL DINAS   is perched on a commanding hilltop in the Black Mountains, overlooking the A479 between Bronllys and Tretower. At 1476 feet up it is the highest castle site in Britain. It has been likened to Castell Dinas Bran, but is even more fragmentary. The ascent from Pen-y-Genffordd is a steep one, though amply rewarded by the magnificent view. The large, ditched enclosure is actually an Iron Age hillfort. When it was re-occupied in the Middle Ages a cross-ditch was dug to divide the enclosure into two, the southern half forming an outer bailey to the stone castle in the northern half.

The defences which filled the sloping northern bailey may have been raised by the redoubtable William de Braose, lord of Brecon and Gower, who rebuilt several of his castles in stone. Castell Dinas was the most ambitious of the group, suggesting that the castle was new (and perhaps incomplete) when William was forced into exile in 1207. Unfortunately the masonry has collapsed into grassy ramparts through which many stones still peek. Evidently the mortar was of the same poor quality here as at several other elevated castle sites in mid-Wales. At the highest point a mound of rubble marks the site of an oblong keep, with what appears to have been a concentric surrounding wall. A small inner bailey was formed between the keep and the west curtain. Along the west curtain mounds of rubble mark two small mural towers. These were square in the Norman manner, supporting the attribution to William de Braose. Only on the east does the curtain still rise several feet high. The arch of a postern is buried in the debris.

Despite its formidable setting and the successive lines of defence, the castle fell to Richard Marshal, earl of Pembroke, in 1233. He had rebelled against Henry III in alliance with Llywelyn the Great, but he was soon forced to flee to Ireland. Owain Glyndwr is said to have used the derelict castle as a base.

> *Access:* Freely accessible (uphill walk).
> *Reference: Brycheiniog* (X).
> *Relations:* Hillfort castles such as Cefnllys and Castell Dinas Bran. Castles of William de Braose at Brecon, Hay, Abergavenny and Oystermouth.

CASTELL DU,   the Black Castle, overlooks Sennybridge and is also known as Sennybridge Castle. In 1271 it was held by a Welsh lord, Einion Sais, who was an ally of Llywelyn the Last. It thus appears to be a native Welsh castle, possibly built by Llywelyn himself after he overran the lordship of Brecon in the 1260s. Unfortunately the castle has fallen victim to later stone-robbing. It was a small, oblong enclosure, but only a U-shaped flanking tower and an adjoining fragment of curtain survive. One patch of smooth ashlar facing survives high up, but otherwise the tower is a featureless lump.

> *Access:* On private land.
> *Reference: Castles of the Welsh Princes* by P. R. Davis.
> *Relations:* Castell Meredydd and Castell Morgraig are other native castles of south-east Wales.

CRICKHOWELL CASTLE, by the River Usk, was founded in Norman times by the Turbevilles, sub-tenants of the lords of Brecon. Their oval motte is still prominent, with the buried footings of a Norman shell keep on the summit. Sir Grimbald Pauncefoot built the rest of the stone castle towards 1300, but most of his work has perished. The only substantial feature is part of a double tower, comprising the curved front of a semi-circular tower and one wall of a narrow oblong tower which projects more deeply beside it. It is curious how this fragment survives to full height, with lancet windows and parapet, when almost everything else has been torn down. It has been suggested that the rounded tower was one of a pair forming a typical Edwardian gatehouse, but there is no trace of the gateway. The only other survivor is the precarious fragment of a round turret, one of two which flanked a gateway at the foot of the motte. St Edmund's Church, contemporary with the stone rebuilding of the castle, contains Pauncefoot effigies. The castle was garrisoned in 1403, at the height of Owain Glyndwr's revolt, but it fell into decay after the Herberts built a new mansion (now vanished) nearby.

Access: Freely accessible (LA).
Reference: GAHW *Clwyd and Powys.*
Relations: The Turbevilles also built Coity Castle.

HAY CASTLE Hay-on-Wye was founded by the Norman lords of Brecon. Their first castle was the low motte which is visible behind a wall near the parish church. The move to the present hilltop site, overlooking the River Wye, must have taken place by 1200, because a Norman window survives in the keep. This is probably the work of William de Braose, lord of Brecon and Gower, who is infamous for the 'Abergavenny Massacre'. Tradition ascribes the castle to his formidable wife Maud, who rebuked King John for the murder of Prince Arthur. Hay Castle probably fell when John invaded the lordship of Brecon in 1207. William escaped to France but Maud was carried off into captivity, eventually starving to death at Windsor Castle. John captured the castle a second time in 1216 during his war upon those barons – including Reginald de Braose – who had forced him to sign the Magna Carta. Hay saw further fighting during Simon de Montfort's revolt, changing hands twice. Castle and lordship subsequently passed to the Bohun earls of Hereford (1241) and the Stafford dukes of Buckingham (1372). It was garrisoned against Owain Glyndwr.

The oval summit of the hill made a natural bailey, but the curtain which surrounded it has largely disappeared. All that survives is portion of the northern circuit, facing the town. It comprises an embattled stretch of wall, a gateway, and the ruin of an oblong tower. This tower is rather small to be called a keep, but several diminutive Norman 'keeps' in South Wales were positioned to command the entrance. The Norman window (its mullion missing) overlooks the courtyard. In the late fifteenth century the keep was remodelled, its outer front being rebuilt entirely. The rebuilding may have been necessitated by a Yorkist slighting in 1460. Alternatively the castle may have been damaged by Richard III during the revolt of Henry Stafford, duke of Buckingham. Buckingham's sudden betrayal of a monarch he had just helped to place on the throne may reflect his revulsion at the fate suffered by the legitimate princes in the Tower of London, though Richard's apologists regard him as the real instigator of the murders.

Immediately beside the keep is the gate arch (thirteenth century), which is still closed by its original wooden gates. The gateway is deep enough to contain a small portcullis chamber above. On the other side of the keep stands a house with a line of Dutch gables, built in the 1660s to replace the medieval domestic quarters and now itself half ruined after a fire. Hay was a fortified town in the Middle Ages, but only a short fragment of the town wall survives off Newport Street.

Access: The castle is open daily as one of Hay's second-hand bookshops.
Reference: BOW *Powys. Country Life* (XXXVI).
Relations: For William de Braose see Brecon, Castell Blaen Llynfi, Castell Dinas, Abergavenny and Oystermouth.

LLANDDEW PALACE   lay two miles north of Brecon. Llanddew was one of the centres of the Celtic church, and the bishops of St David's established an episcopal palace beside the parish church in the twelfth century. In the vicarage garden is the ruin of a hall attributed to Bishop Henry de Gower (d.1347). The crumbling, ivy-covered walls do not tell us much, but if his palaces at Lamphey and St David's in Pembrokeshire are anything to go by it would have been a building of some splendour. Those palaces, unusually for medieval Wales, were not fortified, but this one stood within a defensive wall probably built by one of Gower's predecessors. Only a fragment of curtain now remains, with a well recessed into it.

Access: On private land.
Reference: **Archaeologia Cambrensis** (4th series, IV).
Relations: The bishops' castle at Llawhaden and their fortified close at St David's.

SCETHROG TOWER   is a rare example of a later medieval Welsh tower house. It stands beside the River Usk, five miles south-east of Brecon. The tower is square, rising to four storeys including the low basement. Nevertheless it is difficult to visualise as a tower now, because the top storey has been turned into a gabled attic. All the windows are later insertions, creating the impression of a normal farmhouse. It is unclear whether the tower stood alone or formed part of a manor house. The tower, probably dating from the fourteenth century, was occupied by a branch of the Picard family of Tretower.

Access: Private.
Reference: **Brycheiniog** (XI).
Relations: Tower houses such as Talgarth, Candleston and Llandough. For the Picards see Tretower.

TALGARTH TOWER   is a curious sight among the buildings of Talgarth. This square structure is a medieval tower, perhaps fourteenth century, beside the bridge over the little River Ennig. Its history and purpose are obscure. The present windows are much more recent insertions and the tower has later adjuncts on three sides. Most tower houses, such as nearby Scethrog, were the defensive homes of minor lords, but a few in England served as administrative centres and court houses. Talgarth belonged to the lords of nearby Bronllys Castle, so the tower may have been intended to keep watch over the little town. It was later used as a prison.

Access: Exterior visible.
Reference: Brycheiniog (X).
Relations: Nearby Bronllys. Small tower houses at Scethrog, Broncoed and Candleston.

TRECASTLE   This is a fine earthwork in the grounds of nineteenth-century Castle House. Its tree-clad motte is an impressive one – large, oval, and surrounded by a deep ditch. The castle lies in the village of the same name, three miles west of Sennybridge. Positioned on the edge of the lordship of Brecon and lacking any recorded history, its builder is a matter for conjecture. It may have been raised by the Cliffords after the Lord Rhys captured Llandovery Castle.

Access: Visible from the road.
Reference: GAHW Clwyd and Powys.
Relations: The motte-and-bailey castles at Brecon, Bronllys, Builth and Crickhowell.

TRETOWER CASTLE AND COURT   Although quite ruinous, Tretower is the best preserved of the castles of Breconshire. It has the added attraction of a late medieval mansion close by, still with certain defensive features. Tretower Castle and Court were successive centres of one of the dependent baronies within the lordship of Brecon. The castle was founded after Bernard de Newmarch's invasion by a Norman knight known to us simply as Picard. He raised a castle of the motte and bailey type, but the 'motte' here is just a low platform encased in stone.

Perhaps his grandson John Picard erected the large shell keep towards the end of the twelfth century. This is a rare example of a shell keep being built to fit the residential buildings within. The south and west walls are straight because a Norman hall and solar stood against them. These two walls still stand almost to full height, the narrow gap at the corner resulting from the collapse of the spiral staircase as recently as 1947. The shallow projection in the south wall contained a small kitchen, its fireplace visible within. On the other sides the polygonal wall of the shell keep has collapsed, while the gate tower which guarded the entrance is reduced to foundations.

In the thirteenth century the interior of the shell keep was transformed, possibly by Roger Picard who was here in the 1230s. The Norman hall and solar were pulled down except for their outer walls, and the windows which lit them were blocked. This cleared the interior to make room for an inner tower keep of the fashionable

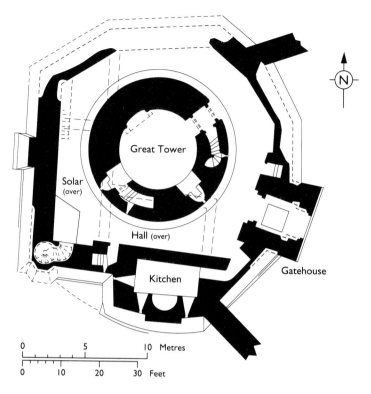

TRETOWER CASTLE KEEP

circular type. Brecon Castle once had a similar double keep and probably provided the inspiration. It is an early if small-scale example of concentric planning, the round keep rising higher than the closely-surrounding shell keep so that attackers could be fired upon from both parapets.

The round keep survives intact except for its parapet, though it is now a shell. It is similar to the Cliffords' keep at Bronllys – perhaps the same master mason was responsible. Like Bronllys it contained four storeys, the entrance being placed as usual on the first floor at the top of a wooden stair. However, the two keeps are not identical. The basement here contained a well instead of a prison, and the stair connecting the upper floors of the keep was a spiral rather than straight. All three upper floors are lit by pairs of windows. The entrance hall at Bronllys was not heated, but the corresponding hall at Tretower has the remains of a grand hooded fireplace. Above is the solar. The doorway attached to a window embrasure in this room connected via a drawbridge with the parapet of the shell keep. It is the third floor of this tower which lacks a fireplace and therefore cannot have provided comfortable accommodation. As at Bronllys, this top floor is a later thirteenth-century addition, and the shell keep wall was heightened at the same time.

The keep forms one angle of a triangular bailey which was also walled during the thirteenth century. Today the curtain is very ruinous. So are the round towers which project at the other two angles, one being reduced to its footings though the other still stands to a reasonable height. Residential buildings no doubt existed in the bailey, but the castle was later abandoned for a more comfortable manor house outside. The architectural details suggest that the north range of Tretower Court already existed before the Picard family died out in 1305. This does not necessarily mean that they had already abandoned the castle. It was garrisoned against Owain Glyndwr in 1403 but was perhaps already in decay, since Tretower had languished in the hands of absentee owners for a century.

Sir Roger Vaughan decided to live at Tretower Court in the mid-fifteenth century. He remodelled the north wing and added a longer range at right-angles. Although his half-brother, Sir William Herbert, was enlarging Raglan Castle at that time, there was nothing defensive about Roger's mansion. However, his son Thomas Vaughan created a courtyard in the 1480s by building an embattled wall on the other two sides. This wall is thick enough to be regarded as a curtain, with arrow slits in the battlements. The wide wall-walk (later roofed over to form a covered gallery) is supported by arches on the courtyard side. It must be admitted that the wall is not especially high, while the squat gate tower has separate archways for horse and foot traffic – a common convenience in the fifteenth century but not very secure. No attempt was made to strengthen the other two sides of the mansion and there was no moat. The whole composition seems to be an example, more common in England, of the sham castellated architecture favoured by barons during the Wars of the Roses.

Nevertheless Tretower Court is one of the few evocative Welsh examples of a late medieval baron's residence, even if it is somewhat restored. Although the north range may go back to the Picards it was extensively rebuilt by Sir Roger Vaughan. He added the restored wooden gallery which overlooks the courtyard at first-floor level. A hall occupied the middle of the upper floor, with chambers on either side. The disappearance of the original partition walls on both floors is misleading, but the arch-braced roof is original.

Roger Vaughan's west range formed a new and grander house, relegating the north range to his heir or important guests. The first apartment formed the solar – its large oriel window is another restoration. Next comes the great hall, no longer than the hall in the north range but loftier, because it rises the full height of the range. Its roof is similar but more finely moulded. The altered area further south contained domestic offices, followed by a separate hall for the Vaughans' retainers. Large windows inserted around 1630 have altered the character of this range. In keeping with the vanity of that time false windows were even inserted into the court-yard face of the curtain, to give the impression of an additional wing which doesn't exist.

Access: Tretower Court and the castle keep are open daily except in winter (both Cadw). The castle bailey can only be seen from outside.

Reference: Guidebook by C. A. R. Radford.

Relations: Brecon's shell keep and the circular keep at Bronllys. There are other concentric keeps at Raglan, Ewloe and Launceston (Cornwall).

OTHER SITES   Norman motte-and-bailey sites can be seen at:

Aberllynfi Castle

Aberyscir Motte (near Cradoc)

Alexanderstone Motte (near Brecon)

Caer Beris (near Builth Wells)

Cilwhybert Motte (near Llanspyddid)

Llandefaelog Fach Motte (near Pwllgloyw)

Madoc's Castle (near Lower Chapel)

Maescelyn Motte (near Crickhowell)

Tredustan Motte (near Talgarth)

Trefecca Motte

Twmpan Motte (near Pennorth)

Vaynor Castle

Two ringworks survive at *Crickadarn* and there is another at *Llysdinam* (near Newchurch). *Hen Castell* (near Llangattock) and *Llanleonfel Castle* (near Beulah) are the square, ditched enclosures of later medieval strongholds. A castle of the Mortimers overlooked the River Usk at *Pencelli*. Once a strong stone enclosure with a twin-towered gatehouse, it is reduced to one collapsed corner of a square Norman keep behind a Tudor farmhouse.

Caernarfonshire

Mountainous Arfon formed the heart of the Welsh principality of Gwynedd. Castles were introduced during a brief occupation by the earl of Chester around 1088. His motte survives at Abergwyngregyn. Gruffudd ap Cynan drove out the Norman invaders a few years later and founded a dynasty which would keep this corner of Wales independent for two more centuries. Although his biographer says that he 'delivered the land of Gwynedd from castles', the Welsh soon copied the Normans by raising mottes. Their oldest masonry castles are some collapsed remains at Castell Garn Fadrun and Castell Dinas Emrys. Llywelyn the Great was the real instigator of native stone castles in Gwynedd. He copied English trends by building an oblong keep at Dolwyddelan, a round keep at Dolbadarn, and – most advanced of all – an early twin-towered gatehouse at Criccieth. These castles are all spectacularly sited. Henry III turned another of Llywelyn's castles at Deganwy into an important royal stronghold, but little remains on its two natural mounds.

The native Welsh castles are inevitably overshadowed by the two mighty strongholds which Edward I built after he conquered Gwynedd in 1283. Caernarfon and Conwy, with their accompanying town walls, are among the finest medieval fortifications in Europe. Of the native castles, only Criccieth was retained long term for an English garrison. The magnificent castellated sham of Penrhyn Castle incorporates something of its late medieval fortified predecessor, built by a Welsh lord.

ABERGWYNGREGYN CASTLE   Hugh d'Avranches, earl of Chester, raised a castle 'at Bangor' about 1088, during his brief occupation of Gwynedd. In fact it was probably this site beside the Afon Anafon, five miles east, commanding the entrance to the Menai Strait opposite Castell Aberllleiniog on Anglesey. His conical, flat-topped motte, known as Pen-y-Mwd, stands behind the houses of the village (the name is often contracted to Aber). No trace remains of a bailey. Gruffudd ap Cynan expelled the Normans in 1094. There is no evidence of later occupation, but according to tradition Llywelyn the Last was here when he rejected a summons to attend Edward I's coronation.

Access: On private land.
Reference: GAHW *Gwynedd.*
Relations: Earl Hugh's castles of Caernarfon, Castell Aberlleiniog and Tomen-y-Mur.

CAERNARFON CASTLE AND TOWN WALL Caernarfon's military history goes back a long way. Half a mile inland can be seen the foundations of the Roman fort of Segontium. Even the present castle is not the first on the site. Hugh d'Avranches, palatine earl of Chester, overran the north Welsh coastline around 1088 and built a motte-and-bailey castle here, where the River Seiont flows into the Menai Strait. His conquests were soon lost and the castle then became a residence of the Welsh princes of Gwynedd, though nothing from their period is visible.

Edward I chose Caernarfon as the capital of his new principality in 1283. It is possible that he was motivated by Welsh legend, according to which Caernarfon had been the birthplace of Constantine the Great and the seat of the emperor Macsen Wledig. Edward thought his alien rule would be more palatable if he presented himself as their legitimate successor. The polygonal towers which distinguish Caernarfon from his other castles, and the bands of darker masonry on the mighty south front, were probably inspired by the imperial walls of Constantinople. It is likely that someone in the royal entourage had seen them at first hand.

Caernarfon is unquestionably the greatest of Edward's castles, despite the stiff competition from the other three which he built to encircle Gwynedd. James of St George was no doubt the architect, since he was Master of the King's Works in Wales with overall responsibility for the vast building programme. As Constantinople shows, polygonal towers were nothing new and James himself had built some in his native Savoy. What is odd is the irregular layout, long and narrow like Conwy but completely lacking the symmetry which characterises James' other castles. The plan of the castle resembles an hourglass, with a narrow middle separating the two courtyards or wards. Straight lengths of curtain connect the seven main flanking towers and the two gatehouses. The polygonal layout of the eastern or upper ward was determined by the Norman motte which was curiously retained.

In common with Edward's other fortifications, Caernarfon was undertaken with tremendous speed. Work began in June 1283 and the town wall was finished in just over two years. The southern half of the castle, overlooking the river, stood complete to the outside world by the end of 1287. The Pipe Rolls record a direct cost of £6,610 in those years, and Caernarfon can also perhaps claim a chunk of the £9,400 spent at various unspecified places in Wales. By contrast the north side of the castle, within the protection of the town wall, hardly stood above the foundations. At this point the impetus wore off. A slackening of expenditure from 1288 suggests that it

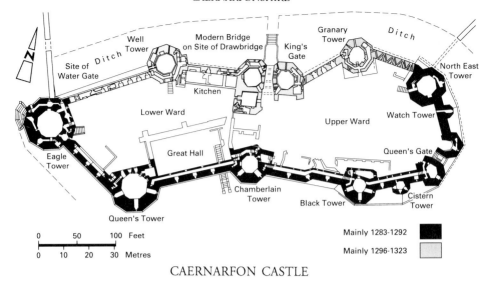

CAERNARFON CASTLE

had been decided to put the rest of this ambitious project on hold. One wonders if building would ever have resumed had Wales truly been pacified.

In 1294 came the setback of Madog ap Llywelyn's rebellion. His followers sacked the new town, killing the constable and damaging the half-built castle. When they had been driven out construction continued in earnest on the missing northern front. A further £5,698 was spent in the next seven years, despite Edward I's invasion of Scotland. Although building halted temporarily as the war dragged on, it resumed in 1304. By Edward's death in 1307 the castle was broadly defensible. Work continued at a slower pace throughout Edward II's reign. The Eagle Tower was heightened and the courtyard fronts of the other towers were built (these had been omitted in the haste to construct the outer walls). This final phase accounted for at least another £7,584. The accounts end in 1330, after Edward's deposition and murder. Approximately £25,000 had been spent on the castle and town wall in total, representing more than a quarter of the Edwardian expenditure in Wales. The castle was its present majestic self on the outside but much had been left incomplete within.

Today the castle is an unspoilt example of medieval military architecture at its peak. This is because its later history was one of quiet neglect but not total decay. Although intended as a fitting seat for a prince of Wales and his retinue – truly the 'Windsor of Wales' – the princes rarely came here and the castle served chiefly as an administrative centre and gaol. The only opportunity to demonstrate its strength came during Owain Glyndwr's revolt, and Caernarfon rose to the challenge. With Gwynedd firmly in Owain's hands, the castle survived years of isolation when it was often under siege. Supplies and reinforcements were tenuously brought in by sea. At the height of the blockade in 1403, a mere thirty-seven archers (the castle's normal complement) withstood two attacks by Owain's French allies. Caernarfon's involvement in the Civil War was less distinguished, castle and town changing hands without much resistance three times. Nevertheless it was still considered a potential threat. At the Restoration parliament ordered the demolition of the castle, but thankfully this mammoth task was not attempted. It decayed for two more centuries until repairs began. Today the castle is still intact externally, though many of the battlements are Victorian restorations.

To appreciate the castle's strength one should first examine the exterior. A good starting point is the Eagle Tower, overlooking the quay at the west end of the castle. It differs from the other towers owing to its decagonal plan and the special distinction of three surmounting turrets, which rise 128 feet. The Eagle Tower has its own postern leading into the ground-floor store room. Beside it, a torn-off projection with doorways leading nowhere is evidence for a walled dock by which the castle could be provisioned. All the other mural towers are surmounted by a single watch turret. The Queen's Tower – the next one along on the south – is almost as big as the Eagle Tower, but the others are smaller. They reach approximately the same height, though the sloping ground (a legacy of the motte) results in towers of two, three and four storeys. The banded south front of the castle is handsome but uncompromisingly military. Its curtain is fifteen feet thick at the base, pierced by numerous arrow slits but no windows.

Beside the Chamberlain Tower, in the middle of the south front, steps ascend to a postern through the curtain. The smaller Black Tower is beyond, followed by a low, projecting turret which contains a cistern. Here the immense stone plinth encasing the Norman motte is most apparent. At the eastern apex is the Queen's Gate, its slim flanking towers united by a tall arch above the entrance. This gateway is impossibly high up now, demonstrating the ground level within, but was once reached by a stone ramp as at Conwy. The wall continues past a higher projecting turret to the North-East Tower, where we reach the junction with the town wall and the end of the 1280s building campaign.

We now move onto the second phase of construction, from 1295. Walter of Hereford was now in charge of operations and the banded masonry which characterised the south front disappears. Military severity is relaxed somewhat, several traceried windows from the royal apartments looking out from high up. The curtain, interrupted by the Granary Tower, the King's Gate and the Well Tower, gets thinner from east to west as economies were made. Consequently the two western sections are a mere eight feet thick, and the final stretch was finished off lower than the rest. Doorways high up in the Well and Eagle towers show the intended height of the curtain. The Well Tower itself was never quite completed, and had to wait until Victorian times to receive its watch turret. Unfortunately the wide ditch which separated the castle from the town has been supplanted by a road.

The King's Gate is much the larger of the two gatehouses. Its shallow polygonal towers flank a tall drawbridge recess, crowned by a much-weathered statue of Edward II in a decorative niche. The archway leads into a gate passage which was defended by a drawbridge, a pair of gates and three portcullises. However, the existing passage is only half its intended length. The rear portion of the gatehouse was never built, except for the porter's lodge on the west side. Foundations stretching towards the Chamberlain Tower suggest that the gatehouse was originally planned to fill the narrow middle of the castle, dividing it into two. Had it been completed the gate passage would have led into a central hallway, with further passages leading left and right into the upper and lower wards. A simplified version of this can be seen at Denbigh Castle.

At first-floor level the King's Gate had living rooms in the flanking towers. Between them, above the gate passage, is a chapel which would have been inconvenienced by the raising of the portcullises and the large murder holes in the floor. This narrow chapel faces north – a rare departure for military reasons from the normal orientation. The top stage of the gatehouse is just a facade towards the town, because plans for a large hall at this level did not materialise. Hence the King's Gate never assumed the keep-gatehouse role intended for it.

The profusion of spiral staircases, wall-walks and passages makes Caernarfon a very extensive castle to explore, and it is inevitable that something will be missed in the course of a single visit. Most of the towers have been given roofs and floors again. One significant contrast with the other Edwardian castles is found at parapet level. Instead of a continuous wall-walk, the flanking towers interrupt each section. Attackers who gained one stretch of wall-walk would have been trapped until they could batter down the doors of the adjacent towers. Within the thickness of the south curtain is an archers' gallery which continues around the towers. A second gallery higher up was meant to be identical, but only the stretch between the Queen's and Chamberlain towers was ever covered over.

Although the castle is chronologically divided into south and north, within the great girdle of walls the division between west and east is more significant. The western or lower ward formed the garrison's half of the castle. It is empty now, but much of it was occupied by buildings. Between the Queen's and Chamberlain towers thick foundations mark the site of an immense great hall, while opposite are the footings of the kitchen. All the towers were intended to house officials and the garrison in addition to their defensive function. This explains the profusion of fireplaces and latrines, and mural chambers containing small bedchambers and chapels. The Well Tower – the only one still open to the sky – contains a large well once serving the adjacent kitchen.

The Eagle Tower at the west end is so named because of the stone eagles (now badly eroded) which crown the turrets. Its four storeys, with numerous wall chambers and passages, provided ample accommodation for the king's justiciar, who was also constable of the castle. Because of this role and its three watch turrets, the Eagle Tower may be regarded as a keep, though the King's Gate would no doubt have supplanted it as the constable's residence had it ever been completed. The Queen's Tower probably housed another important dignitary.

On the other side of the King's Gate we are in the upper ward, once filled by the Norman motte. This was only flattened in 1870, and it still accounts for the higher ground level within. It has been suggested that the motte was retained to carry a tower which would have dominated the castle, but if so the intention was never carried out. The north curtain of the upper ward has two experimental types of arrow slit at ground level, designed to improve the archer's range of fire. One stretch contains triple slits emanating from a single embrasure, while another stretch has three narrow apertures merging into a single slit through the outer wall. Windows higher up show that important lodgings stood in the shadow of the motte. These were the private royal apartments, but it is likely that they were only built of timber. The upper ward of Caernarfon would thus have corresponded to the inner ward of Conwy, reached from outside the town through the Queen's Gate. From here it is apparent that the Queen's Gate is just a facade, since its rear wall was never built.

While the castle is justly celebrated in its own right, it is perhaps more famous now for the princely investitures which have taken place within its walls. Like many royal ceremonies they are a recent invention, starting in 1911. Few of the English princes of Wales have had much to do with Caernarfon. Admittedly the first of their line was born here in April 1284, when Edward I and Queen Eleanor were visiting the newly-started castle. According to tradition the birth took place in the Eagle Tower, but building cannot have been advanced enough. Just as improbable is the story that the king presented the baby Edward to the Welsh as a prince born in Wales who could speak no English. If this colourful event took place at all it probably happened at Rhuddlan.

The medieval town of Caernarfon was surprisingly small in comparison with Conwy – nature imposed the limits. To the west is the Menai Strait, to the south the castle with the Seiont behind, while the Cadnant brook flowed to the north and east, leaving just a narrow isthmus opposite the Queen's Gate. The Cadnant is no longer apparent because it has been driven underground. Within the walled area is the little grid of streets laid out by Edward I's planners. The establishment of boroughs for English settlers was as much a feature of Edward's conquest as the building of castles, so the town wall (unusually) was also financed from the royal coffers. It failed to prevent Caernarfon from being taken by surprise during Madog's rebellion, and £1,195 was subsequently spent on the town wall alone. This is a big sum, suggesting that a great deal of damage had been wrought, but there is no obvious patching. The records show that the town as well as the castle held out against Owain Glyndwr.

Although the walled circuit is short even by medieval standards, extending just half a mile, it is a complete example of a medieval town wall, second only to Conwy. Seven semi-circular bastions are spaced along the line of the wall, as well as one complete round tower at the north-west corner of the circuit and two twin-towered gatehouses at opposite ends of the High Street. The wall begins close to the castle's North-East Tower, the gap between them denoting the original width of the castle ditch. Just before the first bastion the wall is pierced by an original postern. The East Gate is mutilated. It retains its rounded flanking towers, but the gate passage was replaced by a wider archway in 1873. At the third bastion the wall turns north-west. This stretch preserves much of its embattled parapet, with merlons pierced by arrow slits, but the three archways are recent insertions to ease traffic flow.

The round tower at the north-west angle of the circuit was soon adapted as the bell tower of St Mary's Church. It was erected against the town wall in 1307, though the traceried windows are Victorian insertions. Here begins the long western stretch of the town wall, overlooking the quay. Its two flanking towers and the West Gate have houses built into them. A diminutive square barbican remains between the flanking towers of the West Gate. The town wall rejoins the castle at the Eagle Tower. Beside the junction is a rebuilt gateway which led from the walled dock into the castle ditch. Provisions could thus have gone direct to the castle kitchen via the postern in the Well Tower.

It is worth looking at the town wall from within where this is possible. From here it is clear that the bastions are open-backed. The gaps along the wall-walk were originally crossed by wooden bridges, which could be thrown down to hinder the progress of besiegers if they gained control of one section of wall. However, these bridges soon rotted and were replaced by stone archways, two of which survive. Also notice the stone stairways which led to each section of parapet.

> *Access:* The castle is open daily and the town wall can be closely followed (both Cadw).
> *Reference:* Guidebook by A. J. Taylor. RCAHMW *Caernarvonshire* (II). *HKW* (I).
> *Relations:* Edward's castles at Conwy, Beaumaris and Harlech. Caernarfon inspired the polygonal towers and gatehouse of Denbigh Castle. As well as Conwy there are substantial town walls at Denbigh, Chepstow and Tenby.

CASTELL DINAS EMRYS

occupies a tree-covered hill overlooking the A498, a mile north-east of Beddgelert. It is primarily a Dark Age site. A causeway ascends to the entrance at the northern apex of a large, roughly D-shaped enclosure. This is surrounded by overgrown drystone ramparts dating from the sixth century, when the insecure inhabitants built a hillfort like their Iron Age ancestors. Legend has it that this was the place where King Vortigern tried to build a strong tower as a refuge, but it collapsed every night until Merlin exposed two battling dragons who symbolised the struggle between Saxons and Celts.

Later on Dinas Emrys was a residence of the princes of Gwynedd. At the highest point of the enclosure, overlooking the entrance, are the buried footings of an oblong structure. When discovered in 1910 it was romantically identified with Vortigern's tower. In fact it is a medieval keep, probably built by one of the feuding sons of Owain Gwynedd. The interior was found to be full of charcoal from a subsequent burning, suggesting that there was just a stone base with a timber superstructure. Presumably the castle was abandoned before the English conquest.

> *Access:* Freely accessible (NT). The approach begins at Craflwyn.
> *Reference:* *Archaeologia Cambrensis* (CIX).
> *Relations:* Dinas Powys is another Dark Age castle site. Owain Gwynedd's sons also raised Castell Garn Fadrun.

CASTELL GARN FADRUN

The commanding hill of Garn Fadrun, six miles west of Pwllheli, offers magnificent views up and down the Lleyn Peninsula. The strenuous ascent begins at Garnfadrun village which shelters on the south side of the hill. This is one of three striking Iron Age hillforts on the Lleyn, each preserving its surrounding drystone ramparts. Just below the summit (1,170 feet) are the collapsed remains of a more massive drystone wall, enclosing a narrow courtyard on the edge of the precipice. No doubt the summit formed a natural motte to this bailey. The primitive enclosure probably represents the oldest stone castle in Gwynedd of which something still survives. Giraldus Cambrensis, in his *Itinerary through Wales*, tells us that a stone castle here was newly built when he passed by in 1188, drumming up support for the Third Crusade. It must have been built by Rhodri, one of Owain Gwynedd's feuding sons.

Access: Freely accessible (uphill walk).
Reference: RCAHMW *Caernarvonshire* (III).
Relations: Compare the hillfort sites of Castell Dinas Bran, Cefnllys and Castell Dinas.

CONWY CASTLE AND TOWN WALL Although they are both military masterpieces of James of St George, Master of the King's Works in Wales, the contrasts between Caernarfon and Conwy are striking. It might be said that Conwy Castle is less architecturally distinguished. In contrast to Caernarfon's banded stonework, the masonry of Conwy looks rough and ready. Originally the whole castle gleamed white in a coat of limewash, and some patches still remain. Although smaller than Caernarfon, its stunning position on a rock overlooking the River Conwy estuary and the well-preserved residential buildings within are ample compensations. Furthermore, the medieval town was larger and its town wall is nearly a mile in length. So while Caernarfon may hold the crown as the greatest Edwardian castle, Conwy's town wall is undoubtedly the finest in Wales and ranks among the best preserved in Europe.

Edward I reached Conwy with his army in March 1283 and immediately chose it as the site for a new castle and borough. He thus abandoned his father's castle at Deganwy, its twin peaks visible on the other side of the estuary, which had been destroyed by Llywelyn the Last twenty years before. In the main years of construction 1500 masons, carpenters and labourers were employed. Castle and town wall rose simultaneously and were substantially complete by the end of 1287. This was an astonishing rate of progress which did not run out of steam, unlike Caernarfon. Afterwards there is a trickle of expenditure down to 1292. According to the Pipe Rolls the whole enterprise cost £13,760, and to this should be added a portion of the £9,400 spent at a number of Welsh sites in 1283-84. This represents considerably more expenditure than Caernarfon over the same period, though Caernarfon eventually cost more.

Edward I visited the castle in 1295 and immediately found himself in danger. He had arrived to quell the revolt of Madog ap Llywelyn, but a winter flood cut off the bulk of his army while the king was besieged by the Welsh. Several tense days passed before Conwy was relieved. It was 1399 before the castle received another royal visitor, again in difficult circumstances. Richard II, returning from his expedition to Ireland, took refuge in the castle when he discovered that Henry of Bolingbroke had returned from exile and was coming to meet him. Richard was enticed out by promises of safe conduct, and took the road which led to his deposition and death. Owain Glyndwr's revolt broke out soon after. On Good Friday, 1401, a band of his supporters tricked their way into the castle while the garrison was worshipping in St Mary's Church, but they were soon persuaded to withdraw. After that the castle remained aloof from the rebellion.

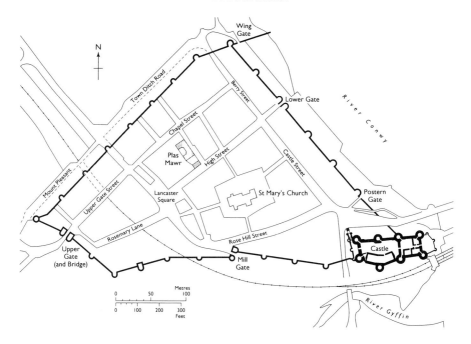

CONWY TOWN WALL

These colourful incidents cannot hide the fact that the castle's history was normally that of a gloomy outpost, decaying fast in the inclement weather. The problem was exacerbated by the wooden roofs. To save money none of the buildings – not even the undercrofts – had been vaulted in stone. As early as 1343 a survey of the Black Prince's Welsh castles revealed what a bad state it was in, and this led to the construction of eight stone arches to support a new roof over the great hall. By 1635 a visiting nobleman found the castle too dangerous to enter. John Williams, archbishop of York and a native of Conwy, repaired the defences at considerable expense to help secure Charles I's supply route to Ireland. Conwy was garrisoned for the king throughout the Civil War and only surrendered to Major-General Thomas Mytton in August 1646, when the Royalist cause was irrevocably lost. Thankfully no serious slighting was attempted but the remaining lead and timber in the castle were sold.

Conwy Castle shares with Caernarfon an elongated plan with no concentric defences, a layout dictated here by the narrow outcrop of rock on which it stands. Its design is very simple: an oblong enclosure surrounded by a mighty curtain, with eight tall, cylindrical towers presenting formidable and uniform fronts to north and south. The towers are all of equal size – this is one of the few Welsh castles lacking any kind of keep. Nor is there a gatehouse, though the entrances at each end of the castle are guarded by barbican enclosures. The gateway high up at the western end of the castle is now inaccessible. It was once reached by a stone ramp, but only the massive block which formed its summit remains. From here a drawbridge crossed

26

the gulf to the gateway, which is flanked by twin round turrets. The present approach ascends the rock and enters the castle through a rough opening cut alongside the original gateway. We are now in the West Barbican, a narrow enclosure with three projecting turrets.

Immediately in front is the main west wall of the castle, its two corner towers flanking the entrance gateway between them. It is odd that the western towers and the gateway are quite separate. Since this was the age of the great gatehouse, and Edward's other Gwynedd castles had at least one, the temptation must have existed to build a gatehouse across the narrow west end of the castle. It is difficult to say why it was resisted, unless James of St George was more concerned with overall symmetry.

Nevertheless it would be wrong to suggest that the absence of a proper gatehouse constitutes a source of weakness. Reaching the barbican would have been a major challenge to attackers in the first place. Once in this narrow space, they would be under attack from the main curtain. As a further compensation, this wall carries the boldly-projecting corbels of a machicolated parapet. Together with those on the east wall, they are probably the oldest machicolations in Britain. The gate passage is no longer than the thickness of the curtain, but that is still twelve feet, and thus ample space to have housed a portcullis and two pairs of gates. Together the two western towers probably formed the constable's residence, enabling him to control the main entrance to the castle as in a conventional gatehouse.

Inside, the castle is divided into two unequal parts by a cross-wall, the western two-thirds forming the outer ward. This courtyard is not quite oblong, because the south curtain bows outwards to embrace the summit of the rock. Since the great hall is built against this wall, it forms an oddly curved apartment. Conwy is the only one of Edward I's castles to have preserved its domestic buildings intact. The great hall, which was used by the constable and the thirty-strong garrison, survives intact although roofless. The original wooden roof rotted in the course of half a century, and the surviving stone roof arch is one of the eight inserted after 1343. Owing to the drop in ground level there is a narrow cellar beneath the southern half of the hall. The tower at the apex of the bend is aptly called the Prison Tower, its basement forming a grim prison which must have been reached by a trap-door from the floor above. Against the loop-holed north curtain are the foundations of a large kitchen, with the Kitchen Tower rising behind it. Originally the outer ward would have been a narrow passage between the kitchen and the hall. Even now it has a claustrophobic air, and the whole castle is very compact.

The ditch in front of the cross-wall is interrupted by an unusually large well which sinks ninety feet into the rock. A small barbican protects the gateway leading into the inner ward. This is a small quadrangle occupying the eastern third of the castle, and containing the royal apartments. They take up most of the available space, the only free corner once being occupied by a subsidiary building. Again the buildings are roofless but otherwise complete. They show that this strong castle accommodated a miniature palace, even though royal visits proved to be rare.

Edward's palace consists of two ranges at right-angles to each other, the main rooms standing above undercrofts. A private hall – much smaller than the great hall

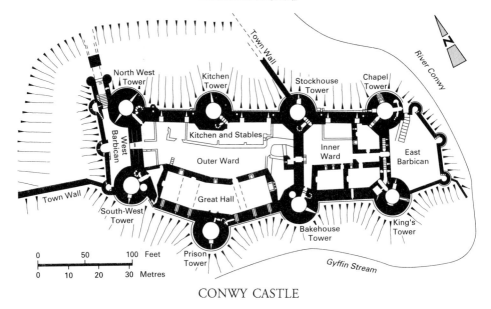

CONWY CASTLE

– occupies the south range, with a solar alongside. The east wing is believed to have housed the royal audience chamber. These rooms were lit by tall windows which preserve the stumps of intricate tracery. Extra accommodation was provided in the adjacent towers. The King's Tower at the south-east corner contained a suite of four private apartments leading off the solar (the other towers are three-storeyed). The Chapel Tower houses a round chapel at the level of the audience chamber, its sanctuary formed by a decorative recess in the thickness of the wall. At the western angles of the quadrangle are the Stockhouse and Bakehouse towers, their names revealing that this was the service end of the palace.

The palace could be reached without having to pass through the outer ward. A passage leads from the east wing into the Eastern Barbican. The main east front of the castle mirrors the west, with a central gateway closely flanked by the twin eastern towers of the castle. Machicolation corbels again threaten the ground, but a row of windows was allowed high up in this wall to light the audience chamber. The East Barbican, again with three flanking turrets, is more spacious than the western. It contained the royal garden. Steps descend to an entrance beside one of the turrets. Old drawings show that a wall descended the rock to a point of embarkation on the river bank. This was the private approach for kings and princes. In times of siege the castle could also have been supplied by sea this way. The steep drop at this end of the castle is obscured by the three bridges which now span the estuary. Thomas Telford's suspension road bridge of 1826, and Robert Stephenson's railway bridge built two decades later, are both castellated in deference to their surroundings.

Fortunately the castle is so well preserved that the wall-walk and most of the tower tops are accessible. From here there are spectacular views of the walled town, the estuary and the surrounding hills. The eight towers preserve their battlements.

Unlike Caernarfon the wall-walk is continuous, skirting around the towers to allow mobility under siege. At this level there is no significant barrier even between the two wards. The towers at the four corners of the inner ward are capped by watch turrets, a conceit which the four towers of the outer ward do not possess.

The upper floors of all the towers contained residential chambers, so they are well provided with latrines and fireplaces. Large windows lit these chambers with impunity, well out of reach of siege towers. Today only the Chapel Tower has a roof and floors, and these are modern replacements. The other towers are empty shells, but the only one to have sustained serious damage is the Bakehouse Tower. Much of its outer front collapsed long ago, but it is a testimony to the masonry that the upper part of the tower remained intact all round. The gaping hole was filled up in 1875, to prevent any further collapse onto the railway line below.

Conwy's excellent town wall encloses a roughly triangular area which seems to have been deliberately laid out in the shape of a Welsh harp. The wall is regularly flanked by twenty-one towers, mostly of the semi-circular, open-backed type which are usual on medieval town walls. They rise higher than the wall. In addition there are three gatehouses with twin flanking towers. The construction of the wall reflected the urgent prioritising which attended the foundation of a town for English settlers in hostile territory. First came the north-west and south-west sides of the circuit, which are undefended by nature. Then followed the south wall, afforded some natural protection by the Gyffin Brook. Finally the north-eastern stretch was built, overlooking the quay and the wide River Conwy estuary.

The castle occupies the east corner of the town enclosure. Springing from the Stockhouse Tower, the town wall descends the castle rock but is immediately interrupted by the only gap in the circuit. Sadly this was made as recently as 1958 to make way for a new road. Beyond a counterfeit tower added by Telford, the quayside wall begins in earnest. There is a postern beside the first genuine tower. A picturesque jumble of buildings lines the quay and obscures the wall to a large extent. We pass the Lower Gate, which has a house built into it. At the end of the quayside stretch a thick spur wall projects from the circuit and descends to the river, thus shielding the quay from the outside world. This spur wall, embattled on both sides, is pierced by a gateway which preserves its portcullis groove. Beyond the broken end of the spur wall a round tower once rose from the estuary, like the Water Tower at Chester, but was ultimately swept away by the current.

From here the wall-walk is accessible and can be followed all the way along the north-west side of the town. The wooden bridges spanning the gaps across the towers are modern, but they recall the original arrangement. In contrast to the castle, each tower broke the continuity of the wall-walk, as at Caernarfon. If attackers reached the parapet, the tower bridges on either side could be pulled away to isolate that portion of wall. On the inner face stone stairways ascend to each section of wall-walk.

All the gateways along this north-west stretch, including one cut through a flanking tower, are recent insertions. One tower has cracked badly owing to the railway tunnel beneath. Below the wall the broad ditch survives. The wall gradually climbs to its highest point, a circular tower crowning a rock at the acute west angle of the circuit. Then the wall descends steeply to the Upper Gate, the flanking towers of which are set at different levels owing to the slope. This gatehouse in preceded by one side wall of a barbican, while the gate passage preserves the evidence for a draw-bridge, a portcullis and a pair of gates. At this point the accessible stretch of wall-walk comes to an end. The wall continues to descend dramatically. This south-western stretch is particularly well preserved, its battlements still intact.

The town wall changes direction at the bottom of the hill. From here to the castle it fronts the Gyffin Brook, which skirts the castle rock before flowing into the estuary. The first tower along this southern stretch, unlike the other mural towers, has a back wall. It formed the chamber block of Llywelyn's Hall, which is attested by three windows cut through the town wall. This Welsh manor house was refurbished as a residence for Edward, the first English prince of Wales, after his investiture in 1301. The presence of a royal manor house in the town suggests a shortage of accommodation in the compact castle.

Beyond, the wall has been pierced to let the railway into the town, though the continuity of the parapet is maintained by an embattled Victorian arch. From here, the town wall has the railway line as its neighbour. The parapet of the next section is distinguished by twelve projections which look like individual machicolations. They are actually latrine chutes, built to serve the office of the King's Wardrobe which lay against the wall here. Next comes the Mill Gate, set in a re-entrant angle of the circuit. Because of its position, one tower is U-shaped but the other is round in order to flank the adjacent stretch of wall. The wall can be mounted again here, continu-ing past more open-backed towers until it rejoins the castle at the West Barbican.

The extent of the town suggests that Conwy was intended as the chief borough of Edward I's new principality, even if Caernarfon became the seat of government. Before its foundation the site was occupied by the abbey of Aberconwy, where Lly-welyn the Great was buried in 1240. Edward transferred this shrine of the Welsh princes to a new site at Maenan, further up the Conwy valley, and adapted the abbey church as the parish church of St Mary. It occupies the centre of the walled area. Aberconwy House is the only survivor of the merchants' dwellings which lined the streets of the medieval town, while Plas Mawr is an opulent town house of the Eliza-bethan period.

> *Access:* The castle is open daily. Long sections of the town wall parapet are accessible. (Both Cadw.)
>
> *Reference:* Guidebook by A. J. Taylor. RCAHMW *Caernarvonshire* (I). *HKW* (I).
>
> *Relations:* Its predecessor, Deganwy. The Edwardian castles in Gwynedd at Caernarfon (with accompanying town wall), Beaumaris and Harlech. Compare the spur wall at Chester.

CRICCIETH CASTLE crowns the summit of a rounded headland which juts into the sea, proudly looking down upon the little seaside town below. The castle is dominated by a twin-towered gatehouse, now all the more so owing to the complete ruination of the rest. There are sweeping views of the coastline up and down the Lleyn Peninsula, with Snowdonia in the distance.

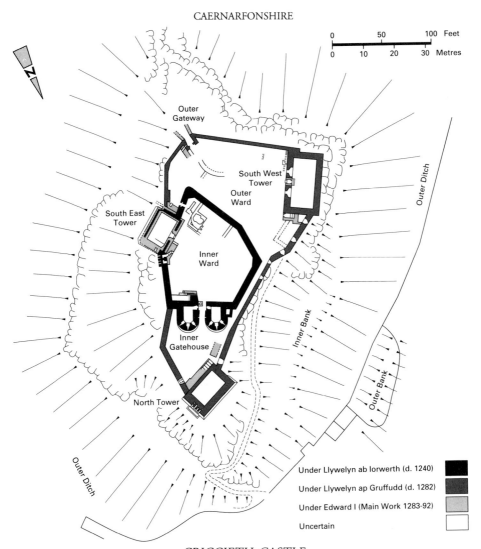

■	Under Llywelyn ab Iorwerth (d. 1240)
▨	Under Llywelyn ap Gruffudd (d. 1282)
▧	Under Edward I (Main Work 1283-92)
□	Uncertain

CRICCIETH CASTLE

Criccieth is no doubt one of the castles founded by Llywelyn the Great to consolidate his power in Gwynedd. It existed by 1239, when Llywelyn's son Gruffudd was imprisoned here. Edward I captured Criccieth in March 1283, during his invasion of Gwynedd. Although a series of new and grander castles was already under construction, Edward retained Criccieth as a link in the mighty chain around Gwynedd, complementing Harlech across Tremadog Bay. Its coastal position saved it from the abandonment suffered by the other native castles of Gwynedd. An English borough was founded to accompany the castle. In 1285–92 £319 was spent here – a trifling sum compared with Caernarfon, Conwy and Harlech. Another £245 followed during Edward II's reign.

The castle consists of a long, triangular enclosure with a small inner ward built across the middle, resulting in three courtyards. Much of the plain inner curtain still stands, but the outer wall has collapsed. Little more is left of the three oblong towers which guarded the outer curtain. On the east, overlooking the sea, the inner and outer curtains coalesce, but on the west there is a narrow corridor between them. The ascent from the town passes below the stump of the Engine Tower, named after a catapult which once stood on the roof. The gatehouse rises behind it, but there is no original entrance here. Although you can now jump over the foundations, it was originally necessary to run the gauntlet of the castle's long curtain and enter the outer ward through a small gate tower at the rear. To reach the inner ward, one then had to pass through the corridor between the two curtains, before reaching the small northern enclosure in front of the gatehouse. The castle was thus exceptionally tortuous to enter.

Criccieth is a mixture of different building campaigns, but there has been much debate about its construction. One theory is that the triangular enclosure formed Llywelyn the Great's original castle, into which the inner ward and gatehouse were inserted by Edward I. There are good reasons for supposing this, despite Edward's low recorded expenditure. The Mountfort Tower at the south-west corner is the largest and would have resembled Llywelyn's keep at Dolwyddelan. Furthermore the gatehouse, with its U-shaped towers closely flanking a long gate passage, is a smaller version of the keep-gatehouses of Harlech and Beaumaris. This kind of gatehouse was still rare in the 1230s, and Llywelyn's other castles have simple entrance gateways. Finally, the positioning of one courtyard within another is a loose example of concentric planning, which seems Edwardian. The main objection to this theory is that the Leyburn Tower, situated at the junction of the inner and outer curtains, is aligned with the inner curtain. Surely this would not have been the case had the outer curtain come first.

A study of the masonry confirms that the inner ward in fact represents Llywelyn the Great's original castle, probably built in the 1230s. Henry III's Montgomery no doubt inspired the gatehouse. Along with the round keep of Dolbadarn, it shows that Welsh castle building advanced a long way under Llywelyn. The outer ward and its towers were added later, probably under Llywelyn the Last. Square towers may seem old-fashioned for the mid-thirteenth century, but the masonry is of good quality and Llywelyn also built an oblong keep at Dolforwyn.

Edward I only heightened the oblong towers, so his contribution has vanished. The gatehouse was heightened under Edward II. Clearly discernible near the top is the original walled-up parapet, with arrow slits in the merlons. Thus strengthened, the castle held out during Madog ap Llywelyn's rebellion in 1294, obtaining supplies by sea. Circumstances were different during Owain Glyndwr's revolt. When the French blockaded the Irish Sea in 1404, relief was impossible and the castle was forced to surrender. Owain made nearby Harlech his capital, but Criccieth was superfluous to his needs. He seems to have slighted the castle to deny it to the English, and it was never re-occupied.

Access: Open daily in summer (Cadw).
Reference: Guidebook by R. Avent. RCAHMW *Caernarvonshire* (II). *HKW* (I).

Relations: Castles of the two Llywelyns at Dolbadarn, Dolwyddelan, Castell-y-Bere, Dol-forwyn and Ewloe. Compare the round-towered gatehouse at Montgomery.

DEGANWY CASTLE is marked by two splendid rocks to the east of the River Conwy estuary. This naturally defensive site was a seat of the Dark Age kings of Gwynedd. Robert de Rhuddlan established a castle here during his advance along the north Welsh coastline, perhaps as early as 1075. As a castle Deganwy had a chequered history, reflecting its position on the frontier between Gwynedd and the debatable lands to the east. Three times the Welsh destroyed the castle to prevent its use by the English. Llywelyn the Great first destroyed it in 1212, when King John invaded. Llywelyn recovered the site after John withdrew, and Deganwy became one of his new stone castles. He imprisoned his rebellious son Gruffudd here.

In 1241 the advancing English prompted Llywelyn's son Dafydd to dismantle the castle again. Henry III had it rebuilt in 1245–53. The substantial sum of £7,441 recorded in the Pipe Rolls includes the cost of the garrison, but building was also financed from the revenues of Ireland and the earldom of Chester. Known to the English as Gannock Castle, it was left incomplete. Llywelyn the Last failed to capture the castle when he overran the lands east of the Conwy in 1257, but he succeeded in 1263 as a result of the baronial unrest in England. He did not attempt to hold it, and so the castle was destroyed for a third time. Edward I camped in the ruins when he invaded, but he decided to build Conwy Castle on the other side of the estuary.

The two natural 'mottes' flank a lower ward which is bounded by a ditch. Unfortunately the substantial stone defences have been reduced to a few fragments. Henry III's mighty gatehouse, guarding the southern entrance to the lower ward, is represented by a fragment from one of the twin flanking towers. There is a chunk of a smaller gate tower on the north, but excavations have shown that this side was never walled in stone. Henry built a large, U-shaped keep (Mansell's Tower) on the conical eastern hill, but it has disappeared. The western hill is much the larger of the two. A hazardous climb is rewarded by fine views of Conwy and the estuary. This upper ward was surrounded by a low curtain, which survives in a very ruinous state on the north and west. It dates largely from Henry III's rebuilding, but the stretch containing a solid, half-round turret is a relic of Llywelyn the Great's castle. A fine carved head found here (now in the National Museum of Wales in Cardiff) may represent Llywelyn.

Access: Freely accessible.
Reference: RCAHMW *Caernarvonshire* (I). *HKW* (II).
Relations: Its successor, Conwy. Compare Robert de Rhuddlan's original castle at Rhuddlan and Henry III's Montgomery.

DOLBADARN CASTLE stands at Llanberis on the edge of Snowdonia, guarding the route through the Pass of Llanberis. The site is a narrow outcrop of rock with steep falls on all sides, especially the east, where there is a sheer drop to the Llyn Padarn. The outcrop forms a wide triangle with a slightly concave main axis, so that the plan resembles a boomerang. Like the other native castles of Arfon we have no record of its construction. Two main building phases are evident, but it is likely that the whole castle is the work of Llywelyn the Great. The circular keep, still virtually complete, contrasts with the drystone curtain and residential buildings, which are now reduced to their footings.

The keep is an addition, so we will ignore it temporarily and examine the low walls covering the rest of the site. They consist of unmortared layers of slate. The outcrop is enclosed by straight lengths of curtain, which are thicker on the comparatively vulnerable west side. An oblong structure, rather thin-walled for a tower, stood at the southern apex of the castle. A more substantial rectangular tower guarded the middle of the long west curtain. A third tower may have crowned the rock at the northern tip, but nothing remains here. The hall lay across the north end of the courtyard. Another large domestic building, near the keep, is a later insertion because it projects beyond the original line of the curtain. There is no trace of the original entrance – it may have occupied the destroyed portion of the western curtain. By and large the enclosure seems to be an early work of Llywelyn (before 1200). It is built as crudely as his uncle's Castell Garn Fadrun.

Llywelyn's years of alternately fighting and allying with the English barons are reflected in the keep. It was added on the line of the east curtain, probably in the 1230s. The keep is a worthy companion to those being erected by both English and Welsh lords in South Wales. Admittedly it should be compared with the smaller round keeps and not with the great tower of Pembroke. The keep is a perfect cylinder except for a projecting latrine turret. A restored flight of steps against the plinth curves up to the first-floor entrance. The doorway was defended by a portcullis – an unusually sophisticated touch in a keep.

All three floors of the keep were equipped with fireplaces and latrines. It is strange that the basement has these features, since no windows pierce the wall in the vulnerable base of the tower. Presumably this chamber was reached by a ladder from the floor above. Windows light the two upper floors, notably the large pointed window in the top storey which gives the keep its peculiarly forlorn appearance. A narrow spiral stair (the only one in a native Welsh tower) connects these two floors and continues to the vanished parapet. The walls rose high enough to conceal the roof and protect it from combustible missiles.

The keep at Dolbadarn vies with the gatehouse at Criccieth as Llywelyn the Great's finest piece of castle architecture. Llywelyn the Last kept his elder brother Owain Goch prisoner here, following his seizure of sole power in 1255. For twenty-two years he was probably incarcerated in the keep, only being released as Edward I's behest in 1277. Then came the English invasion of Gwynedd. Llywelyn's brother Dafydd was here in May 1283, so Dolbadarn must have been the last Welsh castle to fall. We do not know if it put up any resistance, but there was no role for remote Dolbadarn in Edward's principality. In 1284 timber was taken away for use in the new works at nearby Caernarfon, and the castle came to the end of its short life. It is a testimony to the improving skill of Llywelyn the Great's masons that the keep has survived such a long period of abandonment.

Access: Always open (Cadw).

Reference: Guidebook by R Avent (includes Dolwyddelan).
Relations: Llywelyn the Great's castles of Criccieth, Deganwy, Dolwyddelan and Castell-y-Bere. Compare the native round keep at Dinefwr.

DOLWYDDELAN CASTLE   is the traditional birthplace of Llywelyn the Great c. 1173. The oblong keep looks typical of the Norman keeps which prevailed in England at that time. However, stone castle building came late to Gwynedd under its native rulers and the existing castle cannot have stood then. In the valley to the south-east is a rocky knoll known as Tomen Castell. Excavations have revealed a primitive square tower on its tree-clad summit. This may have been built by Llywelyn's father Iorwerth, and is thus more likely to be the birthplace.

There can be little doubt that it was Llywelyn who made the move to this stronger site. The castle, midway between Betws-y-Coed and Blaenau Ffestiniog, overlooks the winding A470 which cuts through Snowdonia. It occupies a ridge, with deep ditches cutting off the gentler slopes to north and south. The small, D-shaped courtyard was enclosed by a curtain which is now largely reduced to its footings. Thankfully the keep, dramatically perched on the edge of a precipice, is more substantial. It was probably built soon after 1200 and was thus becoming old-fashioned by English standards. Although other Welsh princes continued to build oblong keeps, Llywelyn himself later adopted the new trend for round towers.

As usual in the native Welsh castles, the entrance was a simple gateway through the curtain. Beside it are the ruins of a second rectangular tower (the West Tower). Only its courtyard front still stands. This tower housed a great hall at first-floor level, and the large fireplace which heated it can still be seen. It supplemented the rather spartan hall in the keep. The West Tower is an addition, most probably by Llywelyn the Last, although construction of a new chamber is recorded after Edward I captured the castle in January 1283. Edward intended to retain the castle as an English outpost. However, it wasn't garrisoned for long, perhaps only until the revolt of 1294, since relief under siege must have proved impossible in the wilds of Snowdonia.

The keep is still intact, but only as the result of a drastic restoration in 1848. At this time Welsh nationalism was rekindling after centuries of suppression, and Llywelyn the Great's traditional birthplace had become a national shrine. The keep is entered through a doorway at first-floor level, reached by a staircase against the wall. A small porch (forebuilding) guarded the entrance but only the stump remains. At the top of the steps a wooden bridge crosses a gap which was originally spanned by a drawbridge. Within the keep the entrance floor forms a single large hall. The wall furthest away from the entrance contains a narrow passage leading to a latrine, though this side has largely been rebuilt. The room beneath was a dank cellar, presumably reached by a trap-door and ladder from the floor above.

Llywelyn's keep was a squat affair of only two storeys. Later, perhaps under Edward I, the parapet was raised to shield the roof from combustible missiles. It was probably here in 1402 that Owain Glyndwr imprisoned his old enemy, Reginald de Grey of Ruthin. Then in 1488 the Welsh nobleman Maredudd ap Ievan re-occupied the derelict keep and converted the roof space into a third floor. Maredudd did not try to make the keep more accessible, because life was still dangerous here at the end of the Middle Ages. The intervening floor was not restored in 1848 so the interior is now one tall room, crowned by a Victorian roof. A straight stair leads in the thickness of the wall to the parapet. The battlements which give the keep its distinctive profile, and the projecting drains, date entirely from the restoration.

Access: Open daily (Cadw – uphill walk).
Reference: Guidebook by R. Avent (includes Dolbadarn).
Relations: Llywelyn's castles of Criccieth, Deganwy, Dolbadarn and Castell-y-Bere.

PENRHYN CASTLE   This immense castellated pile, just outside Bangor, is a neo-Norman mansion built in 1827–37 by Thomas Hopper for George Dawkins Pennant. The wealth he had accumulated in the slate industry is evident in the incredibly opulent interior, while the exterior of this romantic revival castle is dominated by a square 'keep' with corner turrets. It is modelled on the great Norman keep at Rochester Castle and much grander than any genuine Norman keep in Wales. However, the castle incorporates something of the fifteenth-century fortified manor house which preceded it. This house, extolled in a contemporary poem, was built by Gwilym ap Gruffudd, the foremost Welsh nobleman of his day. His widow Joan obtained a licence to crenellate or embattle Penrhyn in 1438 – a rare example of a licence being granted to a woman. The house was built around a square courtyard, which is now represented by the grand staircase. Much of the masonry of the surrounding state rooms is old beneath a nineteenth-century veneer, and an original spiral staircase can be seen off the drawing room. Despite the licence it is likely that the only defensive feature was a tower house (now vanished) in one corner.

Access: Open regularly in summer (NT).
Reference: NT guidebook.
Relations: The surviving Welsh tower house at Broncoed and the Norman keep at Rochester (Kent).

OTHER SITES   Some native Welsh earthworks should be mentioned. The motte at *Dolbenmaen* was probably the seat of the lords of Eifionydd before Criccieth Castle was built. Likewise the motte known as *Ty Newydd*, west of Llannor, may be the forerunner of Castell Garn Fadrun. Another is *Bryn Castell*, above the River Conwy facing Tal-y-Cafn, while *Tomen Fawr* (near Llanystumdwy) is a ringwork. Some drystone walling on the rock of *Pen-y-Castell*, near Maenan, may represent a crude masonry stronghold contemporary with Castell Garn Fadrun.

Cardiganshire

Gilbert de Clare invaded Ceredigion in 1110, raising earthwork castles at Aberrheidol, Cardigan and Ystrad Meurig. They were taken over by the Welsh of Gwynedd during the Anarchy. Caer Penrhos is a striking native ringwork, though Norman motte-and-baileys such as Castell Gwallter are more common. A brief Norman revival ended when the Lord Rhys recovered the lost territory of Deheubarth. After his death Deheubarth fragmented and Ceredigion again came under the sway of Gwynedd. Cardigan was much fought over, but the remains of the Marshals' stone castle there are not very telling. The only other masonry castle is Aberystwyth, one of those built by Edward I to consolidate his conquests of 1277. Though a good example of concentric fortification, it is unfortunately the most ruined of Edward's mighty chain of castles.

ABERRHEIDOL CASTLE   This is what the forerunner of Aberystwyth Castle is usually called, owing to a single documentary reference. However, there has been a curious transposition of names, because its grassy ramparts look down from a ridge above the Afon Ystwyth, not the Rheidol which paradoxically runs through Aberystwyth. It is a ringwork-and-bailey site. The castle is one of several raised by Gilbert de Clare when he invaded Ceredigion in 1110. His dynasty would play a leading part in the invasions of Wales and Ireland.

Excavations have shown that the ramparts, originally lined with timber, were later cased in stone. The history of the castle is a stormy one, reflecting the tenuous existence of this Norman enclave in a resolutely Welsh part of Wales. Owain Gwynedd destroyed the castle in 1136 after defeating the Normans at Crug Mawr. Roger de Clare re-occupied the site in 1158, only to lose it to the Lord Rhys six years later. The castle changed hands at least five times in the early thirteenth century, in struggles between Deheubarth, Gwynedd and the English. It was finally captured by Llewelyn the Great in 1221. He probably destroyed it, since the record is then silent until Edward I commenced the new Aberystwyth Castle a mile to the north.

> *Access:* On private land.
> *Reference: Archaeologia Cambrensis* (CXXVI).
> *Relations:* Its successor, Aberystwyth. Gilbert de Clare's castles at Cardigan and Ystrad Meurig.

ABERYSTWYTH CASTLE   Standing as it does at the mouth of the Afon Rheidol rather than the Ystwyth, the town seems inappropriately named. The name Aberystwyth was probably derived from the Norman ringwork nearby, which is now confusingly known as Aberrheidol. It only came to be applied to the present castle and town in the fifteenth century. Prior to that they were known as Llanbadarn, after the inland church of Llanbadarn Fawr. This was one of the royal castles of

Edward I's invasion of 1277. His brother Edmund 'Crouchback', earl of Lancaster, arrived in July and immediately began building. It was intended to contain Gwynedd from the south just as Flint and Rhuddlan would from the east. These castles suffered a heavy slighting after the Civil War, but Aberystwyth is the most ruined of the three. Of all Edward's Welsh castles only Builth has fared worse.

Like Rhuddlan, Aberystwyth is a concentric castle. Furthermore, it is the only one of Edward's first group to have a fully developed Edwardian keep-gatehouse. Such features are associated with Edward's famous master mason, James of St George, but he was engaged at Rhuddlan and Flint during the main years of construction and seems to have played no part in its design.

The building of the castle was hampered by delays and complaints of shoddy workmanship. It was still incomplete when Dafydd ap Gruffudd's rebellion broke out in 1282. The Welsh burnt the new town and stormed the castle in a surprise attack. James of St George, now Master of the King's Works in Wales, did visit to assess the damage, but left reconstruction in the hands of his compatriot, Giles of St George. Work dragged on until 1289. If the reported destruction is to be believed much needed to be done, but most of the £3,885 recorded in the Pipe Rolls comes before 1282. Even this figure is surprisingly low compared with the cost of Flint and Rhuddlan. Aberystwyth may have received a portion of the £9,400 spent at various un-named sites in Wales after the conquest of Gwynedd. The expenditure must be stretched still further because, alone among the new boroughs founded in 1277, Aberystwyth was given a stone town wall. Nothing remains of it now, but chance finds have confirmed its existence.

After the repairs of the 1280s the castle was ready for its next test. It held out for several months in 1294 when blockaded by Madog ap Llywelyn, who briefly threatened to overturn Edward's conquest. However, the most intense military activity took place during Owain Glyndwr's revolt, when the castle was besieged four times. Having resisted an attack by Owain in 1401, it fell after a long siege three years later, when supply by sea had been thwarted by a French fleet in the Irish Sea. Harlech fell around the same time, making Owain the master of central Wales. Aberystwyth resisted a pounding from the primitive cannon of the young Prince Henry in 1406 – the first recorded use of firearms in Wales. However, prolonged sieges resulted in the recovery of both castles during the winter of 1408–09. The castle distinguished itself in another long siege during the Civil War, but it was eventually compelled to surrender to the overwhelming might of parliament (April 1646). It suffered a severe slighting a few years later.

As befits this seaside town, the castle overlooks the beach. Owing to the slighting only a few fragments stand to any appreciable height, but considerable portions have been excavated and the footings left exposed. They reveal a diamond-shaped castle with a double line of walls. Much of the concentric outer wall survives, though it is just a low screen wall designed to shield the main curtain from attack. Round towers guard the acute north and south angles. The entrance from the town is through a twin-towered gatehouse on the east, a miniature version of the main gatehouse immediately behind. As usual in a concentric castle, the outer ward is just a narrow strip of ground between the two curtains.

The inner curtain was a much more massive construction. It was basically four-sided, but the eastern half of the enclosure formed a curved front with the keep-gatehouse in the centre. The gatehouse must have resembled Edward's later gatehouse at Harlech, comprising a long gate passage between round-fronted towers. Its upper floors no doubt contained the constable's residence. Unfortunately most of the gatehouse is reduced to its footings, with only the front of one of the flanking towers standing high. Between the gatehouse and the round South Tower are the foundations of the hall. Midway along the south-west curtain is the base of a U-shaped tower. The other two angle towers have disappeared, but a half-round tower between them survives intact because it was preserved as a landmark for shipping. It is pierced by a gate passage, in line with the base of a twin-towered gateway through the outer curtain. This leads onto a promontory, where the war memorial now stands.

Access: Freely accessible (LA).
Reference: The Castle and Borough of Aberystwyth by C. J. Spurgeon. *HKW* (I). GAHW *Dyfed.*
Relations: Castles of Edward I's 1277 campaign at Builth, Flint and Rhuddlan. Rhuddlan is concentric, along with his later castles of Harlech and Beaumaris.

CAER PENRHOS is a mighty ringwork set astride the rampart of an Iron Age hillfort. Its elevated position above Llanrhystud is a good example of the defensive sites favoured by native Welsh castle builders. The *Chronicle of the Princes* tells us that the castle was raised in 1148 by Owain Gwynedd's brother, Cadwaladr ap Gruffudd, showing that the rulers of Gwynedd already had territorial ambitions beyond their principality. Its short and stormy history reflects the in-fighting among the Welsh as much as their conflict with the Normans. Owain's son Hywell wrested it from his uncle, only to be ejected by the Lord Rhys of Deheubarth. He in turn was forced to withdraw during Roger de Clare's campaign of 1158. Although the Lord Rhys soon recovered Ceredigion, there is no further mention of the castle.

Access: On private land.
Reference: Ceredigion (III).
Relations: Hillfort castle sites such as Castell Garn Fadrun, Cefnllys and Castell Dinas.

CARDIGAN CASTLE, once an important stronghold, is now a disappointment. Arnulf de Montgomery raised a castle nearby on his expedition to Pembroke in 1093. This is the Old Castle earthwork, which still survives a mile further down the River Teifi. Gilbert de Clare re-established Norman rule in 1110, only to lose it after Owain Gwynedd's victory at Crug Mawr in 1136. His grandson Roger took possession again in 1158. It may have been at either date that the present site was chosen. However, six years later Roger was ejected by the Lord Rhys. He skilfully ruled an independent Deheubarth and made Cardigan his chief seat. Rhys rebuilt the castle in stone (1171), but nothing survives of this first native stone castle of Wales. The golden age of Welsh rule ended when Rhys' son Maelgwn, motivated by fear of Llywelyn the Great, sold the castle to King John. It fell to Llywelyn during the Magna Carta war, but was retaken in 1223 by William Marshal the Younger. Llywelyn's supporters captured the castle again in 1231, using catapults to batter the walls. Its recovery by the Marshals in 1240 brought to an end more than a century of hotly-contested ownership.

Henry III assumed control of this strategically important castle, spending £684 here during the ensuing decades. This sum cannot account for much more than the round keep which Henry is known to have built here. It is likely that the curtain had already been built by the Marshals before the siege of 1231. The royal constable, Robert Waleran, also claimed £150 for providing a wall around the town, but nothing of that remains. Cardigan Castle was substantial enough to warrant no improvements under Edward I, but was in a deplorable condition when the Welsh royal castles were surveyed in 1343. Nevertheless it was garrisoned strongly enough to deter Owain Glyndwr, and substantial repairs were carried out after the collapse of his revolt. The castle was slighted after its capture by parliamentary forces in 1644. Castle House was built into the ruins in the nineteenth century, the bailey becoming its garden.

One might have expected more in this pleasant old town, but the castle is a sadly neglected site. It was an elongated enclosure, probably once divided into inner and outer baileys. A long stretch of curtain still delimits the south end of the enclosure, but this plain wall is now capped by phoney battlements. In places it is shored up by steel braces. One tapering, semi-circular bastion projects near the bridge over the Teifi. The outer bailey is an overgrown wilderness, while the inner is marked by the derelict Castle House. Attached to it is the stump of a round mural tower rising from a square base. This cannot be the 'great round tower' built by Henry III. It seems that Cardigan had a round keep second only to Pembroke, but its site awaits discovery. Excavations would reveal a great deal.

Access: No admission, but the curtain is visible from the road.
Reference: The History and Antiquities of the County of Cardigan by S. R. Meyrick. *HKW* (II).
Relations: The Marshal castles of Cilgerran, Pembroke, Chepstow and Usk. See Henry III's work at Deganwy and Montgomery.

CASTELL GWALLTER is an impressive motte-and-bailey castle, commandingly sited half a mile west of Llandre. The motte is isolated by a ditch and a surrounding rampart. Beyond the small inner bailey there is an outer enclosure, naturally defended by steep slopes to the north and east. The castle is attributed to Walter de Bec, one of Gilbert de Clare's tenants. Owain Gwynedd captured the castle in 1136, but lost it to the young Lord Rhys and his brothers in 1153. They may have destroyed the castle because there is no further record of it.

Access: The castle is reached via a public footpath.
Reference: Archaeologia Cambrensis (XCIX).
Relations: Motte-and-bailey castles such as Tomen-y-Bala, Tomen-y-Mur, Castell Allt-y-Ferin and Pencader.

YSTRAD MEURIG CASTLE occupies a promontory overlooking the village church. The vulnerable north-east side is cut off by a ditch. A substantial oblong keep commanded the approach, its buried foundations still visible in the turf. Gilbert de Clare raised a castle here when he invaded Ceredigion in 1110, although that may have been the motte of Cwm Meurig a mile to the east. It is not certain when the move to this site occurred. In 1136 the Welsh stormed whichever castle was then in use, and Roger de Clare's re-occupation in 1158 was brief. The castle fell into the hands of the Lord Rhys, who founded nearby Strata Florida Abbey, but his son Maelgwn destroyed it in 1208 to thwart Llywelyn the Great. The keep may have been built by the Clares or the Lord Rhys, or even by one of Rhys' grandsons who re-fortified the site.

> *Access:* Visible from the road.
> *Reference: Ceredigion* (I).
> *Relations:* The de Clare castles of Aberrheidol, Cardigan and Pencader.

OTHER SITES A number of motte-and-bailey sites recall the struggle for dominance between Deheubarth, Gwynedd and the Normans:

Caerwedros Motte
Castell Gwythan (Blaenporth)
Castell Pistog (near Henllan)
Cwm Meurig Motte (near Ystrad Meurig)
Dinierth Castle (near Aberarth)
Domen Las (Abereinion)
Humphrey's Castle (near Pontshaen)
Lampeter Castle
Llwyndyris Motte (near Llandygwydd)
Manian Fawr Motte (near St Dogmaels)
Tomen Llanio (near Tregaron)
Ystrad Peithyl Castle (near Aberystwyth)

Cardigan Old Castle, raised by Arnulf de Montgomery during his invasion in 1093, is a rectangular earthwork on the Teifi estuary, a mile from the later castle and town. *Castell Gwynionydd* (near Llandysul) and *Tomen Rhydowen* at Rhydowen are ringworks. Some earthworks overlooking Llanilar mark the site of *Pen-y-Castell*, raised by one of the Lord Rhys' grandsons.

Carmarthenshire

Henry I encouraged Norman and Flemish settlers to south-west Wales. They established a chain of castles at the river mouths, venturing with less success further inland. St Clears, Pencader and Castell Allt-y-Ferin are good examples of the numerous motte-and-baileys, while Norman ringworks underlie the later stone castles of Kidwelly and Llansteffan. A royal presence was maintained in the important but now incomplete castle at Carmarthen. Further up the River Tywi lay the remaining native part of Deheubarth, which the Lord Rhys made a force to be reckoned with. His successors divided the principality between themselves in the thirteenth century.

They emulated their English neighbours by building stone castles. Dryslwyn and Newcastle Emlyn are now fragmentary, but Dinefwr, with its circular keep and towered curtain, is the best preserved of all the native Welsh castles.

Nevertheless the most ambitious castles in the county date from the Edwardian period, when Marcher territory expanded at the expense of conquered Deheubarth. Kidwelly is the finest of the group, the original towered quadrangle being strengthened by the earl of Lancaster with a concentric outer wall and a mighty gatehouse. He also walled the little town. Llansteffan is nearly as impressive, while the ruins of Laugharne have been Tudorised. John Giffard rebuilt two of the native strongholds: Llandovery is now very ruinous but his great castle of Carreg Cennen, crowning a rock, is one of the strongest castles in Wales. The other native castles were strengthened by the king. At both Dryslwyn and Newcastle Emlyn the best-preserved portions are Edwardian additions, while Dinefwr was given a new hall. Carmarthen's gatehouse was rebuilt after Owain Glyndwr's revolt.

CARMARTHEN CASTLE Unusually for South Wales, this castle was founded by an English king and remained a Crown possession for most of its history. The first castle of Rhyd-y-Gors, raised in 1095 after the Normans first stormed into Deheubarth, stood further down the Tywi estuary. It had a brief life, being destroyed when the Welsh counter-attacked the following year. Henry I established the present castle beside an abandoned Roman town soon after 1100. Although it changed hands several times during the Anarchy, the castle resisted the Lord Rhys in three sieges. Henry II spent £170 on improvements in 1181–83 – a sum large enough to imply some masonry. Llywelyn the Great captured Carmarthen along with much of Deheubarth during the Magna Carta war. It remained in his hands until the younger William Marshal, earl of Pembroke, recovered the territory in 1223. Ten years later William's recalcitrant brother Richard failed to take the castle when he joined forces with Llywelyn.

The castle was walled under William and Gilbert Marshal, with additions by Henry III after he resumed royal control in 1241. Edward I made it the seat of the justiciar for South Wales. English rule suffered an interruption under Owain Glyndwr. Its capture in 1403 prompted Henry IV to recover it in person. Owain took Carmarthen again with the help of his French allies in 1405 and held it for four years, after which £380 was spent under Henry IV as part of a general strengthening of the royal castles in the south-west. Town and castle fell to the Lancastrians during the Wars of the Roses, then changed hands twice in the Civil War. Although the defences were slighted by parliament, the castle retained its administrative role. The bailey housed the county gaol for centuries and is now filled by the grandiose County Hall (1938).

Overlooking the bridge across the River Tywi, the castle comprised a large, roughly square bailey. Three sides have disappeared and only some ruins of the west front remain – even these are largely obscured by later buildings. Such accretions were once common in decaying urban castles, but they have usually been cleared away. Best preserved is the gatehouse in the middle of the front. This is actually the latest part of the defences, rebuilt by Henry IV after the recovery of the castle in 1409. Externally it is complete up to the corbelled parapet, with a row of machicolations projecting on corbels above the gateway. Though still a round-towered gatehouse in the Edwardian tradition, it is a comparatively modest structure which cost no more than £100 to build.

The other remains can only be seen from a narrow passage behind the curtain. It is bounded by an inner wall which was added for greater security when the castle was used as a gaol. A stretch of the Marshals' curtain links the gatehouse to an irregular keep at the north-west corner of the bailey. This is a small enclosure of the shell keep type, though here the keep encases the Norman motte instead of rising from its summit. It is usually attributed to the Marshals because of the two rounded projections, but the form of the keep makes Henry II just as likely a builder. South of the gatehouse the curtain has perished, but the circular south-west corner tower survives. It rises from a massive square base with pyramid spurs. Such spurs are a feature of Edwardian castles in South Wales, so this tower is probably a result of Edward I's expenditure in 1288. Close by are the footings of a square mural tower.

Carmarthen and Caerwent were the only two Roman towns of Wales. It is likely that the Roman town wall still stood when Henry I established his castle, and a new town grew up within it. Rebuilding took place from 1233, making Carmarthen the first medieval Welsh town to invest in stone defences. Nothing remains of the town wall now, but west of the castle can be seen part of a larger earthwork circuit raised by the Royalists during the Civil War. The borough was wealthy enough to have several monastic houses, but St Peter's is the only medieval church remaining.

Access: Freely accessible (LA).
Reference: RCAHMW *Carmarthenshire* (under St Peter's). GAHW *Dyfed. HKW* (II).
Relations: Compare Henry II's work at White Castle, and Henry IV's at Kidwelly. Llawhaden has a similar gatehouse.

CARREG CENNEN CASTLE, five miles south-east of Llandeilo, is a powerful Edwardian fortress. It is all the stronger for its breathtaking situation on the edge of a great limestone crag in the foothills of the Black Mountains. Such a setting is more typical of native Welsh castle building. The princes of Deheubarth had a castle on the site, though nothing is left of it. It may have been established by the Lord Rhys. A castle certainly existed here by 1248, when his grandson Rhys Fychan wrested it from the English. It frequently changed hands between Rhys and his uncle Maredudd, who were fighting for control of Deheubarth, then succumbed to Edward I during the invasion of 1277. Later risings in 1282 and 1287 resulted in temporary seizures by the Welsh.

In 1283 Edward granted the castle and its lordship to John Giffard, who had commanded the English at the skirmish of Cilmeri where Llewelyn the Last was killed. It is perhaps surprising that he should choose to build his new castle here, when other inaccessible Welsh castles were being abandoned, but its impregnable position must have appealed to this hardened soldier. As a baronial stronghold we

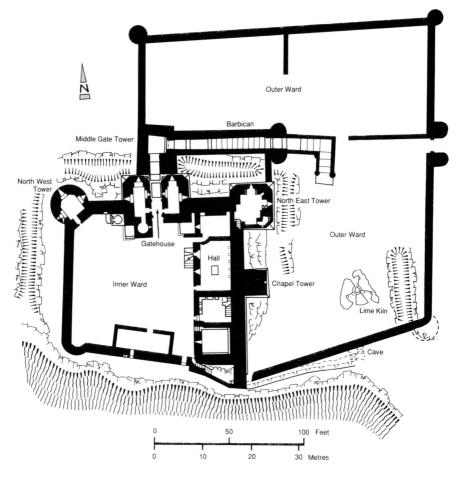

CARREG CENNEN CASTLE

have no record of its construction, which is a pity, because building a major stone castle here must have been quite an achievement.

John Giffard's inner ward, square and compact, stands on the summit of the crag. It was probably complete by the time he died in 1299. Though still impressive, the ensemble is quite ruinous and presents an erratic skyline. On the north and east, where the approach is merely steep rather than sheer, the main castle is fronted by an outer ward. This is an early addition to the fabric and may be the work of Giffard's son, another John. The outer curtain is now reduced to its footings, along with the round turrets which guarded the corners and the outer gate. It is parallel to the inner curtain, but the walls are too far apart to be classed as a concentric defence.

The mural towers of the inner curtain are also concentrated on the comparatively vulnerable north and east. Rising from the rock at the north-west corner is the only circular tower, now rather squat because it has lost its upper part. A short stretch of curtain connects with the gatehouse, which bore the brunt of the later slighting.

Hence one of its semi-octagonal flanking towers survives almost to full height but the other has been broken down. For the north-east corner tower John Giffard departed from Edwardian convention in favour of a square plan, though the corners are canted off. Both this and the gatehouse towers have pyramid spurs at the bases. Such spurs were a common feature in the Edwardian castles of South Wales, designed to be proof against mining. Midway along the east front projects the smaller Chapel Tower, again square but solid in its lower half. There is no tower at the south end of this eastern front, the high curtain terminating abruptly at the cliff. No windows were permitted through the towers or curtain, but there are numerous cross-slits.

Carreg Cennen has the most elaborately defended entrance of any Welsh castle, because the gatehouse can only be reached by a long stone ramp forming a complex barbican. Attackers would have needed to beat down the outer gate in the shadow of the North-East Tower, before turning a corner and ascending the ramp, exposed all the way to arrow-fire from the parapet. Modern bridges cross the two drawbridge pits. The ramp ends in a square gate tower (now very ruinous), from which there is another right-angled turn across another drawbridge pit before reaching the gatehouse proper. This gatehouse has the usual long entrance passage, once guarded at either end by gates and a portcullis. It could thus be sealed off from the rest of the castle in true keep-gatehouse style. However, defensive mobility was catered for, because mural passages link the gatehouse with the corner towers.

Internally the castle seems rather empty, though no doubt there were once buildings on all sides. Only meagre ruins survive of the main residential apartments against the east curtain. A central hall was flanked by the solar and kitchen. The main rooms stood at first-floor level above cellars – note the flight of steps which led to the hall entrance. All the windows must have faced the courtyard. Even the little chapel in the upper part of the Chapel Tower was lit, appropriately enough, only by cross-slits. A second chamber beyond the solar survives, with a window facing the courtyard and another overlooking the cliff. Described in a survey of 1369 as the King's Chamber, the room probably housed important guests.

The south and west sides of the curtain are thinner and lack mural towers, except for a shallow projection at the junction. On these sides nature offered the chief defence – a low cliff on the west and a precipitous drop of three hundred feet to the south. The south curtain survives up to its corbelled parapet. Steps descend from the south-east corner of the courtyard to a long, vaulted passage on the edge of the precipice. It leads to a natural cavern in the rock. There must have been a good reason for this passage but it has been forgotten. A theory that the cavern held the castle's main water supply seems unfounded. Even the cleft in the cliff face was walled up to deny this toe-hold to assailants.

The second John Giffard was executed in 1322 for joining the Marcher barons' attack on the king's favourite, Hugh le Despenser the Younger. Ironically the forfeited lands were awarded to Hugh, but only until Edward II's overthrow a few years later. In 1340 the castle was granted to the earl of Lancaster, becoming royal with Henry of Bolingbroke's usurpation in 1399.

So far John Giffard's castle had never been put to the test, and when the time came there was no will to defend it. The castle was abandoned to Owain Glyndwr, who appears to have deliberately dismantled it. It was reported to be 'completely destroyed and thrown down'. No doubt this was an exaggeration, but Henry V spent over £500 on repairs, which implies some considerable patching up. A single gun port in the circular tower may belong to this restoration. At that time there were fears that the French might land in south-west Wales and foment another revolt. However, Carreg Cennen's revival was short-lived. After Edward IV seized the throne the castle became a refuge for Lancastrian outcasts. As a result of their raids, Sir William Herbert sent five hundred men to demolish the castle once again in 1462. This slighting was achieved with picks and crowbars.

Access: Open daily (Cadw).
Reference: Guidebook by J. M. Lewis.
Relations: John Giffard's castle at Llandovery. Towers with spur bases at Carew, Caerphilly, Chepstow and Goodrich (Herefordshire).

CASTELL ALLT-Y-FERIN occupies the end of a ridge above the River Cothi, two miles north of Llanegwad. The triangular enclosure, divided into two by a cross-ditch, is naturally defended by steep falls on two sides. A ditch and rampart cut off the level approach, overlooked by a conical motte which is encircled by its own ditch. This impressive earthwork may be the castle of Dinweiler, raised by Gilbert de Clare, earl of Pembroke, in 1145 during a brief period of Norman expansion into Welsh Deheubarth. The castle does not appear in recorded history after that, although it may have been occupied by the princes of Deheubarth until nearby Dryslwyn Castle was built.

Access: On private land.
Reference: RCAHMW *Carmarthenshire.*
Relations: The de Clare castles at Pencader, Aberrheidol and Ystrad Meurig.

DINEFWR CASTLE, a mile west of Llandeilo, occupies a crag overlooking the River Tywi. Here lay the ancestral 'capital' of the princes of Deheubarth. The ruins constitute the best-preserved native castle in Wales. A castle existed here by 1163 and the surrounding curtain is sometimes attributed to the Lord Rhys, but the masonry looks rather accomplished for a native prince of the twelfth century. In any case Rhys made Cardigan his chief seat, and Dinefwr only returned to prominence under his feuding sons. One of them, Rhys Grug, was driven out of the castle by the English, but Llywelyn the Great restored him. In 1220 Rhys Grug ungratefully dismantled the castle to prevent it falling into Llywelyn's hands. It is likely that the present round keep and curtain were built by his grandson, Rhys Fychan, in the mid-thirteenth century. He fought with his uncle, Maredudd ap Rhys, for mastery over Deheubarth despite the growing threat from both Gwynedd and the English. Dinefwr shows that Rhys was learning the art of castle building from his Marcher neighbours. He even took the alien step of planting a native town outside.

By 1257 the castle was substantial enough to alarm Henry III, who despatched

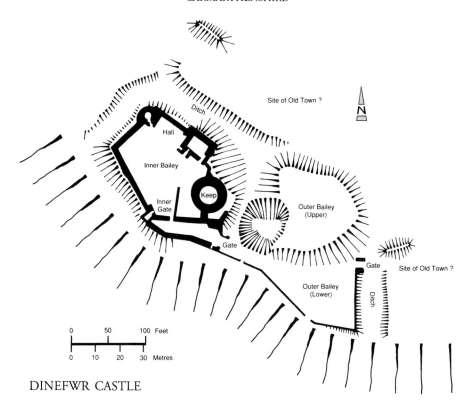

Site of Old Town ?

N

Ditch

Hall

Inner Bailey

Inner
Gate

Keep

Outer Bailey
(Upper)

Gate

Gate   Site of Old Town ?

Outer Bailey
(Lower)

Ditch

0   50   100 Feet

0   10   20   30 Metres

DINEFWR CASTLE

an army to destroy it. The Welsh united and routed the invaders at Coed Llathen nearby. However, in 1277 Dinefwr surrendered to Edward I's invaders without a fight. Some repairs were carried out at the modest cost of £60, and a new English borough was established. This town has quite disappeared and even its site is uncertain. Edward had to recapture the castle during Rhys ap Maredudd's revolt of 1287, though the main fighting took place at nearby Dryslwyn Castle. Anglicised as Dynevor, the castle normally remained in royal hands for the rest of the Middle Ages. However, Edward II granted it to his favourite, Hugh le Despenser the Younger, who built up a huge estate in South Wales. It was probably Hugh who added the new hall – the only significant addition to the native fabric. His arrogance incited the other Marcher barons to rise up against him in 1321, and Dinefwr was one of numerous Despenser castles sacked. Though restored to power, Hugh was executed in 1326 when his royal master was overthrown.

Ironically for a castle of native origin, and unlike Dryslwyn, Dinefwr resisted an attack by Owain Glyndwr in 1403. Henry VII's supporter Rhys ap Thomas modernised the accommodation, but the castle was later abandoned for Newton House which stands half a mile to the north. The decaying castle was restored in the eighteenth century as a romantic ruin in Dinefwr Park, which was landscaped by 'Capability' Brown.

An outer bailey guarded the comparatively gentle approach from the east. This was once walled in stone, but only some foundations remain. Ahead is the inner bailey on the summit of the hill. It is separated from the outer enclosure by a rock-cut ditch. A long barbican was formed on the ledge between the inner curtain and the steep drop to the river. Only some footings of its loop-holed outer wall can be seen. It may be a rare example of a native Welsh barbican, though the addition of a new gate is recorded under Edward I. A simple gateway through the curtain leads into the pentagonal inner bailey. Intact up to its parapet, the curtain is rather lacking in flanking towers. Apart from the square turret at the back of the barbican, there is just a single round tower guarding the northern angle of the curtain.

The keep vies with Llywelyn the Great's Dolbadarn as the best-preserved example of a native circular keep. It stood just inside the enclosure, but the curtain has collapsed down the slope at this point. As usual the ground-floor entrance is a later insertion. Originally the keep was reached by a wooden stair through a doorway (now blocked) on the floor above. The keep is powerful but rather squat in appearance, because the main structure is now only two storeys high, a tall plinth accentuating the horizontal. Surely Rhys Fychan intended a third storey to dominate the castle. Perhaps it was removed after 1343, when the Black Prince's survey reported that the keep was in danger of collapse. The recessed stage which now crowns the keep was a Georgian summer house, its large windows once giving guests panoramic views across the park. To reach it, a staircase was constructed to the parapet of the curtain, from which a stone bridge crosses the narrow gap to the keep.

Only three arrow slits lit the first floor of the keep, so the accommodation can best be described as spartan. No doubt Rhys had wooden domestic buildings in the bailey, but Hugh le Despenser built a new residential range on the north-east, supplanting the older curtain on this side. His hall is intact except for the wall facing the courtyard. Next to it is the solar block, built in the form of an oblong tower. Both chambers are now largely early Tudor in appearance owing to a thorough remodelling by Rhys ap Thomas, who restored a number of castles in south-west Wales.

Access: Open regularly except in winter (Cadw / NT).

Reference: Guidebook by S. E. Rees (includes Dryslwyn). *HKW* (II).

Relations: Castles of the princes at Dryslwyn, Newcastle Emlyn and Cardigan. Compare the native round keeps at Dryslwyn, Dolbadarn and Castell Meredydd.

DRYSLWYN CASTLE, five miles west of Llandeilo, crowns the summit of a great round hill, offering a commanding view along the Tywi valley. Maredudd ap Rhys, grandson of the Lord Rhys, died here in 1271, and it seems likely that he built the castle. It was probably under construction at the same time as nearby Dinefwr Castle was being built by his nephew, Rhys Fychan. The two castles must have been uncomfortably close considering their builders' rivalry for control of Deheubarth. Both castles were similar in conception, consisting of a round keep and a small walled courtyard. However, whereas Dinefwr remains largely intact, Dryslwyn is now very ruinous. The two fragments which still stand high post-date the Edwardian conquest. Little of the native Welsh castle remained visible until excavations in the 1980s uncovered the footings.

The keep was about as large as Dinefwr's and more massively built. Only the stump remains, a crowning pile of stones representing the basement vault. Little of the original, tower-less curtain stands to any height, but Dryslwyn does preserve some low ruins of its native domestic buildings. They consist of a large hall, with the base of a central hearth still in place, and a cross-wing which housed the solar. These apartments left only a small open space in the inner ward. Beside the keep are the foundations of a gate tower. Beyond lay two outer courtyards occupying the elongated summit of the hill. A fragment of masonry at the far end marks the site of an outlying tower which commanded the approach.

Maredudd's son Rhys sided with Edward I against Llywelyn the Last. However, the lands promised to him were not forthcoming, and Dryslwyn remained occupied by a royal garrison. In 1287 he rebelled, seizing Dryslwyn and raiding as far as Gower. Edward I was on campaign in Gascony at the time, but he despatched his cousin Edmund, earl of Cornwall, with an army of eleven thousand men. Their attempt to undermine the walls failed when the mining tunnel collapsed prematurely. Eventually the curtain was breached with the aid of a large catapult. Rhys ap Maredudd escaped to continue his resistance (no more successfully) at Newcastle Emlyn.

After the siege Edward I spent £300 on repairs, the south side of the castle being rebuilt. It has been suggested that this side was breached during the siege, but the steep drop to the Tywi makes this improbable. It is more likely that the Welsh curtain had already begun to slide down the slope. Much of Edward I's massive replacement curtain has followed it, but one chunk still stands, the windows showing that a chamber lay against it. The other standing portion is a square tower which was added behind the solar. A row of three lancet windows high up suggests that this was the chapel.

Like Dinefwr, Dryslwyn was retained in royal hands. Hugh le Despenser the Younger held it under Edward II, and the castle was ransacked by the other Marcher barons in 1321. In 1403 the Welsh constable declared for Owain Glyndwr. The castle disappears from history after that, and was probably dismantled on Owain's withdrawal. Even the borough which accompanied the castle did not survive. It lay on the slope to the north of the castle – some of its surrounding bank and ditch are still visible.

Access: Freely accessible (Cadw).
Reference: Guidebook by S. E. Rees (includes Dinefwr).
Relations: Nearby Dinefwr, and Maredudd ap Rhys' Newcastle Emlyn. Edward I also strengthened the native castles of Castell-y-Bere, Criccieth and Dolwyddelan.

KIDWELLY CASTLE AND TOWN WALL   Although mildly ruined, Kidwelly is one of the best-preserved castles of South Wales. The parapets can still be walked and some of the original battlements remain in place. Attractively placed on a ridge above the River Gwendraeth before it flows into Carmarthen Bay, it is one of a group of castles established by the Norman invaders early in the twelfth century. Like the later Edwardian castles of North Wales, they were positioned on river mouths for supply by sea.

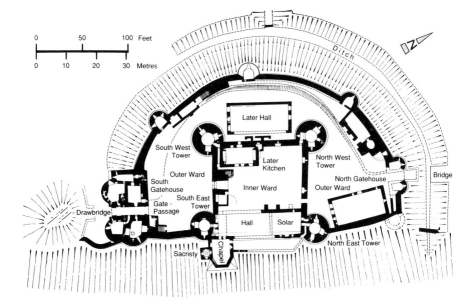

KIDWELLY CASTLE

First mentioned in 1114, the castle was founded by Roger de Caen, bishop of Salisbury. It may be surprising to find a bishop taking part in the invasion, but Roger was the king's chancellor and an ambitious prelate. His English castles were notable stone structures for their time, but Kidwelly began as a frontier outpost of earth and timber. It is a half-ringwork, its bank and ditch enclosing a semi-circular area against the steep river bank. This determined the shape of the later stone castle. Roger brought the civilising influence of the Church with him, founding a priory on the opposite bank of the river.

Over the next century the castle frequently changed hands between Normans and Welsh. It finally fell to the English when Patrick de Chaworth captured it from the Lord Rhys' grandson in 1244. The castle seems to have been entirely of wood throughout this period. The present stone castle is Edwardian, marking the final conquest of Deheubarth. It is unusual because the semi-circular outer curtain, following the line of the ringwork, closely surrounds a square inner ward. Kidwelly is thus a concentric castle, except on the riverside where the walls coalesce. Another curiosity is the placing of the main gatehouse on the outer curtain rather than the inner. The castle is not all of one build, and the pattern of ownership suggests a considerable interval between the construction of the inner and outer curtains.

The inner ward – a rare example of a keep-less castle with uniform corner towers – was probably begun in 1274, when Payn de Chaworth accompanied his king home from crusade. Payn died two years after leading Edward's troops into Welsh Deheubarth in 1277. He left a baby daughter, Matilda. It is likely that the inner curtain was complete by then, except for the naturally protected east front overlooking the river. The great hall closing this side may have been built during Matilda's minority.

To compensate for the purely domestic nature of the hall, the Chapel Tower was then constructed to command the eastern side of the castle. The military character of this work suggests a new lord in residence. In 1298 Matilda married Henry, the younger son of the earl of Lancaster. Henry went on to build the outer curtain, along with the mighty keep-gatehouse at the south end, overlooking the river.

Henry of Lancaster's munificence extended beyond the castle to walling the little town in stone and rebuilding the fine priory church beyond the river. This survives as the parish church of St Mary. However, his building campaign ground to a halt after he became earl of Lancaster, following the execution of his brother Thomas in 1322. He thus lived his later years as one of the greatest barons of the realm, but succumbed to blindness. The gatehouse was still incomplete when Owain Glyndwr's supporters descended in 1403. Owain burnt the town and besieged the castle for three weeks until it was relieved. As a duchy of Lancaster stronghold, Kidwelly now belonged to the Crown. Henry IV and Henry V spent over £600 here, chiefly on completing the gatehouse, at a time when the estuaries of south-west Wales were vulnerable to a French landing. The gatehouse was finally roofed in 1422. Sir Rhys ap Thomas, Henry VII's supporter, added some new domestic buildings. After that the castle sank quietly into decay. Though garrisoned in the Civil War there is no record of a siege.

The handsome keep-gatehouse forms the entrance to the castle. It was once preceded by a barbican which is now reduced to a scrap of wall. As usual, round-fronted towers flank the entrance to the gatehouse. A drawbridge recess frames the gate arch. At the top a row of machicolations marks the completion of the building early in the fifteenth century. Both ends of the long gate passage were closed by a portcullis and wooden gates. Doorways on either side of the gate passage lead to vaulted porters' lodges and store rooms. In one chamber is a circular opening which looks like a well, but is in fact the entrance to a sinister pit prison.

Both storeys above the gate contained several rooms, providing an extensive residence for the constable. On the first floor the hall runs nearly the full length of the gatehouse, with a small kitchen walled off at the east end. There was inevitably some inconvenience in placing the hall just above the entrance. A long slot in the middle of the floor is a murder hole poised above the gate passage, while the inner portcullis was operated from the recess overlooking the courtyard. The small room between the flanking towers contained the winding gear for the outer portcullis and the drawbridge. Another murder hole slot can be seen in the floor here. Two private chambers occupied the towers, and there were further rooms in a narrow annexe at the west end. From the kitchen a doorway leads onto a stretch of curtain connecting with the South-East Tower of the inner ward. This curtain had a parapet on both sides. It would thus have been possible to maintain contact with the gatehouse if the outer ward was overrun.

On the upper floor the layout is similar. The large room directly above the hall perhaps formed the constable's solar, with bed chambers in the towers. Henry of Lancaster abandoned work at this level and it was only completed by the Lancastrian kings. The handsome windows overlooking the courtyard are theirs, and so are the stone vaults which cover the tower rooms. A new stair turret was added towards the courtyard.

Once through the gatehouse, Payn de Chaworth's inner ward lies immediately ahead. Its entrance is just an archway with a portcullis groove, which seems rather feeble for the Edwardian period. However, the gateway is flanked quite closely by the adjacent corner towers – an arrangement also seen at Conwy. The loop-holed inner curtain is dominated by its four circular corner towers, which project boldly and rise much higher than the curtain. The South-West Tower was singled out for special treatment. Each floor is covered by a domed vault, recalling the keep at Pembroke. This protection against fire suggests that the tower may have been intended as a last resort in emergencies, or as a treasury. It is hardly a keep, however, because it is no larger or better appointed than the other three towers. The chambers within all of them are quite small owing to the thickness of the walls. Although there are fireplaces and latrines for habitation, the rooms are lit only by arrow slits.

As first built the corner towers had three storeys – the original walled-up battlements can still be seen. All four were given an extra storey by Henry of Lancaster, with stair turrets (inspired by Edward I's castles) rising a little higher. The heightening of the towers enabled archers on the parapet to shoot over Henry's outer curtain.

Unfortunately the main residential range on the east side of the ward is now mostly reduced to foundations. It once contained the great hall and solar above cellars. Henry of Lancaster built the Chapel Tower, which projects boldly from the steep slope. This semi-octagonal tower rises from a square base with exceptionally tall pyramid spurs. Above the arrow slits the tower contains a fine apsidal chapel, which was reached from the hall. Note the lancet windows, the priest's seat and a double piscina (a wash basin for sacred vessels). A projecting turret contains a sacristy and, below, a tiny bed chamber for the priest. No doubt there were lesser buildings on the other three sides of the ward. The only survivor now is Rhys ap Thomas' kitchen, added against the west curtain in conjunction with his new hall in the outer ward.

A postern beside the North-East Tower leads back into the outer ward. Beyond a gabled building added by Rhys ap Thomas is the North Gate. It was a twin-towered gatehouse matching the great gatehouse on the south, but much smaller and now fragmentary. From here Henry of Lancaster's outer curtain follows the line of the Norman ringwork, encircling the inner curtain and returning to the main gatehouse at the south end. Three semi-circular towers project from it, though the central one has collapsed into the ditch. Rhys ap Thomas' new hall stands between the western towers of the inner curtain. Its position outside the curtain shows an indifference to defensive considerations by the early Tudor period.

The fortified town was no larger than the outer bailey of some castles. Much of the Norman town ditch still survives. Kidwelly soon overspilled onto the other bank of the river, and the portion within the defences was abandoned after Owain Glyndwr's attack. Henry of Lancaster's stone town wall has vanished except for the fragment visible from the fallen middle tower of the outer curtain. Otherwise, the only portion now surviving is the South Gate, a simple rectangular building with a central gate passage.

Access: The castle is open daily, while the town gate is freely accessible (both Cadw).

Reference: Guidebook by J. R. Kenyon. *HKW* (II).
Relations: Compare Roger de Caen's English castles at Old Sarum and Sherborne. There are concentric castles in South Wales at Caerphilly and St Donat's, and keep-gatehouses at Llansteffan and Caerphilly.

LAUGHARNE CASTLE is a romantic ruin overlooking the estuary of the River Taf. A Norman castle occupied the site. It casts some light on the fluid nature of the Norman conquest that as early as 1116 Henry I entrusted a Welshman with the constableship of the castle. Henry II drew up his treaty with the Lord Rhys here in 1172. Rhys burnt the castle after Henry's death, and it was sacked again by Llywelyn the Great in 1215. Evidence of the destruction has been found in excavations – a stone hall perished during one of these attacks. Even the Norman earthworks are no longer visible, though they determined the irregular layout of the later castle.

The existing castle is a monument to the de Brian family – an unbroken succession of lords called Guy. The first Guy de Brian was here by 1248. It is likely that he built the compact inner ward, with its twin towers facing the town. Work may have been in progress when Llywelyn the Last's supporters stormed the castle and dragged Guy off into captivity, following their victory over an invading English army at Coed Llathen (1257). His son continued building later in the century, adding the inner gatehouse and walling the large outer ward in stone. During his long tenure the fourth Guy de Brian patched up the older walls and improved the accommodation. He was the most illustrious member of the family, carrying the royal standard at the battle of Crecy and commanding the English fleet against the French. However, he was the last of his line to hold Laugharne, and after his death in 1390 the castle was neglected.

It was temporarily rescued by Sir John Perrot, lord lieutenant of Ireland. After renting the castle in 1575 he upgraded it to the standards of Elizabethan comfort – a rare conversion in Wales. Like his Tudorised castle at Carew, the alterations are surprisingly sympathetic to the original structure. Work was still incomplete when Sir John was arrested on a trumped-up charge of treason. He died in captivity in 1592. The ruin of the castle began immediately and was completed during the Civil War. In 1644 it was bombarded by parliamentary forces under Major-General Rowland Laugharne, a native of the town, then stormed in a night attack. Evidently the castle was slighted. In the eighteenth century the ruins became the centrepiece of a landscaped garden after the fashion of the time.

From the town the castle is entered through a twin-towered outer gatehouse, part of the second Guy de Brian's work. Its outer front was blasted down at the slighting. A low stretch of curtain survives alongside. The rest of the outer ward is now bounded by a Georgian garden wall on the line of its medieval predecessor.

Ahead lies the inner ward. Facing the outer gatehouse are the two circular towers built by the first Guy de Brian. They are identical in circumference but the ruinous North-East Tower was once lower than its partner, the top having been added by Sir John Perrot. The four-storey North-West Tower has vaulted rooms, its entrance placed securely at first-floor level. Because of this the tower may perhaps be regarded as the keep, though the rooms are spartan, with just one fireplace on the top floor and no latrines. The tower is still complete although the battlements are restorations. Sir John Perrot replaced the short stretch of curtain between the towers with a new domestic range. This embattled structure blends with the medieval work. A tall, semi-circular stair turret projects midway along like a mural tower. A long gallery occupied the top floor, extending into the North-West Tower.

The second Guy de Brian added the inner gatehouse to his father's curtain. Although a product of the Edwardian age, it is an oblong gate tower with shallow, rounded turrets. As first built it was only half as tall, though it would have looked more formidable when the ditch lay in front. The fourth Guy heightened this gatehouse, while Perrot is responsible for the distinctive Tudor gate arch, the column of oriel windows above it and the surmounting gable. A sign of economy is the absence of a back wall – the courtyard facade of the gatehouse must have been of timber.

Within, the castle is very much a shell. When the residential buildings stood the inner ward would have been reduced to a narrow space. Apart from foundations, these buildings are only attested by the scars they have left on the surrounding curtain. The accommodation was largely rebuilt by the fourth Guy de Brian and again by Sir John Perrot. The main apartments stood at first-floor level against the south wall, on the low cliff overlooking the estuary. At the south-west corner, beside the large kitchen fireplace, is a slender round tower rising from a square base. Further east is the site of the hall, a gaping hole in the curtain marking the position of an Elizabethan oriel window. Beside it, a thin square turret contains a postern leading onto the cliff. The east side of the castle was presumably levelled at the slighting.

Access: Open daily in summer (Cadw).

Reference: Guidebook by R. Avent.

Relations: Compare the vaulted towers at Kidwelly and Pembroke, and Sir John Perrot's additions at Carew. The de Brians also built Woodsford Castle in Dorset.

LLANDOVERY CASTLE   guarded the upper end of the Tywi valley. It overlooks a tributary, the River Bran, which flows through the town. The castle is a small ruin on the summit of a motte raised by Richard Fitz Pons, founder of the Clifford family. It was probably new when the Welsh of Deheubarth attacked in 1116, burning the bailey but failing to storm the motte. The Cliffords were driven out in 1158 when the castle was sacked. Henry II intervened and repaired it, but the Lord Rhys took possession in 1162. The castle remained Welsh for over a century, though it changed hands several times in squabbles between Rhys' descendants.

Edward I's invasion of 1277 restored English control. Edward granted the castle to John Giffard and the existing masonry is his. He built a small enclosure on the summit of the motte – in effect an Edwardian shell keep. The main survival is a semi-circular tower which still rises almost to full height. A chunk of the north wall also survives, with a smaller tower projection containing a well. There would have been very little room inside the walls and the main domestic buildings must have occupied the bailey below, but there was never a stone curtain around it. John Giffard was more preoccupied with building his great castle at Carreg Cennen.

Work was probably still in progress when the castle was temporarily lost during Rhys ap Maredudd's rebellion in 1287. Llandovery last saw action in 1403, when it withstood an attack by Owain Glyndwr.

Access: Freely accessible (LA).
Reference: GAHW *Dyfed.*
Relations: John Giffard's castle at Carreg Cennen. Richard Fitz Pons also founded Bronllys Castle.

LLANSTEFFAN CASTLE magnificently crowns a hilltop overlooking the estuary of the River Tywi. It is still an impressive stronghold despite its ruinous condition. An Iron Age hillfort occupied the site. On the west, which is the comparatively easy approach, its double ditch can still be seen. The Normans created a D-shaped bailey on the summit, with a ringwork at the highest point on the west. It was probably one of the chain of castles erected to guard the river mouths in the early years of the twelfth century, but it is not mentioned until 1146. In that year the castle was captured by the three young princes of Deheubarth, including the future Lord Rhys. Rhys' brother Maredudd repelled an attempt to recapture it, hurling down the Normans' scaling ladders, but the castle did eventually fall.

Half a century later the Lord Rhys came again. During his invasion of 1189 he seized a number of the coastal castles but was unable to hold on to them. A few years later the castle was in the hands of William de Camville. Five generations of de Camvilles lived here until they died out in 1338, and they transformed the castle into a powerful stone fortress. William made a start by walling the Norman ringwork, having borrowed money from the royal coffers for that purpose. His curtain is a thin retaining wall against the rampart. Not much survives above courtyard level, and the section facing the outer bailey was later demolished.

The castle fell again when Llywelyn the Great swept through Deheubarth in 1215. Llansteffan remained in Welsh hands until William Marshal the Younger's campaign of reconquest in 1223. Geoffrey de Camville then strengthened the inner bailey. A circular tower, too small to be a keep, was built on the line of the curtain to command the outer bailey. Owing to the later destruction of this side only its excavated base can be seen. Fortunately Geoffrey's inner gatehouse stands almost complete. It is a square tower with two storeys above the gate passage.

After the Welsh victory at Coed Llathen in 1257 the depleted garrison succumbed to another attack. Again the English soon recovered their lost ground. The second William de Camville, grandson of the first, set about greatly strengthening the castle by building an outer curtain. Work probably continued into the time of his son, another Geoffrey. The thick curtain has two U-shaped towers and a strong outer gatehouse between them. The West Tower is now very ruinous, but the larger North Tower still rises impressively. Its three storeys contained comfortable accommodation. Two turrets, one housing latrines and the other a spiral stair, mark the junctions with the curtain. Owing to the steep drop the south curtain is tower-free, but the south-east angle projects to give the impression of a tower. At this time the vulnerable west side of the older inner curtain was thickened with a series of arches designed to carry a wider wall-walk.

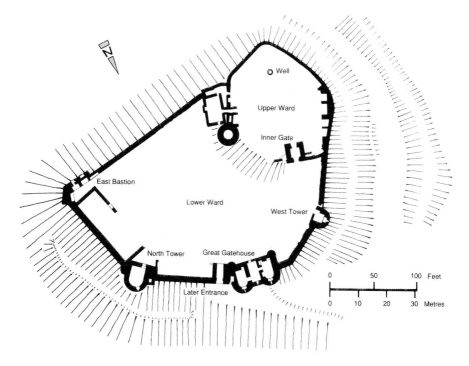

LLANSTEFFAN CASTLE

The centrepiece of the outer defences is the twin-towered gatehouse. It is a smaller version of the main gatehouse at Caerphilly Castle, so it probably dates from 1270 at the earliest. As at Caerphilly there is a narrow slot through which water could be poured if attackers tried to set the wooden gates ablaze. Guard chambers flank the entrance passage, which had murder holes in the vault and a portcullis at each end. The gatehouse looks odd now because both ends of the gate passage have been walled up. At some later date it was decided to eliminate the inconvenience caused by portcullis winding gear in the hall above by inserting a new entrance alongside. Unlike the larger gatehouse at Kidwelly, the two upper floors were fully occupied by the hall and the solar. On the wall towards the courtyard both rooms have a fireplace and a large pair of windows, compensating for the arrow slits in the towered outer face. Consequently this keep-gatehouse, like others of its class, was less secure from the bailey. Round stair turrets clasp the inner corners of the building.

Like Kidwelly, the main gatehouse is situated on the outer perimeter of the castle rather than the inner core. Indeed, the outer curtain was the more formidable defence. At some point the portion of inner curtain facing the outer bailey was demolished. This may have happened once the outer curtain was complete, in which case it represents a deliberate if mystifying decision to create a single large enclosure. Alternatively it may reflect changes wrought from 1367, when Edward III ordered the repair of the castle owing to fears of a French invasion. It is too uniform to be the result of damage inflicted by Owain Glyndwr when he briefly occupied the castle. The blocking of the gatehouse is usually attributed to Jasper Tudor, earl of Pembroke (d.1495). He was granted the castle by his nephew, Henry VII, and seems to have been the only later lord to occupy the castle. The gable ends of a large barn against the outer curtain may also date from his time.

Access: Always open (Cadw).
Reference: Guide by P. Humphries. RCAHMW *Carmarthenshire.*
Relations: Compare the keep-gatehouses at Kidwelly and Caerphilly. Jasper Tudor repaired the walls of Tenby.

NEWCASTLE EMLYN   The fragmentary ruins of this castle occupy a promontory surrounded by a loop of the River Teifi. There is only a narrow level approach from the town of the same name. The Lord Rhys' grandson, Maredudd ap Rhys, built the 'new castle' of Emlyn about the year 1240 to guard his frontier with the earl of Pembroke's lordship of Cilgerran. He also built Dryslwyn Castle. Maredudd's castle consisted of two baileys in line, but only some foundations remain of his plain curtain around the triangular inner bailey. Unlike the other native castles of Deheubarth, there is no trace of a round keep. Maredudd's son Rhys sided with Edward I against Llywelyn in 1282, then rebelled five years later while Edward was away in Gascony. Having escaped the fall of Dryslwyn Castle, he seized Newcastle Emlyn from the English and continued his resistance. However, the castle surrendered in 1288 once the large catapult used at Dryslwyn had been brought here. Rhys was hanged and the castle was taken over by the king.

The most prominent feature of the castle now is the gatehouse. Even this is very ruinous, but its outer front is still two storeys high with semi-octagonal flanking towers. Perhaps it never rose any higher. Close by a tall finger of masonry represents a flanking tower, also polygonal. Together they represent a strengthening of the castle on its vulnerable landward side by Edward II. The gatehouse was under construction in 1321, though there is little royal expenditure to account for it. By the time of the Black Prince's survey in 1343 the rest of the castle was in a precarious condition.

From 1349 the castle was granted to a succession of absentee lords. They neglected it, and Owain Glyndwr inflicted damage when he raided in 1403. The castle enjoyed a reprieve under Henry VII's supporter, Sir Rhys ap Thomas. He improved the domestic amenities at a number of castles in South Wales. Large windows replaced the arrow slits in the gatehouse, and the depressed gate arch may also date from his time. In 1645 a siege of the castle was broken by a Royalist relieving force, but the Roundheads stormed it at the end of the year. That the Royalists put up some resistance is shown by the earth ravelin which shielded the gatehouse from direct bombardment. However, then or soon afterwards the rest of the castle was reduced by slighting to its current melancholy state.

Access: Freely accessible (LA).
Reference: Carmarthenshire Antiquary (XXIII). GAHW *Dyfed. HKW* (II).
Relations: Castles of the princes at Dinefwr and Dryslwyn. Edward II completed Caernarfon and Beaumaris castles.

PENCADER CASTLE   is an imposing motte overlooking the confluence of two streams, three miles north of Alltwalis. Away from the steep slope there is a ditch in front, but the bailey has been cut off by a disused railway line. This is probably the castle of Mabudryd erected in 1145 by Gilbert de Clare, earl of Pembroke, when he penetrated deep into Deheubarth. The Welsh soon regained control, and Henry II came to Pencader to receive homage from the Lord Rhys in 1162. Henry was admonished by an old man who assured him that the Welsh would still be here to answer in their native tongue on the Day of Judgement.

> *Access:* On private land.
> *Reference:* RCAHMW *Carmarthenshire*.
> *Relations:* Gilbert de Clare also raised Castell Allt-y-Ferin.

ST CLEARS CASTLE,   known locally as Banc-y-Beili, lies beside the Afon Cynin near its junction with the Taf. The Norman founder of the castle is unclear. A Norman chancel arch in the parish church survives from a small priory which accompanied the castle. The Lord Rhys twice captured St Clears, and Llywelyn the Great overran the castle during his campaign of 1215. It was still defensible during Owain Glyndwr's revolt. The French expeditionary force which landed in 1405 attacked the castle, but they were driven off by an army from Pembrokeshire. Today the site is just an earthwork, consisting of a grassy motte and a square bailey surrounded by a ditch, but it once had at least a stone keep on the motte.

> *Access:* Freely accessible (LA).
> *Reference:* *Carmarthenshire Antiquary* (XIX). GAHW *Dyfed*.
> *Relations:* Motte-and-baileys such as Castell Allt-y-Ferin, Llandovery and Pencader.

OTHER SITES   The stump of a round turret just outside Laugharne marks the site of *Roche Castle*, a fortified manor house of the family who built Roch Castle in Pembrokeshire. *Green Castle*, overlooking the River Tywi below Carmarthen, is the ruin of a Tudor manor house on an older castle site. *Abercywyn Castle* (near Laugharne) and *Castell Garn Fawr* (near Bronwydd) are Norman ringworks. *Llanelli's* Norman castle lies submerged in a reservoir, the summit of its motte forming an islet in the water. Other motte-and-bailey castles surviving from Norman times are:

Ammanford Castle	*Castell Meurig* (Llangadoc)
Banc-y-Bettws (near Llangendeirne)	*Llanllwni Mount*
Castell Bach (near Cwmbach)	*Pant Glas Motte* (near Bronwydd)
Castell Du (near Pencader)	*Pen Castell* (near Pentre Cwrt)
Castell Mawr (Llanboidy)	*Talley Mound*
Castell-y-Domen (near Pontantwn)	*Tomen Llawddog* (near Cwmpengraig)
Domen Fawr (near Felindre)	*Twmpath Motte* (near Burry Port)
Llanegwad Castle	*Ystum Enlli Castle* (near Llangennech)

Denbighshire

Prior to the Edwardian conquest this area of the Four Cantrefs was a no-man's land, disputed between Gwynedd, Powys and the Normans. Some motte-and-bailey castles can be seen, though there are few compared with central and southern Wales. Owain Gwynedd raised Tomen-y-Rhodwydd to consolidate his hold on newly-conquered territory. Tomen-y-Faerdre is probably another native Welsh effort, while Sycharth is remembered for its later occupation by Owain Glyndwr. Masonry castles made an exceptionally late appearance. The earliest, panoramically sited in the native Welsh manner, is Dinas Bran, built in the mid-thirteenth century by a lord of Powys.

Edward I awarded this area to some of his chief supporters in the invasion of 1282. It was partitioned into four baronies, thus becoming Marcher lordship territory unlike the rest of North Wales. Each new lord built a castle inspired by Edward's royal fortresses, though they are all inland rather than coastal. Denbigh Castle, the largest of the group, is interesting for its complex gatehouse. The accompanying walled town demonstrates the resources of its builder, the powerful magnate Henry de Lacy. Reginald de Grey's castle at Ruthin is now quite ruinous while Holt is fragmentary. By contrast, Chirk Castle – left unfinished by Roger Mortimer – has undergone a rare Welsh transformation into a mansion.

CASTELL DINAS BRAN is magnificently sited on a great hill overlooking the River Dee and Llangollen. Little wonder that it was believed to be the Grail Castle of Arthurian romance. A steep ascent beginning at the medieval Dee Bridge is rewarded by spectacular views from the summit. The castle occupies the highest point of an Iron Age hillfort. There is no record of its construction, but this area was ruled by the Welsh lords of Ial, who frequently had to change their allegiance between Gwynedd and Powys. The castle is attributed to Gruffudd ap Madog. He was Llywelyn the Last's ally, and probably sought to emulate his prince by building a stone castle.

The castle is very ruinous and little rises to any great height, but enough remains to show its layout. In contrast to earlier native Welsh castles it has a regular, oblong plan. On the south, where the ground does not fall away so steeply, the castle is fronted by a rock-cut ditch. Several chunks of the surrounding curtain survive. Two gaping holes represent windows which lit the hall. Alongside are fragments of the kitchen, in a U-shaped tower which projected midway along the south curtain. There were no angle towers, but the north-east corner is occupied by a gatehouse with round flanking turrets. Narrow guard chambers flanked the long gate passage. The southern chamber retains its vault, but the northern chamber and turret are reduced to foundations. Apart from Llywelyn the Great's mighty gatehouse at Criccieth this is the only gatehouse in a native Welsh castle.

Two sides of an oblong keep survive in a bold position, projecting from the east front to command the approach to the gatehouse. The keep probably contained a single apartment above a cellar. A ditch separates the keep from the castle bailey, and there is the base of a stairway which led to the first-floor entrance. Because of its shape it has been suggested that this keep is older than the rest, but native Welsh castle builders could be conservative – Llywelyn the Last built an oblong keep at Dolforwyn a few years later.

Gruffudd ap Madog died in 1270 and was buried in the nearby abbey of Valle Crucis, which his father had founded. Dinas Bran proved to be another short-lived native castle owing to the Edwardian conquest. In 1277 the Welsh burnt and abandoned the castle when Edward I's forces approached. Henry de Lacy, who led the expedition, recommended that this formidable site should be refortified. However, the new lord, John de Warenne, built the more accessible castle at Holt instead. There is a tradition that the English defended the castle against Owain Glyndwr in 1402, but afterwards it sank into ruins.

> *Access:* Freely accessible (LA – uphill walk).
> *Reference: Archaeologia Cambrensis* (CXXIII). GAHW *Clwyd and Powys.*
> *Relations:* Its successor, Holt. Hillfort castles such as Castell Garn Fadrun and Castell Dinas. Compare the native Welsh castles of Caergwrle, Dolforwyn and Powis.

CHIRK CASTLE is known in Welsh as Castell-y-Waun. Most of the castles of North Wales, grand as they are, survive as empty shells or battered ruins. Only Chirk and Powis have made the transition to stately homes. The magnificent interiors and lush gardens of Chirk contrast with the towered curtain. This retains its Edwardian severity, though it is not quite as original as it appears.

In 1282 Edward I created the barony of Chirk and gave it to Roger Mortimer, in reward for his services during the Welsh wars. He later became justiciar of Wales. We have no record of the castle's construction. Its resemblance to Beaumaris Castle has led some scholars to believe that it was begun after Madog ap Llywelyn's rebellion was crushed in 1295. James of St George, the architect of Beaumaris, may well have designed the castle, though no royal expenditure is recorded here. Unlike the other Edwardian castles of North Wales no accompanying borough was established. The castle stands aloof in landscaped parkland, two miles west of the present town of Chirk. Evidently Roger's scheme was too ambitious. He left the castle far from complete in 1322, when he was imprisoned for his part in the war against the Despensers. Roger died in the Tower of London in 1326. His nephew, the more famous Roger Mortimer, escaped from the Tower to overthrow Edward II. Roger appropriated Chirk along with much else. However, his brief taste of power ended with his execution in 1330, when the young Edward III asserted himself.

After that Chirk was seldom in the hands of the same family for very long. It seems to have been an unlucky lordship, considering the number of holders who came to a bad end. They include two Fitzalan earls of Arundel, both beheaded in the fourteenth century; the duke of Somerset, killed at the battle of St Albans in 1455; the future Richard III, of whom no more need be said; and Sir William Stanley, who lost his head for supporting the Yorkist pretender Perkin Warbeck. Stability finally came with the purchase of Chirk by a London merchant, Sir Thomas Myddelton, in 1595. His family have occupied the castle ever since.

The second Sir Thomas Myddelton captured Powis Castle for parliament during the Civil War, but lost Chirk to the Royalists while he was away (1644). Reluctant to bombard the castle with artillery, he eventually bribed his way back in. Having saved his home from serious harm, the disillusioned parliamentarian undid his good work by prematurely declaring for Charles II in 1659. Major-General Lambert, conducting the last siege of the Civil Wars, slighted the castle after its surrender. Considerable rebuilding was financed by £30,000 compensation which Sir Thomas received after the Restoration. A lavish remodelling of the interior followed under Richard Myddelton a century later, and the architect Pugin made further alterations in the 1840s.

Roger Mortimer's castle was planned as a mighty oblong surrounded by a thick curtain, with round towers at the corners and a semi-circular tower in the middle of each side. Only the northern half of this castle stands, as far as the mid-wall towers. It is likely that the castle was left in this half-finished state when Mortimer was imprisoned in 1322. The alternative possibility, that the entire southern half soon collapsed down the slope to the Afon Ceiriog, seems improbable. A plain curtain now closes off the south side of the quadrangle. This is later medieval, though its date is a matter for conjecture.

The intermediate towers of the castle are reminiscent of Beaumaris, but the similarities should not be overstated. Chirk had no concentric outer wall and no opposing pair of gatehouses. There is just a plain gateway through the north curtain, recessed within a taller arch which contains the portcullis groove. The mural towers flank it quite closely, nevertheless it is not a true gatehouse in the Edwardian sense.

Since they rise no higher than the curtain, the five flanking towers appear rather squat. No doubt they were left incomplete (another affinity with Beaumaris), but only one of the towers survives in its original state. That is Adam's Tower, the semicircular tower on the west side. It contains four storeys, including a basement prison. Both the North-West Tower and the northern mid-wall tower have been hollowed out on the upper floors to create more space internally. The North-East Tower and the middle tower on the east are thin-walled throughout. This side of the castle was levelled during the slighting. It was rebuilt on the old foundations by the second Sir Thomas Myddelton – a remarkable piece of antiquarianism for the time. Even on the north and west the curtain has been altered, with inserted Jacobean windows and restored battlements.

Owing to the later transformations nothing can be said about the original domestic buildings. No doubt they surrounded the courtyard like their successors. Nothing stands against the west curtain now, but two mural latrines suggest that this was not always the case. The present north range was erected by the first Sir Thomas Myddelton, but its interior is a result of later restorations. Beyond Pugin's entrance hall, a grand staircase in the hollowed-out North Tower leads to the state apartments. These are Richard Myddelton's contribution and a fine example of Georgian elegance, notably the grand Saloon with its coffered ceiling. The east wing was rebuilt after the slighting. Its panelled Long Gallery is little altered since 1678, but the courtyard front with its projecting corridor is Pugin's.

It has been suggested that the plain south curtain was hurriedly built by Thomas Fitzalan during Owain Glyndwr's revolt. If so, its defensive purpose was soon negated by the Perpendicular-style windows which light the chapel at the east end. The antiquary John Leland says that Sir William Stanley made improvements to the castle, so the chapel may belong to his tenure (1483–95). The rest of the south range dates from 1529, when the castle was held by Henry VIII. It consists of a series of Tudor lodgings divided by timber-framed partitions.

> *Access:* Open regularly except in winter (NT).
> *Reference:* NT guidebook. BOW *Clwyd.*
> *Relations:* James of St George's Beaumaris. Roger Mortimer also built Narberth Castle. Compare the inhabited castles of Powis, Cardiff, St Donat's and Picton.

DENBIGH CASTLE AND TOWN WALL

DENBIGH CASTLE AND TOWN WALL Denbigh Castle crowns a hill overlooking the Vale of Clwyd, accompanied by a medieval ghost town which is still surrounded by most of its defensive wall. Like many other hilltop castle sites in Wales, Denbigh was first fortified in the Iron Age. Llywelyn the Last's treacherous brother, Dafydd ap Gruffudd, was awarded the Four Cantrefs after Edward I's Welsh campaign of 1277. He may have built a castle here – the site was strong enough to resist Edward I's forces for a month during his revolt in 1282. Dafydd abandoned Denbigh to Henry de Lacy, earl of Lincoln, who received this territory as a reward from Edward. Henry was a capable soldier who played a major part in the Welsh invasion. He also founded Lincoln's Inn, the first of the law schools in London, and assisted the king with his legal reforms.

Denbigh was the most ambitious of the new Marcher lordship strongholds, especially as Henry de Lacy went to the expense of enclosing his new borough within a stone wall. This was a remarkable gesture, since even Edward I only built stone walls around two of his new towns in North Wales – Conwy and Caernarfon. Edward visited soon after Denbigh's capture and gave Henry £22 to help with the initial works. James of St George, Master of the King's Works in Wales, was present, which suggests that the overall design of the fortifications may have been his.

At Caernarfon and Conwy the castles and town walls rose simultaneously, since new boroughs for English settlers were an essential feature of the Edwardian conquest. Henry de Lacy went further by devoting his initial efforts entirely to the town wall. A castle must have been intended from the outset, and it is likely that the narrow south end of the town enclosure was always reserved as the site. It is the highest part of the hill, yet it is only here that the town wall is regularly flanked by towers. Nevertheless in height and thickness this southern stretch matched the rest of the town circuit. It is thus very different to Caernarfon, where the south side of the castle was built first to complete the town enclosure, but was of a much more massive character.

The town wall did not prevent Madog ap Llywelyn from capturing Denbigh during his rising in 1294. Henry de Lacy's relieving expedition was defeated. He

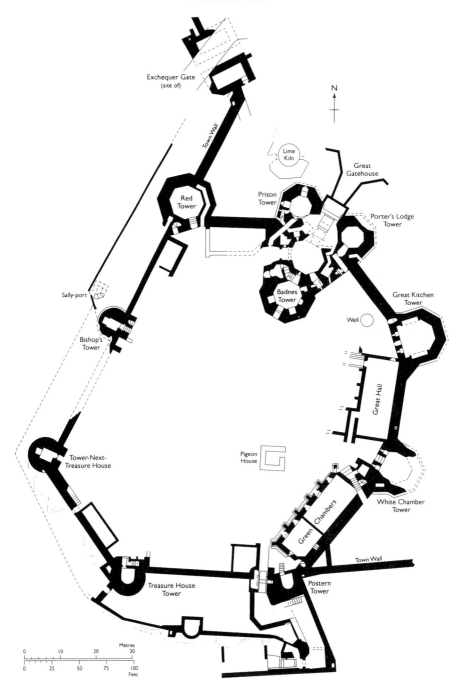

DENBIGHSHIRE

Exchequer Gate
(site of)

Town Wall

Red
Tower

Prison
Tower

Lime
Kiln

Great
Gatehouse

Porter's Lodge
Tower

Sally-port

Bishop's
Tower

Badnes
Tower

Well

Great Kitchen
Tower

Great Hall

Tower-Next-
Treasure House

Pigeon
House

White Chamber
Tower

Green Chambers

N

Treasure House
Tower

Town Wall

Postern
Tower

Metres
0   10   20   30

0   25   50   75   100
Feet

DENBIGH CASTLE

only recovered his lordship after Edward I put down the insurrection the following year. Evidently the town wall was strengthened after this episode. It is possible that the castle was only begun after the revolt. John Leland records the tradition that Henry de Lacy abandoned the castle unfinished in 1308 when his son drowned in the well. On Henry's death three years later the extensive Lacy estates were inherited by Thomas, earl of Lancaster. After the latter's execution in 1322 Denbigh passed through the Despensers, the Montagus and the Mortimers, who made sporadic attempts to complete it.

Owain Glyndwr failed to capture the castle on the outbreak of his rebellion in 1400, and it withstood two sieges by the Lancastrian Jasper Tudor in the 1460s. However, on each occasion the town was stormed and burnt. According to tradition the burgesses withdrew to the valley below to avoid further sieges, but in fact Denbigh had expanded beyond the walls at an early stage. During the Civil War Colonel William Salusbury repaired the decaying castle and town wall for the king. A six-month siege ended in their surrender to Major-General Thomas Mytton in October 1646. Parliament used the castle as a prison and garrison post, but its present battered state suggests that it was blown up at some point. The most likely explanation is that the castle, now regarded as a Roundhead stronghold, was slighted after the Restoration.

In its heyday the castle must have been on a par with the mighty Edwardian castles of Gwynedd, but unfortunately it is more ruinous than those four. The castle is entered through a handsome gatehouse which, though itself ruined, is still the most impressive part of the complex. Its outer front is typically Edwardian, with a lofty gate arch flanked by twin towers. That on the right (the Prison Tower) is more or less complete, but the left tower has been blasted down to its foundations. Their polygonal shape was inspired by Caernarfon Castle. Another affinity with Caernarfon is the weathered statue of the king in a niche above the gateway. Enough is left to show that the entrance passage was defended by a drawbridge, two portcullises, two pairs of gates and murder holes.

A surprise awaits within the gatehouse. Instead of running directly through to the courtyard, the gate passage ends in an octagonal hallway. From here, a second passage to the right leads to the courtyard, the exit being flanked by a third polygonal tower at the back of the gatehouse. So the gatehouse is a triangular composition, consisting of three towers around a central lobby from which defenders could fire upon assailants. It is the most elaborate of the Edwardian keep-gatehouses, although the King's Gate at Caernarfon would have been similar had it been completed to the original design.

The central hallway would have been a death-trap to any attackers who managed to get that far. There was originally no access to the gatehouse rooms from here. All three towers are reached by separate doorways from the courtyard. A long passage leads to the Prison Tower, which had a dismal prison in its basement. The upper floor of the gatehouse was reached by a spiral staircase in the rear tower. It formed a spacious residence for the constable. All three towers had residential chambers at this level, but his hall occupied the room above the octagonal lobby. A doorway leads onto the eastern curtain, but the present wall-walk here is deceptive. It was actually the floor of a mural gallery (another affinity with Caernarfon), the curtain originally rising to a higher parapet.

Straight sections of curtain surround the roughly oval courtyard of the castle. There is a stark contrast between the older town wall on the south and west, and the more massive curtain enclosing the castle on the north and east. Two semi-octagonal towers flank the east front, with the footings of the great hall between them. The Kitchen Tower, nearest the gatehouse, has two enormous fireplaces at ground level. Two residential chambers occupied the upper floors where Charles I lodged during a three-day visit in 1645. Henry de Lacy's private rooms lay in the White Chamber Tower on the other side of the hall, but the outer front of this tower has fallen. Against the next stretch of curtain is the ruined undercroft of the Green Chamber, a new solar added later in the fourteenth century.

Just beyond the Green Chamber is the junction with the older town wall. Here a gateway cuts through the curtain and descends to a complex barbican. A wide staircase descends steeply through three turns. It emerges at the base of the rock, where it is commanded by a semi-circular flanking tower. This tower is not on the main curtain of the castle – it belongs to a parallel outer wall, added when the castle was built. Hence Denbigh became a concentric castle, but only on those sides where the weaker town wall doubled up as the castle wall. Apart from the stretch commanding the barbican, little of this outer wall now remains.

Four semi-circular towers project from the town wall portion of the castle enclosure. They are much smaller than the polygonal towers of the east front, resembling those which flank the town walls of Conwy and Caernarfon. This whole section is now badly ruined, one stretch of wall having collapsed. At the north-west corner of the courtyard stood the Red Tower. This octagonal structure is now reduced to foundations. It was being roofed in 1374, though whether this represents a repair or a belated completion is unclear.

The town wall continues beyond the Red Tower. Beside Ffordd Newydd are some footings of the Exchequer Gate, a twin-towered gatehouse which resembled the Burgess Gate further on. Houses obscure the north-western part of the town wall. After the concentration of towers on the castle sector it is curious how few towers flank the rest of the circuit, which extends for three-quarters of a mile. At Caernarfon and Conwy towers were provided at frequent intervals, but Henry de Lacy built more economically. We soon reach the empty shell of the Burgess Gate, which was added as part of the general strengthening following the siege of 1294. It is a small Edwardian gatehouse. The semi-circular flanking towers rise from square bases, a rare motif in North Wales but common at this period in the Marcher castles of the south. Since there is only one upper storey, the gatehouse appears rather squat.

Beyond the Burgess Gate there follows the only gap in the circuit. This is a good place to contemplate the open space which contained the medieval town of Denbigh. Only two church buildings remain. Looking towards the castle is the tower of St Hilary's Chapel, while close by is the unfinished shell of Leicester's Church. This was built by Elizabeth I's favourite, Robert Dudley. According to tradition it was intended as a new cathedral for the diocese, but St Asaph survived the intended usurpation.

It is worth obtaining the key to walk the parapet of the town wall's north-eastern sector. The wall changes direction twice along this stretch and there are towers guarding these vulnerable angles. Beyond the semi-circular North-East Tower is the Countess Tower, which consists of two square towers placed at right-angles to each other. From this point the original town wall, occupying the summit of the hill, was supplemented after Madog's revolt by an outer salient wall. Clinging to the rock face, this loop-holed wall descends to the polygonal Goblin Tower, which projects boldly at the apex of the salient. This tower not only defended the circuit at its most vulnerable point, it also enclosed a large well which proved to be a vital source of water for the medieval town. The building of this salient suggests that it was a shortage of water which enabled Madog to capture the town in 1294. The Roundheads also concentrated their attack at this point. A steep flight of steps descends to the well in the tower basement. From here the salient wall climbs back up the rock to rejoin the main circuit.

The last stretch of town wall is plain except for a single half-round bastion near the junction with the castle. It belongs with the four bastions on the castle part of the town circuit and suggests that the castle was originally intended to be larger.

> *Access:* The castle is open daily. Much of the town wall can be followed – apply to the key-keeper for the north-east sector. (Both Cadw.)
>
> *Reference:* Guidebook by L. A. Butler.
>
> *Relations:* Caernarfon's gatehouse and polygonal towers. There are other keep-gatehouses at Harlech, Beaumaris and Caerphilly. Compare the Edwardian town walls of Conwy and Caernarfon.

HOLT CASTLE was built by John de Warenne, earl of Surrey. He received the lordship of Ial in 1282 after the young Welsh heir drowned at Holt. Since Warenne was his guardian, this may have been no accident! John abandoned the native stronghold of Castell Dinas Bran in favour of this more convenient site beside the River Dee, five miles north-east of Wrexham. Holt retains the character of the small borough laid out at that time. The main street leads past the church to a medieval bridge, crossing the Dee into Cheshire. It was once protected by a gate tower like that at Monmouth.

The castle stood around a small outcrop of sandstone rock beside the river. This outcrop has been carefully shaped into a pentagon. Its overgrown summit represents the courtyard of the castle, and the sheer sides formed the inner face of cellars which lay beneath the domestic buildings. Only a few chunks of wall now cling to the edge. The most substantial fragment contains a doorway, reached by a flight of steps from the courtyard. Nothing whatsoever survives of the surrounding curtain, which had five angle towers, four round and one square. A print of 1620 shows that the towers were capped by watch turrets in the Edwardian manner. There was also a square gate tower in front of the entrance. During the Civil War the castle withstood a nine-month siege under its governor, Sir Richard Lloyd. It surrendered to General Mytton in January 1647 – a remarkably late date excelled only by Harlech. The subsequent slighting was a thorough one, though later stone-robbing no doubt accounts for the virtual disappearance of the castle.

Access: Exterior visible (LA).
Reference: RCAHMW *Denbighshire*. GAHW *Clwyd and Powys*.
Relations: Its predecessor, Castell Dinas Bran. Compare the Warenne castles in England at Conisbrough, Lewes and Sandal.

RUTHIN CASTLE, on a hill above the River Clwyd, is one of the few Welsh castles to have become a mansion. However, Ruthin is not another Chirk – a castle which has been transformed into a stately home over the centuries while retaining its original character. Rather it is very much a ruin with a large nineteenth-century house grafted onto it. The juxtaposition is an uncomfortable one and confuses the layout of the original castle. As a final twist of fortune the mansion has become a luxury hotel.

Ruthin almost began as one of the royal castles of Edward I. His ditchers were here in 1277, but Edward then granted much of the future Denbighshire to Dafydd ap Gruffudd as a reward for his support against Llywelyn the Last. Dafydd built a new castle at Caergwrle, but it is uncertain if work continued at Ruthin. The existing masonry is probably the work of Reginald de Grey, lord of Wilton, who was awarded the cantref of Dyffryn Clwyd after Dafydd's rebellion in 1282.

A later Reginald de Grey triggered a disaster for English rule in Wales. He sought to discredit his Welsh neighbour by withholding a summons to serve in a Scottish campaign. That neighbour was Owain Glyndwr, whose great revolt began with an attack on Ruthin in September 1400. He burnt the town but failed to take the castle. Owain finally got his revenge two years later, ambushing Reginald nearby and carrying him off to imprisonment at Dolwyddelan Castle. The ransom of 10,000 marks impoverished the Greys, and they were obliged to sell Ruthin in 1508. During the Civil War the decaying castle was garrisoned for the king. It resisted an assault by Sir Thomas Myddelton of Chirk Castle, but surrendered to Major-General Mytton in April 1646 after a mining tunnel had been dug. The castle was then slighted. It remained a quarry until the Myddelton-West family re-occupied the site in the 1820s. They preserved what was left of the castle as a romantic garden ruin after the fashion of the time. The original house was enlarged into a castellated mansion from 1849.

Ruthin Castle consisted of a roughly pentagonal inner ward and a narrow outer ward to its west. The approach through the grounds skirts the south side of the medieval castle. Little can be seen from here except the footings of a gatehouse, with a neo-Gothic gateway straddling the entrance passage. It was a typical if modest Edwardian gatehouse with rounded flanking towers. Beyond stands the mansion, its two parts connected by a bridge over the castle ditch. The original house occupies one corner of the inner ward, while the grandiose Victorian extension fills the outer ward. Behind the mansion is a round corner tower from the outer ward. It is linked to the inner ward by a length of curtain crossing the wide, flat-bottomed ditch. This wall is pierced by a postern. Defenders could sally into the ditch via a spiral stair in the north-west corner tower of the inner curtain.

The main residential buildings occupied the north side of the inner ward. Externally the north curtain and its two semi-circular flanking towers rise impressively, but the courtyard level is much higher. There are remains of another tower at the eastern angle. The fourth angle was occupied by the gatehouse, which was the main entrance to the castle despite leading directly into the inner ward. The stump of the gatehouse is more interesting than it first appears, because the vaulted basements of the two flanking towers are still complete. They are connected by a corridor beneath the gate passage. Little survives of the south curtain, and the south-western angle tower has disappeared.

Like most Edwardian castle builders, Reginald de Grey founded a town outside the castle. Its earth-and-timber defences failed to keep out Owain Glyndwr. Reginald also built the collegiate church of St Peter, though the magnificent roof commemorates Henry VII's accession. The town preserves some timber-framed houses built after the sacking of 1400.

> *Access:* Now a hotel. Open to non-residents, but obtain permission to visit the ruins.
> *Reference:* RCAHMW *Denbighshire*. Guidebook.
> *Relations:* Edwardian baronial castles at Chirk, Denbigh, Holt and Powis. Compare the Greys' castle at Wilton in Herefordshire.

SYCHARTH CASTLE   lies to the north of the village, six miles south-west of Oswestry. This Norman earthwork consists of a low motte surrounded by a ditch, with a small bailey platform beyond. Its origin is obscure. The castle is famous because Owain Glyndwr lived here before his rebellion. His poet Iolo Goch describes its nine halls and many chambers, no doubt with exaggerated splendour. Excavations have confirmed that these buildings were entirely of wood. It shows that old castle earthworks still made convenient manorial homes in the later Middle Ages. Of course, by Owain's time such a simple castle could offer no serious defence, and the young Prince Henry burnt it down on his first retaliatory raid into Wales in 1403. It was never reoccupied, and Owain spent the best years of his rebellion holding court at Harlech Castle.

> *Access:* On private land.
> *Reference:* *Archaeologia Cambrensis* (CXV).
> *Relations:* For Owain Glyndwr see Ruthin, Harlech and Aberystwyth.

TOMEN-Y-FAERDRE   This motte rises to the east of Llanarmon-yn-Ial, on a crag overlooking the Afon Alyn. Its origin is uncertain, but it was probably raised in the twelfth century by one of the Welsh lords of Ial. If so it is the most impressive of the native Welsh mottes. There is no sign of an accompanying bailey. The castle may have been abandoned when Owain Gwynedd invaded in 1149, because he raised Tomen-y-Rhodwydd a few miles away. However, the castle was refortified during King John's invasion of 1212. Ditchers are recorded here in the Pipe Rolls, so the rock-cut ditch surrounding the motte may date from that time.

> *Access:* Visible from the road.

Reference: RCAHMW *Denbighshire.*
Relations: Nearby Tomen-y-Rhodwydd. Castell Dinas Bran was the later stronghold of the lords of Ial.

TOMEN-Y-RHODWYDD   is an impressive motte-and-bailey earthwork. It rises six miles south-east of Ruthin, overlooking the junction between the A525 and the B5431. A massive rampart surrounds the bailey, while the low motte is protected by a deep ditch with an outer rampart. The site is interesting as a monument to Owain Gwynedd, who revived the power of Gwynedd in the mid-twelfth century. He raised this castle in 1149 to consolidate his hold on a slice of territory annexed from Powys. When Henry II invaded in 1157 his ally, the prince of Powys, took the opportunity to destroy the castle. It is likely that Owain re-occupied it when he regained control a decade later, but no stone defences ever replaced the timber palisades.

Access: Obtain permission to visit at the nearby farm.
Reference: Archaeologia Cambrensis (CXXVII). GAHW *Clwyd and Powys.*
Relations: The Welsh mottes of Tomen-y-Faerdre, Mathrafal and Castell Prysor.

OTHER SITES   Several earthwork castles remain. A large motte-and-bailey on the *Erddig* estate, south of Wrexham, stands on the line of Wat's Dyke. *Tomen Cefn Glaniwrch* and *Tomen-y-Maerdy* are near Llangedwyn, while the motte beside *Chirk* parish church is the predecessor of Chirk Castle. These eastern mottes are Norman efforts, but *Pentre Isaf* (near Llangernyw) is probably native Welsh. Owain Gwynedd may have raised the castle mound of *Hen Foelas* (near Pentrefoelas), which once carried a stone keep. Another motte at *Llys Gwenllian* (near Denbigh) is named after Llywelyn the Great's daughter.

Flintshire

The north-east corner of Wales fell under English control even in Saxon times. Offa's Dyke included the coastal strip as part of the kingdom of Mercia. After the Norman conquest of England Robert 'de Rhuddlan' pushed forward to Rhuddlan, raising a motte near the later castle site. The area formed part of the palatine earldom of Chester for nearly a century. Motte-and-bailey castles such as Hawarden and Mold date from this era. There was then an astonishing change of fortune, with the Welsh dominant here under Owain Gwynedd and Llywelyn the Great. Stone castles made a surprisingly late appearance. In 1241 Henry III invaded and built the vanished castle of Dyserth, but Llywelyn the Last once more recovered the area for Gwynedd. He raised Ewloe Castle with its U-shaped keep to strengthen his grip.

English rule was finally established in 1277 by Edward I. His castles of Flint and Rhuddlan bear witness to the invasion. They are both quite ruinous and not as celebrated as Edward's later castles in Gwynedd. The baronial castle of Hawarden rose on the older earthworks about the same time, while Llywelyn's brother Dafydd erected the hilltop castle of Caergwrle before his rebellion led to the final conquest of North Wales. Not that the Welsh were totally subdued – the tower house at Broncoed was built by a fifteenth-century Welsh lord.

BRONCOED TOWER   This is a rare example (for North Wales) of a late medieval tower house. Two miles south-east of Mold, it is usually referred to simply as The Tower. It was built in the fifteenth century by Rheinallt Gruffudd, and can thus be described as the last native Welsh stronghold. A curious tale is told of a private war he waged with the citizens of nearby Chester about 1470, during the Wars of the Roses. Rheinallt hanged the mayor and defeated a raiding party who came to avenge him. Although complete, the small tower suffered a heavy restoration by the Wynne family in the eighteenth century. All the windows and the picturesque corbelled parapet date from that time. A mural stair descends from the entrance to a low, vaulted basement. The two upper floors, also vaulted, are connected by a spiral stair in a projecting turret. At one corner a thinly-walled annexe contains tiny chambers. The tower may originally have stood alone but it is now attached to a much-altered Elizabethan house.

Access: Private.
Reference: RCAHMW *Flintshire.*
Relations: Small tower houses at Scethrog, Talgarth, Candleston and Llandough.

CAERGWRLE CASTLE   is the last of the native Welsh castles. It was begun in 1277 by Dafydd ap Gruffudd, Llywelyn the Last's treacherous brother. A new Welsh castle so near the English border may seem odd in view of the settlement of that year, in which Llywelyn had been forced back into Gwynedd. However, Dafydd had supported Edward I in his campaign, having been banished from Wales following an abortive attempt to overthrow his brother. Under the Treaty of Conwy Dafydd was rewarded with extensive lands east of the River Conwy.

His castle stands five miles north of Wrexham, overlooking Caergwrle village. Its hilltop position is typical of the castles built by Dafydd's princely family. The name suggests that an ancient hillfort occupied the site, and the rampart surrounding the outer ward may go back that far. Although very ruinous, the remaining portions of the castle are built in ashlar masonry, suggesting that English masons were employed. A ditch and curtain enclose the small inner courtyard at the apex of the hill, with a steep drop at the rear.

The curtain begins at the edge of the cliff and, beyond a pair of latrine chutes in the outer face, joins the boldly-projecting North Tower. Its rounded outer front has mostly collapsed. A gap in the curtain may conceal the site of the entrance gateway. The thick curtain continues to the footings of an eastern angle tower, which resembled the North Tower. An oven has been uncovered alongside, suggesting that the kitchen stood here. A short length of curtain leads back to the cliff, where the foundations of a curved piece of wall have been exposed. It represents a segment of a circular keep, most of its circumference having collapsed down the hill. Whether the precipitous western side was ever walled is open to question, but if it was the curtain has long disappeared over the edge.

Perhaps the castle was incomplete when Dafydd, dissatisfied with his lot, precipitated the final showdown with Edward I. He attacked nearby Hawarden Castle in 1282. Dafydd slighted his own castle when Edward invaded, even filling the well with stones to deny it to the English. Dafydd was later captured and taken to Shrewsbury, where he was hanged, drawn and quartered. Meanwhile Edward repaired the castle and gave it to Queen Eleanor. It was known to the English as Hope Castle, after the other neighbouring village. Edward and Eleanor were here in August 1283, and had a narrow escape when a fire consumed the residential buildings, which were no doubt built of wood. This sealed the fate of the castle. After an active life of just six years it was abandoned and fell into ruins.

Access: Always open (LA – uphill walk).
Reference: Archaeologia Cambrensis (CXXIII). *HKW* (I) – under Hope.
Relations: Compare Llywelyn the Last's castles of Ewloe and Dolforwyn. Queen Eleanor built Haverfordwest Castle.

EWLOE CASTLE, two miles north-west of Hawarden, recalls the brief triumph of Llywelyn the Last. He began the castle in 1257, after re-occupying north-east Wales. It would thus have been under construction in those years when Llywelyn was rapidly expanding his dominions. Of all the native castles in North Wales, this one alone has a less than spectacular setting. Although it stands on a promontory overlooking the junction of two streams, the castle is overlooked by higher ground to the south. Its position was strategic, provocatively close to the English frontier and controlling the road to Chester. It also followed a contemporary English trend in being situated for good hunting. The castle stood within the forest of Ewloe and is still surrounded by woods.

Like all the native Welsh castles, Ewloe is not large, and now it is very ruinous. It consists of two courtyards, with a U-shaped keep occupying the roughly triangular upper ward. The layout suggests that Llywelyn utilised the site of an earlier motte-and-bailey castle, and the curtain around the upper ward forms a sloping stone revetment to the motte. Hence this curtain is still quite substantial outside, whereas little stands above courtyard level. The outer curtain is largely reduced to its footings. At the western extremity of the outer ward a circular tower is perched on a rocky knoll. Part of this tower still stands nearly to full height. There is no doorway from the courtyard, so it can only have been reached at wall-walk level.

Still more curious is the fact that no gate connects the two courtyards. Both were entered from outside the castle by adjacent gateways on the north side. Presumably there was some communication at parapet level. Although both curtains are probably Llywelyn's they are not bonded together, so they are the result of successive building campaigns. Nothing survives of the residential buildings, which were no doubt of timber.

There has been some debate over the date of the keep, which is known as the Welsh Tower. Some authorities regard it as an earlier work by Llywelyn the Great because of the first-floor entrance, reached by a flight of steps. Such an arrangement is typical of Norman keeps, but Llywelyn the Last's castle building was conservative (he later built an old-fashioned square keep at Dolforwyn). U-shaped towers usually project from a curtain, so it is odd to find one standing alone in the centre of an enclosure. Llywelyn built a similar free-standing keep at Castell-y-Bere, and both seem to have been designed to command the most vulnerable approach. The keep overlooks the closely-surrounding curtain, so it is a unique native example of concentric defence.

Although part of the keep has collapsed, the southern half stands almost to full height. From the entrance passage a mural staircase curves up to the parapet. The keep contained a single apartment above an unlit storage chamber, which must have been reached by a trap-door. Most native Welsh towers had just two storeys, the only known exception being the round keep at Dolbadarn. The walls rose higher to shield the roof from burning projectiles. Although the parapet of the keep has vanished, slots for a wooden hoarding are still visible.

There is no record of Ewloe during the 1277 invasion. The rampart immediately south of the castle may be an English siege work. Edward I did not retain the castle, instead building the new castles of Flint and Rhuddlan which could be provisioned by sea. Ewloe was thus another native Welsh castle which had a very short career owing to the Edwardian conquest.

Access: Always open (Cadw).

Reference: Guidebook by D. F. Renn and R. Avent (includes Flint).

Relations: Llywelyn the Last's work at Dolforwyn, Criccieth, Castell-y-Bere and Castell Carndochan. Compare the other U-shaped keeps at Montgomery and Roch.

FLINT CASTLE   was begun by Edward I during his invasion of 1277. Edward reached the site in July, when workmen were already arriving. By August nearly three thousand men were employed, mostly in digging the ditches around the castle and the new town. The next year seems to have been taken up with quarrying, and it was only in 1279 that the walls began to rise. Towards the end of 1280 James of St George, the master mason in charge of operations at Rhuddlan Castle, took over at Flint. That is too late for him to be credited with the design of the castle, although the details are very similar to James' work at Rhuddlan and the later Edwardian castles in Gwynedd. Most of the castle was complete by 1282, but the keep continued at a slower pace until 1286 and may never have reached its intended height. By that time £6,068 had been spent here according to the Pipe Rolls, as well as approximately half of the £1,550 recorded for digging the ditches around Flint and Rhuddlan.

All of Edward I's castles, from Flint to Aberystwyth, were near the coast for supply by sea. Flint Castle occupies a low promontory which juts into the estuary of the River Dee. Although the river now keeps its distance, it once filled the moat at high tide. Beside the keep excavations have found a dock where ships could berth.

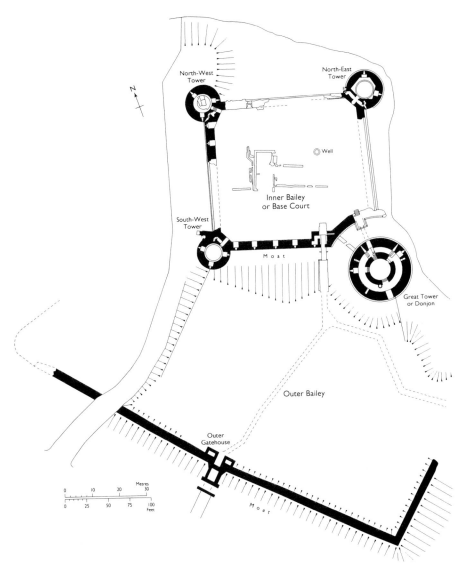

FLINT CASTLE

No doubt this saved the castle in 1282. It resisted an attack by Dafydd ap Gruffudd, though the fledgling borough was sacked. Owain Glyndwr failed to capture the castle on the outbreak of his revolt in 1400. During the Civil War Flint changed hands several times, finally surrendering to Major-General Mytton in August 1646. The castle was heavily slighted the following year and has suffered further as a quarry for the industrialised town.

This explains its very ruinous condition. The outer ward is bounded by a plain curtain which survives only as a low retaining wall for the now-dry moat. A fragment of the outer gate tower remains. Ahead is the inner ward, a square enclosure with circular corner towers, one of them much larger than the others and forming the keep. Most of the inner curtain has perished, its place taken by a more recent retaining wall. Where the curtain does survive – along the south side and for a short stretch on the west – it is pierced by arrow slits as at Rhuddlan.

The North-East Tower is the best preserved of the three mural towers. It contained four storeys, the upper ones polygonal internally as at most of the Edwardian castles. They were linked by a spiral stair and, with their windows, fireplaces and latrines, were intended to be lived in. Note that the curtain wall-walk continued round the backs of the towers – a trait shared by most of the Edwardian castles. Timber residential buildings no doubt stood against the curtain. Surprisingly for an Edwardian castle, there was no gatehouse, the entrance being a simple gateway through the curtain. However, it is immediately flanked by the keep.

Standing isolated from the rest of the inner ward at the south-east corner, the keep is a massive but squat round tower. The inner curtain curves inwards to avoid it. A wooden bridge crossing the moat between them is the successor of the original drawbridge. This isolation recalls certain French keeps, notably Louis IX's Tour de Constance at Aigues Mortes. Edward I would have seen this newly-built tower when he embarked there to go on crusade in 1270. Although round keeps were more fashionable earlier in the century, Edward's vanished castle at Builth also had one.

The entrance passage is surprisingly long, because the keep wall is twenty-three feet thick and encircles a narrow chamber. A vaulted passage is concealed within this great thickness. It runs all the way around the keep, dipping beneath the entrance passage. Though often described as an archers' gallery, foreshadowing the long mural passages at Caernarfon, there are only three arrow slits along it. Three doorways lead down into the central chamber, lending weight to the colourful theory that defenders could have sprung out on unsuspecting assailants if they forced their way into the keep. This might explain why, in contrast to the earlier round keeps of Wales, the entrance was deliberately placed at ground level instead of occupying the floor above.

Higher up, the main reason for the thick surrounding wall becomes apparent. At first-floor level five chambers, now very ruinous, are contained within the great thickness of the wall. It has been suggested that the inner cylinder formed a hall lit only from the roof. However, at least one more storey must have been intended to give the keep a majesty it now sorely lacks. If that was the case then the central space could have served no useful purpose, which seems something of a design flaw. Perhaps the keep rose higher before the slighting. On the other hand, an elaborate timber gallery was built on top of the keep in preparation for a visit by Edward, the new prince of Wales, in 1301. Perhaps this wooden crown was meant to compensate for the lack of height.

One of the five mural chambers faces east and preserves a piscina. This was probably the chapel where Richard II prayed before submitting to Henry of Bolingbroke, who was preparing to lay siege to the castle (1399). Bolingbroke had returned from exile to claim the duchy of Lancaster, but ended up seizing the throne as Henry IV. At Flint, according to the chronicler Jean Froissart, even Richard's favourite greyhound deserted him and went over to Henry. Richard was led away to his deposition and subsequent death at Pontefract.

Access: Always open (Cadw).
Reference: Guidebook by D. F. Renn and R. Avent (includes Ewloe). *HKW* (I).
Relations: The castles of Edward's first Welsh invasion at Rhuddlan, Aberystwyth and Builth. Compare the contemporary round keep at Hawarden and the later isolated keep at Raglan.

HAWARDEN OLD CASTLE is an attractive ruin on a hill in Hawarden Park. It is a baronial castle of the Edwardian period, but the masonry crowns the motte-and-bailey earthworks of a Norman castle established by the Montalt family. They moved to this site from another motte which survives near the parish church. The castle existed by 1205, when it resisted a Welsh attack. In 1264 the victorious Simon de Montfort came here to confer with Llywelyn the Last. He agreed to cede Hawarden to Llywelyn in return for his support. After Simon's defeat and death Llywelyn took the castle by force, but returned it under the terms of the Treaty of Montgomery (1267). Presumably at that time it was still an earth-and-timber stronghold.

Dafydd ap Gruffudd began his revolt with a surprise night attack on the castle in 1282. Roger de Clifford, keeper of Hawarden during the minority of the Montalt heir, was taken prisoner. The attack suggests that the stone castle had already been commenced. It was rare for a lord to undertake significant works at a place he was just holding in wardship, but Edward I perhaps encouraged Clifford to build a castle to complement Flint and Rhuddlan. There may even have been royal assistance, though the Pipe Rolls record no expenditure at Hawarden.

The stone castle consists of a curtain around the bailey and a circular keep on the motte. This keep is the best-preserved part of the castle – Edward I's round keep at Flint no doubt influenced it. Like Flint, but unlike the earlier round keeps of Wales, the entrance is placed at ground level. The entrance passage is flanked by the spiral staircase and a porter's lodge. It leads into the lower floor of the keep, which is lit only by three arrow slits. Another affinity with Flint is the mural passage in the thickness of the keep wall, but here it is placed at first-floor level. Several arrow slits open off it. The vault of the passage recalls the archers' gallery at Caernarfon, suggesting the involvement of the king's master mason, James of St George. The wall passage runs from the spiral stair to a small chapel in the thickness of the wall. A short gap in the passage is occupied by a deep window recess above the keep entrance, from which the portcullis was raised. It is doubtful if the keep rose any higher. The jagged fragments above this level are an eighteenth-century folly, intended to dramatise the keep's silhouette.

In contrast to the keep, the curtain is very ruinous. It was built in straight sections around the older bailey. The curtain is surprisingly tower-less except for the solid base of a semi-circular bastion at the south-east corner. Beside it is the best-preserved piece of curtain, pierced by two tall windows which lit the great hall.

Owain Glyndwr unsuccessfully attacked in 1403. Thomas, Lord Stanley, modernised the castle after 1453. A row of vaulted rooms at the foot of the motte represents new domestic offices. Projecting from the east curtain is the base of a massive rectangular tower. This was a tower house, once housing a lavish set of apartments to replace the limited accommodation in the keep. The ashlar masonry has been thoroughly robbed. Most surprising for this late date was the addition of a long barbican passage to the north of the castle. Its masonry was of similar quality to the tower house and has been reduced to little more than the two drawbridge pits, which are reached by steps.

The castle owes its ruinous state to the Civil War. Having been seized by Charles I's Irish levies in 1643, the Royalists held on to the castle as an outpost of Chester. It finally surrendered to General Mytton in March 1646, after ten months of siege. The old castle was preserved as a romantic landscape feature after the building of the present Hawarden Castle in the 1750s. This castellated mansion was the home of prime minister William Gladstone.

> *Access:* Limited opening times in summer.
> *Reference:* Guide by E. W. Gladstone. RCAHMW *Flintshire. HKW* (I).
> *Relations:* Edward I's castle at Flint. Compare the earlier round keeps at Pembroke, Caldicot, Skenfrith and Tretower.

MOLD CASTLE Bailey Hill, opposite the fifteenth-century parish church at Mold, is a good example of a Norman motte-and-bailey castle. The conical motte stands at one end of an oblong bailey, with a small outwork in front. A bowling green now occupies the bailey. Robert de Montalt may have raised the castle around 1140, but Owain Gwynedd captured it in 1147. Minor royal expenditure is recorded from 1167, after Henry II recovered Mold. Stone walls found in the bailey perhaps belonged to his hall, but there is no later record of the castle.

> *Access:* In a public park (LA).
> *Reference:* RCAHMW *Flintshire.*
> *Relations:* Hawarden Castle also belonged to the Montalts.

RHUDDLAN CASTLES Rhuddlan is dominated by its Edwardian castle, but the little town is older. King Edward the Elder established a 'burgh' or fortified borough here in the year 921. Gruffudd ap Llywelyn used it as a base to devastate the English side of the border during Edward the Confessor's reign. Harold Godwinson – later the ill-fated king – defeated him in 1063. After the Norman Conquest Hugh d'Avranches was installed as palatine earl of Chester, and his kinsman Robert pushed along the north Welsh coastline as far as the Conwy estuary. Robert de Rhuddlan, as he called himself, raised a motte-and-bailey castle here in 1073. It lies to the southeast of the present Rhuddlan Castle, and is reached via a footpath beside the River Clwyd. The motte, known as the Twthill, rises commandingly above the river, and the platform of a bailey can be seen in front.

Its position at the lowest crossing point of the Clwyd made Rhuddlan strategically important, and its stormy history reflects the ebb and flow of Norman and Welsh fortunes. In 1075, just two years after its foundation, the Welsh prince Gruf-

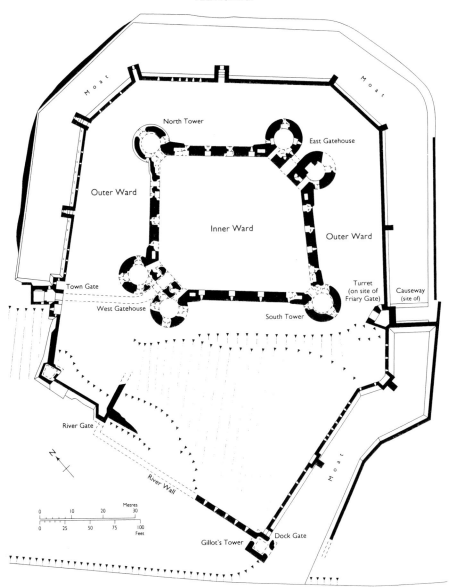

North Tower

East Gatehouse

Outer Ward

Inner Ward

Outer Ward

Moat

Moat

Town Gate

West Gatehouse

Turret
(on site of
Friary Gate)

Causeway
(site of)

South Tower

River Gate

River Wall

Metres
0   10   20   30

0   25   50   75   100
Feet

Gillot's Tower

Dock Gate

Moat

N

RHUDDLAN CASTLE

fudd ap Cynan attempted to capture the castle but was repulsed. Rhuddlan remained firmly in Norman hands until c. 1150, when Owain Gwynedd captured it. The English recovered Rhuddlan under Henry II but lost it again to Owain in 1167, after a three-month siege. It was now the turn of the princes of Gwynedd to hold Rhuddlan for an extended period, terminating when Henry III invaded in 1241. At some point a stone keep (now vanished) appears to have been built on the motte. The wooden bailey defences were repaired by Henry III, despite the erection of a new castle at Dyserth nearby. There was one last period of Welsh rule. Rhuddlan was ceded to Llywelyn the Last in 1267, but recovered ten years later when Edward I invaded.

Edward reached Rhuddlan in August 1277 and decided to build a new castle and borough to the north-west of the Norman site. In September ditchers who had laid out the castle and town at Flint advanced to repeat the process at Rhuddlan. The new town was given a grid of streets which survives to this day. As at Flint, the town had defences of earth and timber only. They have largely disappeared, although the wide ditch – now much shallower than it was – can still be seen at the north corner. Another relic of the Edwardian period is the twin-naved St Mary's Church. It might have been grander if Edward I's plan to make it a cathedral in place of St Asaph had come to fruition. Supply by sea was important for all of Edward's new castles and towns. Rhuddlan is not quite on the coast, so access for ships was made possible by deepening and straightening the River Clwyd for the two miles from Rhuddlan to the sea.

In March 1278 James of St George arrived from Savoy. He took over from the ageing Master Bertram as master mason of the new castle. Thus Edward I's great architect appears for the first time. Although the site must already have been laid out, it seems reasonable to credit James with the design of the castle. It would have been well on its way to completion by the time he was transferred to Flint at the end of 1280. The castle was defensible in time to withstand an attack during Dafydd ap Gruffudd's rising in 1282. Work continued on the courtyard buildings afterwards, the accounts ending in 1285. The Pipe Rolls record an expenditure of £9,202, in addition to the initial cost of digging the ditches around Flint and Rhuddlan which jointly accounted for £1,550.

Rhuddlan served as the main base for Edward I's thrust into Gwynedd in 1283. Here the following year the Statute of Wales was proclaimed, laying down the constitutional framework for the conquered principality. Perhaps it was on this occasion that the king presented his infant son Edward to the Welsh as a prince 'born in Wales who can speak no English'. The later history of the castle is punctuated by several unsuccessful attacks during Owain Glyndwr's revolt and a prolonged Civil War siege, ending with its surrender to Major-General Thomas Mytton in July 1646. Slighted two years later, it was described soon afterwards as a 'wind- and war-shaken castle' – in fact shaken far more by war than wind.

The castle is the best preserved of the royal castles founded during Edward I's Welsh campaign of 1277. Even here the effects of slighting are very apparent, but the castle preserves its majesty. This is especially so from the river, where the south-west facade lacks only its battlements.

Like Aberystwyth, another of Edward's first group, the castle is a concentric fortification. A roughly square inner ward is closely surrounded by an outer curtain except on the south-west, where the ground slopes down to the river and the outer ward widens to meet it. The outer curtain rises out of a broad, flat-bottomed ditch. Today it appears to be little more than a revetment, because not much stands above the level of the outer ward. The main entrance or Town Gate, aligned with the West Gatehouse of the inner curtain, is set between a pair of square turrets.

Heading away from the river, four small, square-fronted towers project from the line of the curtain. Each contains a flight of steps leading down to a postern in the ditch, though so many entrances may have proved to be a weakness during Dafydd's attack because they were soon blocked up. Arrow slits are regularly spaced along the outer curtain, but only near the north corner do they remain complete. Further along the wall is strengthened by buttresses which may have supported corbelled turrets higher up. On the east side of the outer curtain are the footings of a second gatehouse. It is called the Friary Gate because it led to a Dominican friary outside the town. However, this entrance proved superfluous and was blocked in 1300.

From here the outer curtain descends to meet the river. At the angle rises the four-storey Gillot's Tower, guarding a postern where ships could berth. This tower is square, like the others on the outer curtain. Square towers are unusual in the Edwardian period, when the more efficient round tower was generally employed. Beyond a length of loop-holed wall, the curtain was undermined long ago by the Clwyd before it changed course. Indeed, the section of wall further along had to be rebuilt as early as 1300 owing to undercutting by the river.

The inner curtain is much more massive than the outer. It has twin-towered gate-houses at the east and west corners, and circular towers at the other two angles. This design contrasts with Aberystwyth, which had a single gatehouse dominating the rest. Both of the Rhuddlan gatehouses are of equal size and status. The idea of a fully symmetrical castle with twin gatehouses would reach its zenith at Beaumaris, where James of St George designed a larger pair. Neither of those at Rhuddlan can be called a keep-gatehouse, because there was no large courtyard projection for the constable's hall. Hence Rhuddlan is a rare example of a keep-less castle.

Time has contrived to make the gatehouses appear different. The West Gate-house rises to its full height, whereas the East Gatehouse is truncated and one of its towers has collapsed. However, at ground level the East Gatehouse is better pre-served, because it has suffered much less from stone-robbing than its western coun-terpart. There is a similar contrast between the complete South Tower and the broken down North Tower. All six towers were very similar, consisting of three polygonal residential chambers above circular ground-floor rooms. They were served by latrines and fireplaces. The gate passages were defended by a single port-cullis and a pair of gates – not much compared with the multiple barriers of the later Edwardian castles. Two stretches of curtain have also been deliberately breached, such was the determination of the Roundheads to render this castle untenable.

Arrow slits pierce all four sides of the inner curtain, but the open appearance of the ward is misleading. When complete it would have been much smaller, with buildings against the curtain on all sides. These were timber-framed but the accounts show that they were designed on a lavish scale, with separate halls and chambers for king and queen, in addition to the garrison's quarters.

Access: The castle is open daily in summer, while the Twthill is freely accessible (both Cadw).

Reference: Guidebook by A. J. Taylor. *HKW* (I).

Relations: The other castles of Edward's first Welsh campaign at Flint, Aberystwyth and Builth. Aberystwyth is concentric, along with James of St George's later castles of Beaumaris and Harlech.

OTHER SITES *Prestatyn* preserves the earthwork site of a castle raised in 1164 and destroyed by the Welsh just four years later. Unusually for a Norman castle, its low motte is surrounded by a concentric bailey. A motte overlooking St Winefride's Chapel at *Holywell* is attributed to the earl of Chester as late as 1210. Other Norman mottes can be seen at *Bryn-y-Cwn*, south of Flint, and *Tyddin* (near Buckley). Excavations at the moated site of *Llys Edwin* (near Mold) revealed a Norman hall with a keep-like tower and other turrets.

Two pre-Edwardian royal castles have all but vanished. During his invasion of 1157 Henry II raised *Basingwerk Castle* (a few miles from the abbey of the same name) on a spur near Flint. Now known as Hen Blas, this was an earthwork enclosure, though excavations have uncovered a later stone gatehouse. After Henry III invaded in 1241 he built *Dyserth Castle*, complementing his castle at Deganwy further west. Llywelyn the Last destroyed it in 1263, and Edward I chose to build closer to the coast at Rhuddlan instead. Only a stretch of rock-cut ditch survives on a quarried site north of Dyserth village. Its small ward was entered through a twin-towered gatehouse and there may have been a concentric outer curtain – if so, the first in Wales.

Glamorgan

Robert Fitz Hamon invaded Morgannwg around 1091, wresting control of the Vale of Glamorgan from the Welsh. This coastal strip became the lordship of Glamorgan. Heavily settled by the Normans, it is crammed with more castles than any other part of Wales, with particular concentrations around Cardiff, Cowbridge and Bridgend. However, many of these castles have suffered much decay. Cardiff had the chief castle of the lordship. The shell keep on its great motte is an important Norman relic inside a reconstructed Roman fort. Norman tower keeps at Coity, Ogmore and Kenfig are now very ruinous, while those at Fonmon and Penllyn are absorbed by later mansions. Newcastle (at Bridgend) is unique for its elaborate Norman gateway. Alongside these stone castles are the Norman earthworks. Glamorgan is the only Welsh county to have more ringwork enclosures than mottes. A number remain unencumbered by later masonry, such as Llanilid and the first castle site at Dinas Powys.

Surprisingly little survives from the first half of the thirteenth century. St Fagan's and the second Dinas Powys castle are simple, tower-less enclosures which probably date from this period. Otherwise there are some ruins at Castell Tal-y-Fan and Penmark, part of a round keep at Llantrisant and the restored Black Tower at Cardiff.

Moving into the Edwardian period, by far the greatest castle in Glamorgan is Gilbert de Clare's mighty concentric fortress at Caerphilly. It provided the inspiration for Edward I's castles of North Wales and went even further with its artificial lake. The other Edwardian castles have all suffered badly. Gilbert's Castell Coch was reconstructed in Victorian times, while his castles of Morlais and Llangynwyd are reduced to rubble. The Stradling family copied the concentric theme at St Donat's Castle. Neath and St Quintin's are dominated by Edwardian gatehouses, and so is the episcopal palace at Llandaff. Meanwhile, the last prince of Senghenydd built Castell Morgraig, the most formidable of the native Welsh castles. Ewenny Priory is remarkable for its defensive precinct wall, while Cowbridge preserves the only medieval town wall in Glamorgan. Even during this period, there are 'castles' with only token defences at Beaupre and Barry.

Relatively little castle building took place afterwards. Coity, largely rebuilt around the middle of the fourteenth century, is the one later medieval castle of substance. Cardiff Castle's splendid state apartments originated under Richard Beauchamp in the fifteenth century. Candleston and Llandough have tower houses, while St George's retains a late medieval hall. The outer wall of St Donat's Castle now encloses a Tudor mansion.

The beautiful Gower (Gwyr) peninsula formed a separate Marcher lordship established by Henry de Beaumont, earl of Warwick. Its chief castle at Swansea preserves a handsome domestic block in an unsympathetic urban setting. There is a similar emphasis on domestic comfort in nearby Oystermouth Castle, which survives in excellent condition on its coastal hill. Pennard is much more ruinous. All three castles were largely built by the de Braose lords in Edwardian times. Their stewards contributed a fine group of domestic buildings at Weobley Castle and the surviving tower at Loughor. Penrice Castle, replacing an earlier ringwork nearby, is an extensive ruin dominated by a circular keep.

BARRY CASTLE is a small ruin beside the Porthkerry road, on the west side of the town. The de Barris of Manorbier Castle took their name from this place, and it remained a possession of the family until the fourteenth century. Although called a castle, this was in fact a courtyard house with only limited defensive pretensions. All that survives is the ruined south range, which was rebuilt after damage incurred during Llywelyn Bren's revolt in 1316. It contained a spacious hall at first-floor level, but only two walls of the undercroft rise to any height. Better preserved is the slender gate tower alongside. The gateway retains its portcullis groove and the pointed window above may have lit a chapel. Because the gatehouse occupied one corner of the quadrangle, the gable end of the original, thirteenth-century hall is immediately ahead and access to the courtyard involved a right-angled turn.

Access: Freely accessible (LA).
Reference: GAHW *Glamorgan and Gwent.*
Relations: The de Barris' castle at Manorbier.

BEAUPRE CASTLE overlooks the River Thaw, two miles south-east of Cowbridge. It is reached by a path from the road between St Hilary and St Mary Church. The name is a corruption of Beau Repaire – 'beautiful retreat' – which sums up its idyllic setting. Despite its Edwardian origin, this charming ruin is largely an unfortified mansion. Medieval Wales had few manor houses on this scale, and Beaupre is surpassed only by the episcopal palaces of Lamphey and St David's in Pembrokeshire. It was the seat of the Basset family until 1709.

Richard Basset added the picturesque forecourt in Elizabethan times. It is curious for its parapet walk, which cannot have served any genuine defensive purpose but reflects the taste for castellated architecture still prevalent in Elizabethan Wales. The forecourt is entered through a handsome gatehouse dated 1586, but the highlight of Richard Basset's work is a splendid Classical porch in front of the older hall.

The hall, though also remodelled, is part of the original manor house, built soon after 1300. It preserves a splendid fifteenth-century fireplace, which has been moved from its original position. Beside the hall is the original vaulted gate passage, blocked during the Elizabethan conversion. The one defensive feature is the chamber block which projects in front of the gateway. This has thicker walls than the rest and originally served as a tower house, but its character has been altered by Elizabethan gables. The rest of the medieval mansion stood around a large courtyard behind the hall. Some of its buildings remain, intact but much altered, on a farm.

> *Access:* Always open (Cadw).
> *Reference:* GAHW *Glamorgan and Gwent*. BOW *Glamorgan*.
> *Relations:* Tower houses at Candleston, Llandough, Weobley and Scethrog.

CAERPHILLY CASTLE is justly recognised as one of the greatest castles in Europe. It rivals the Edwardian castles of North Wales and was long believed to be an unrecorded work of Edward I. In fact Caerphilly was largely complete by the time those castles were rising, and no doubt provided the inspiration for them. Not only was it the first major concentric castle in Britain, but it was almost unique in its employment of water defences on a grand scale. The whole complex covers some thirty acres. Thus it is surprising to find that this landmark castle was not the work of the king but of a powerful baron. Gilbert de Clare, the 'Red Earl' of Gloucester and Hertford, went to extraordinary lengths to protect and extend his lordship of Glamorgan. Taken with his other castles in Glamorgan, it represents a building programme second only to the king's.

The achievement of building this great castle is all the more remarkable considering the difficult circumstances of its construction. The lands north of Caerphilly Mountain were ruled by the native prince of Senghenydd until 1266, when the young Gilbert de Clare carried him off to captivity in Ireland. Gilbert sought to extend his northern frontier as a buffer against the triumphant Llywelyn the Last, who had become his unwelcome neighbour. Llywelyn claimed overlordship of all lands ruled by the native Welsh, and he complained when Gilbert started building on this annexed territory in April 1268. In 1270 he descended on Caerphilly and burnt the incomplete castle. He came again the following year, but withdrew after

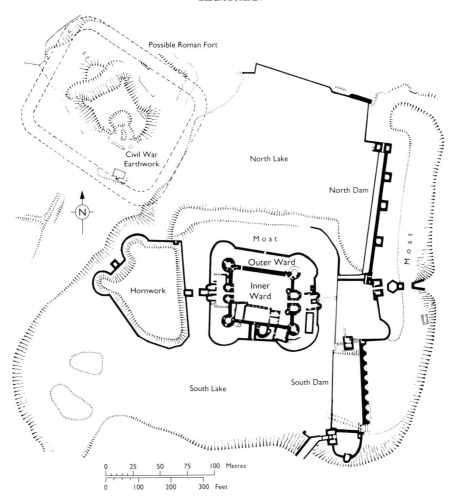

Possible Roman Fort

Civil War
Earthwork

North Lake

North Dam

Moat

Outer Ward

Inner
Ward

Hornwork

Moat

South Dam

South Lake

N

0   25   50   75   100 Metres

0   100   200   300 Feet

CAERPHILLY CASTLE

Henry III offered to arbitrate in the dispute. In the meantime, the castle was to be left incomplete in the custody of two English bishops.

Gilbert's men soon seized the castle from its ecclesiastical guardians, but he seems to have honoured the truce. Consequently there is good reason for assuming that the vast bulk of the castle was built in the period 1268–71. Hence Caerphilly, as well as being on a par with the Edwardian castles of North Wales, was built with the same speed. Unfortunately there are no building accounts for this baronial enterprise and the architect remains a mystery. It wasn't James of St George, who was clearly influenced by Caerphilly. The northern half of the great dam and the domestic buildings are later additions, probably resulting from a resumption of operations after the peace with Llywelyn had broken down in 1276. It is likely that the whole castle was complete by the time Gilbert began his more northerly castle of Morlais around 1287.

In the years that followed 'Giant Caerphilly' – as a contemporary Welsh poet called it – was justly considered to be the most prestigious castle in the lordship, if the constable's salary is anything to go by. Although the new town was sacked in the Welsh uprising of 1295, the castle had to wait until 1316 to be tested, resisting an attack during Llywelyn Bren's revolt even though it was virtually ungarrisoned. After the last Gilbert de Clare fell at Bannockburn, Edward II gave the lordship of Glamorgan to his favourite and possible lover, Hugh le Despenser the Younger. In lavishly remodelling the great hall Despenser contributed the only later modification to the fabric.

Caerphilly is associated with Edward II's downfall in 1326. During his flight from Queen Isabella's supporters he took refuge here for a few days, entrusting the castle with much of his treasure. The constable, Sir John Felton, undertook a valiant resistance against the rebels for several months, despite the execution of the Despensers and Edward's abdication. Ignoring the offer of a free pardon for the garrison, he creditably held out until receiving an assurance that the young Despenser heir would not suffer the same fate as his father and grandfather.

After this time the castle suffered neglect as Cardiff once again became the chief residence of the lordship. There is a tradition that it was damaged by Owain Glyndwr. In the fifteenth century only one tower was regularly maintained to serve as a prison, and when the antiquary John Leland visited around 1539 he described the castle as a massive ruin surrounded by a marsh – so the lakes had already been drained. Although there is no record of activity here in the Civil War, the castle evidently suffered a heavy slighting. All four corner towers of the inner curtain, along with the outer front of the great East Gatehouse, appear to have been blown up.

In this respect Caerphilly is no longer quite the equal of Caernarfon, Beaumaris or Harlech. Its present state of near-completeness is due to an ambitious restoration by the fourth marquess of Bute from 1928. He rebuilt two of the inner ward towers, refronted the East Gatehouse and replaced many of the battlements. All this was done in a scholarly manner, atoning for his father's imaginative reconstructions at Cardiff and Castell Coch. Without it, Caerphilly would be much more of a ruin. Still more important for the impact of the castle today is the reflooding of the lakes in the 1950s.

Although the main castle is concentric, that is merely the central portion. To the west is an outer enclosure, while the eastern approach is closed by a long screen wall which serves as a dam to hold in the lake. There are in fact two lakes, one on the north and one on the south. Gilbert de Clare was no doubt influenced by the great lake which once protected Kenilworth Castle. Gilbert had been present at the siege of Kenilworth in 1266, when the younger Simon de Montfort defied the royal army for months.

Owing to the lie of the land there are no lakes to east and west. However, the western ward and the eastern screen wall shielded the main castle from direct assault, and a succession of moats isolate each element of the castle. The profusion of twin-towered gatehouses is a notable feature. There are seven in all, including three forming a line on the eastern approach. One of these, the East Gatehouse, is the first fully developed keep-gatehouse in Wales. Although the gatehouses on the concentric wall and the dam are comparatively small, they all had drawbridges, portcullises, gates and murder holes to defend them.

Only the southern half of the great screen wall belongs to the first phase of building, so only the south lake can have existed at the time of the truce in 1271. The northern lake was created once building had resumed after 1276. There is quite a contrast in style between the two halves of the dam. The southern half is a wide platform contained by a massively buttressed wall. Conversely, the northern half forms a narrow corridor. Instead of buttresses, the wall here is reinforced by three projecting towers. These towers are semi-octagonal over square bases with tall receding spurs, a feature common in the Edwardian castles of South Wales but not found in the first phase of building at Caerphilly. Near the south end of the screen wall note the arch of the sluice gate, which controlled the water level.

Originally there was just a single gatehouse at the south end of the dam. Its flanking towers are rounded like all the other towers of the first phase, though in its present form this gatehouse is mainly a 1930s reconstruction. It faces west at the edge of the lake, and is commanded by a flanking turret at the southern apex of the platform. At this stage then, the south dam formed an ingenious barbican. Attackers who succeeded in penetrating the gatehouse would be under fire from the main castle as they fought their way along the platform towards the entrance. When the northern half of the dam was built, two further gatehouses were added. They have semi-octagonal flanking towers with tall spurs, like the three mural towers along this section. The northern gatehouse, like the southern, involves a long approach along the dam. However, this squat gatehouse was left unfinished. For the sake of convenience a third gatehouse was built in the middle of the dam, in line with the two eastern gatehouses of the main castle. This must have rendered the north and south gates redundant.

Like Edward I's later concentric fortifications, the main castle is symmetrically laid out on an oblong plan. Round towers flanked the corners of the inner curtain and there are gatehouses in the middle of the east and west sides. Around it, at a lower level, is the concentric wall. Gatehouses to east and west mimic the larger ones immediately behind them, otherwise the outer curtain is plain. It curves outwards in line with the inner corner towers, like the later concentric wall at Harlech.

As seen from the dam, the east front typifies Caerphilly's mixed state of ruin and restoration. The middle gatehouse preserves its flanking towers, but one of them is a rebuilding and the gateway between them has perished. Behind it, the outer front of the East Gatehouse is entirely Lord Bute's reconstruction. Plans to rebuild the fallen tower at the north-east corner of the inner ward were abandoned when restoration came to an abrupt halt in 1939. The south-east corner tower survived the Civil War attempt to blow it up, but only just. It now leans precariously outwards at ten degrees from vertical. The battlements crowning the 'Leaning Tower of Caerphilly' are the only original ones in the castle.

Although the front of the East Gatehouse has been rebuilt from the foundations, the rest of the gatehouse is original except for the battlements. It is a keep-gatehouse of the Edwardian type, intended to house the constable who could thus keep watch over the main entrance. In fact, it was more seriously defensible from within than Edward I's keep-gatehouses. Gates barred access from the courtyard as well as from outside, and the only entrances led into the chambers on either side of the gate passage. Even the doorways leading to the curtain wall-walks were closed by portcullises. Round turrets at the rear corners of the gatehouse contain spiral staircases leading to the upper floors. The first floor is lit by small windows throughout. Only at second-floor level are two large windows allowed, their tracery renewed when the gatehouse was restored. They lit the hall, which was located this high up to prevent disturbance by drawbridge and portcullis gear. Narrow side wings contain small chambers, including a chapel.

In the first building phase the inner curtain was of uniform and modest height all round. After 1276, however, the original wall-walk of the south curtain became a mural passage with a new parapet higher up. This was done to shield the main domestic apartments which lie against the wall. These apartments are unusually well preserved for a Welsh castle but their layout is quite odd.

It is likely that the great hall was permitted to rise in the years of truce 1271–76, since it was built onto the south curtain before that was heightened. The ashlar facade towards the courtyard, contrasting with the rougher masonry of the rest of the castle, belongs to Hugh le Despenser's remodelling. So do the large windows with their delicate hoods. Within, the great hall is a handsome chamber. Carved corbels (several depicting Edward II) once supported a timber roof crafted by the royal carpenter who went on to design the magnificent octagon at Ely Cathedral. In its place there is now a Victorian roof inserted by the third marquess of Bute. A small block containing the solar and chapel is attached to the east side of the hall.

The other domestic buildings, now quite ruinous, all date from Gilbert de Clare's time but represent piecemeal and rather confused additions. First he added a semicircular tower midway along the south wall, containing a vaulted kitchen and residential chambers. Almost immediately, its defensive purpose was negated by the construction of buildings on either side, filling the space between the two curtains. To the east is a large kitchen annexe. On the west the tower is obscured by a walled passage containing a staircase. It descends from the great hall to a water gate in the outer curtain. Supplies could have been brought in here by boat across the lake. Lack of space in the inner ward must have forced the designer's hand, but the foiling of the concentric layout so recently established can only reflect a sense of relaxation after Llywelyn's defeat. Finally, the original modest solar was supplanted by a larger one west of the great hall.

Owing to restoration the west end of the inner ward appears more complete than the east. Both corner towers were rebuilt by the fourth marquess, though fallen portions were painstakingly incorporated in the reconstruction. Of the two the North-West Tower is the more authentic, since only part of its circumference had been blasted down. Between them is the West Gatehouse, smaller than its eastern counterpart with only one storey over the vaulted side chambers. So Caerphilly does not have the curiosity of two keep-gatehouses as seen later at Beaumaris. The West Gatehouse escaped the slighting; so did the smaller gatehouse of the outer curtain in front, its archway framed by a drawbridge recess.

From here a modern bridge crosses the moat to the western enclosure. This has a stone revetment rising out of the moat, but it was never built up into a curtain. A bridge between two low bastions crosses another moat to the outside world. The mound beyond is an artillery redoubt, raised to supplement the castle defences by its obscure Civil War garrison. Excavations have shown that this earthwork occupies the site of a Roman fort.

Access: Open daily (Cadw).
Reference: Guidebooks by D. F. Renn and C. N. Johns. *Caerphilly Castle* by W. Rees.
Relations: The concentric castles with keep-gatehouses at Kidwelly, Aberystwyth, Harlech and Beaumaris. Compare Gilbert de Clare's work at Castell Coch, Morlais and Tonbridge (Kent).

CANDLESTON CASTLE occupies a wooded knoll overlooking sand dunes beyond the picturesque village of Merthyr Mawr, three miles south-west of Bridgend. Its name recalls that it was occupied by a branch of the Cantilupe family. The U-shaped earthwork, which may be Norman, is crowned by some remains of a curtain. One stretch retains its battlements. At the back of the courtyard is the overgrown ruin of a fifteenth-century hall-house. The hall itself stood at first-floor level. Its ornate though damaged fireplace survives high up, but the building suffered many alterations as a farmhouse until the encroaching dunes caused its abandonment in Victorian times. The projecting wing is a Tudor addition. At the south end of the hall rises a small tower house, perhaps a generation older than the hall. It contains a solar at hall level, reached by a straight mural staircase from the vaulted ground floor. Another stair ascends to the plain top floor.

Access: Freely accessible.
Reference: BOW *Glamorgan*.
Relations: Tower houses at Beaupre, Llandough, Scethrog and Talgarth.

CARDIFF CASTLE is an imposing sight in the middle of the big city. It is a unique combination of Roman fort, medieval castle and Victorian mansion. A fort was first established here during the Roman invasion of South Wales, but a new one rose towards the end of the third century. It served as a naval base to intercept Irish pirates who were raiding the coast. As such the fort belongs with the group of 'Saxon Shore' forts erected along the south-east coast of Roman Britain. After the Roman withdrawal the fort site seems to have been abandoned. The Normans utilised it as the setting for a castle, raising a motte in the north-west quadrant. William the Conqueror is said to have first established the castle on his return from a pilgrimage to St David's in 1081. The unusually grand scale of the motte – at forty feet high the largest in Wales – may support this tradition. If not, then it was raised by the Norman adventurer Robert Fitz Hamon. He arrived about the year 1091, ostensibly to arbitrate in a Welsh dispute. He defeated the prince of Morgannwg and estab-

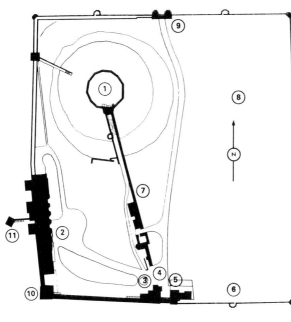

1. THE KEEP
2. CASTLE APARTMENTS
3. BLACK TOWER
4. WELCH REGIMENT MUSEUM
5. BARBICAN TOWER
6. ROMAN WALL
7. BARBICAN WALL
8. OUTER WARD
9. NORTH GATE
10. CLOCK TOWER
11. WEST GATE

CARDIFF CASTLE

lished the lordship of Glamorgan, which for nearly two hundred years would be confined to the narrow coastal strip.

In 1122 Henry I granted the lordship to his illegitimate son Robert, earl of Gloucester. Henry's elder brother Robert Curthose, captured and cruelly blinded in 1106, spent eight years of his long captivity at Cardiff. According to tradition he was incarcerated in the keep, but it is unlikely to be quite that old. Robert of Gloucester went on to become one of the chief supporters of the empress Matilda in her struggle to wrest the Crown from her usurping cousin Stephen. His exploits during the Anarchy are romantically depicted in the Victorian murals of the great hall. Robert's son and successor William was abducted by the prince of Senghenydd, who raided the castle in 1158. William was only released after granting concessions. We do not know if the shell keep already existed at that time – if not, this experience may have prompted William to build it. Another Welsh raid in 1183 left the castle damaged.

Prince John held the lordship of Glamorgan after William's death. He was followed by the de Clare earls of Gloucester and Hertford. After the last de Clare fell at Bannockburn, Edward II granted the lordship to Hugh le Despenser the Younger. Loved by the king but hated by almost everyone else, the Marcher barons ransacked the castle in 1321 and temporarily forced Despenser into exile. Despite his execution on Edward II's downfall, the lordship stayed in the hands of the Despenser family for the rest of the fourteenth century. Owain Glyndwr sacked Cardiff in 1404 but failed to take the castle in a prolonged siege. In 1423 Richard Beauchamp, earl of Warwick, married into the lordship. He was more than an absentee landlord, despite his role as guardian of the young Henry VI and his involvement in the

French wars. Richard built the nucleus of the present state apartments. His Welsh estates descended to Richard Neville (better known as the 'Kingmaker'), Richard III, and Henry VII's uncle, Jasper Tudor. The castle resisted Royalist attacks in 1646 in 1648.

Cardiff is one of the few Welsh castles to have been transformed into an aristocratic mansion. The Herbert family had already enlarged the state apartments in Elizabethan times, and they were further extended in the eighteenth century. However, they are now a testimony to the medieval fantasies of John Crichton-Stuart, third marquess of Bute, and his architect William Burges. Work began in 1867. A stately home in such an urban setting is a rarity, but the Butes were instrumental in transforming Cardiff from a small town into a busy port. As a result their ancestral wealth was massively augmented, and the third marquess ploughed much of it into his grandiose building schemes. The Butes severed their connection with Cardiff in 1947 and returned to Scotland.

The forbidding wall surrounding the castle is both its oldest and newest part. After completing the state apartments, the marquess of Bute began an ambitious reconstruction of the Roman fort wall, which was only completed in 1923. Later Roman forts were very different in character from those of the early empire. With their relatively thick walls and flanking bastions, they show that the Roman army was being forced onto the defensive as barbarian pressure increased. At Cardiff semi-octagonal towers project at regular intervals. The best part of the rebuilding is the twin-towered North Gate. The mural gallery which runs all the way along the wall is more fanciful. Although the existing wall and towers are mostly Victorian, they are built on the ancient foundations which are clearly discernible for much of the circuit. Near the eastern end of the south wall the original masonry remains to a considerable height. This stretch can also be seen from a modern passage within the backing rampart.

Although the reconstructed wall gives us a good idea of what the Roman fort was like, it should be borne in mind that the medieval castle was very different. The fort was divided into two unequal parts by a diagonal cross-wall, and only the smaller inner bailey on the west was ever walled in stone. Elsewhere, in typical Norman fashion, Robert Fitz Hamon had buried the decaying Roman wall beneath an earth rampart. Thus from the Norman conquest until the late nineteenth century, there was an earth bank instead of a stone wall on the north, the east, and half of the south sides – precisely those portions which have been rebuilt. The western half of the south wall is largely medieval, though the covered parapet is a fanciful addition.

No doubt a Roman gatehouse similar to the North Gate occupied the centre of the south front. The existing South Gate and the tower to its right are Victorian – and in medieval vein rather than Roman. However, the tall Black Tower to its left is genuine medieval work, if somewhat restored like most of the castle. This tower marked the south-east corner of the stone inner bailey. Its square plan makes its traditional attribution to the 'Red Earl', Gilbert de Clare, very unlikely. Such an antiquated design does not accord with his Edwardian castles at Caerphilly and elsewhere. It seems more likely that the tower is the work of his grandfather, another Gilbert – one of the barons who forced King John to sign the Magna Carta. Three storeys rise above a gloomy basement prison. Tudor windows have been cut through the walls and there is a projecting latrine turret. The tower contains one of the two regimental museums within the castle.

A cross-wall ran from the Black Tower to the keep, dividing the stone inner bailey from the earthwork outer bailey. This wall was levelled in 1778 by the landscaper 'Capability' Brown to create an uninterrupted lawn within the old fort enclosure. Its site is outlined in modern stone, along with the base of a square tower which flanked the inner gateway. A continuation of this wall forms a wide staircase ascending the Norman motte, which is encircled by a wet moat. On top stands the shell keep.

Only the keep has survived unscathed the later transformation of the castle, successive plans to convert it into a ballroom or a chapel thankfully never coming to fruition. Whether this keep is the work of Robert of Gloucester or his son William is impossible to tell. It is the finest of the few surviving shell keeps in Wales, consisting of a polygonal wall around the summit of the motte. One portion, slightly higher than the rest, represents the outer face of a square tower which was built to command the entrance. In common with some English shell keeps, the entrance was later strengthened with a gate tower. This semi-octagonal projection may have been added by Hugh le Despenser. Presumably there were residential buildings on the confined summit but the interior of the keep is now empty.

Although the keep formed the last resort of the Norman castle, the main residential buildings probably descended into the courtyard at an early stage. They stand against the west curtain. The present library embodies Richard Beauchamp's hall, and the vaulted undercroft beneath it is a rare Welsh example of medieval brickwork. However, everything else is the work of William Burges. His genius is on display in a succession of striking and highly colourful rooms, ranging from the baronial splendour of the present great hall (on the floor above the library) to the Alhambra-style frenzy of the Arab Room.

No doubt the west curtain is still Roman in its core, but the restorer's hand has been heavy. It overlooks Bute Park, sloping down to the River Taff. Between two square towers of the Bute mansion rises the appropriately-named Octagon Tower. This slender tower lies behind the hall and was also built by Richard Beauchamp. Burges added an incongruous spire above the restored machicolations. However, the dominant feature of the castle skyline is the 150-feet high Clock Tower at the south-west corner, built by Burges in a creepy Gothic style which would look more at home in Transylvania.

The streets south of the castle mark the site of the medieval town. Its defensive wall and four gates, probably built in the late thirteenth century when most Welsh boroughs were walled, have perished. They failed to keep out Owain Glyndwr. St John's Church is the only other relic of medieval Cardiff.

Access: Open daily (LA).
Reference: Cardiff Castle by J. P. Grant. *Glamorgan: The Early Castles*. LA guidebook.
Relations: Compare the shell keeps at Brecon, Tretower and Carmarthen. Portchester and Pevensey are English examples of Roman forts converted into castles. William Burges also rebuilt Castell Coch.

CASTELL COCH rises above the River Taff gorge. It overlooks the village of Tongwynlais, just five miles north-west of Cardiff city centre. With its three massive towers capped by conical roofs it is the perfect castle of make-believe. If it appears too good to be true, that is because the existing structure is mainly a romantic reconstruction of Victorian times. In 1875, with the rebuilding of the Cardiff Castle state apartments going on apace, the third Marquess of Bute commissioned his architect William Burges to rebuild Castell Coch as a hunting lodge for weekend parties. Nevertheless it is no fanciful sham. Burges was a scholar of medieval military architecture, influenced by the French castle restorer, Viollet-le-Duc. Furthermore, he was building on the ruins of a genuine medieval castle. Externally at least, he faithfully reproduced it.

The medieval castle is something of a mystery. It dates from the late thirteenth century, comprising a tiny oval courtyard with three circular towers. The walls encase a low Norman motte and there was once an outer courtyard. Owing to the small size of the castle the towers seem disproportionately large. In examining the ruins prior to rebuilding, Burges discerned that the remains belonged to two distinct builds. The Kitchen Tower at the south-west angle, the adjoining hall and the curtain had all been built in a red sandstone rubble (hence 'Red Castle'). Ashlar masonry was then used to thicken the curtain. Two more towers were added on the east front, with a square gate tower adjoining one of them.

According to tradition this is a native Welsh castle begun by Gruffudd ap Rhys, prince of Senghenydd. Like his Castell Morgraig, it overlooks the narrow coastal plain which formed the English lordship of Glamorgan. The completion of the castle is then attributed to Gilbert de Clare after he overthrew Gruffudd in 1266. However, one feature makes Gilbert more likely to be responsible for both phases. The Kitchen Tower, like the so-called keep at the south-east corner, rises from a massive square base with pyramid spurs. Such spurs are a hallmark of Edwardian architecture in South Wales, and seem unlikely to be the work of a native prince.

So how much of the castle is original? The joint between the old and the new is quite apparent outside. Paradoxically, the rough masonry of the first phase survives better. Much of the curtain, the hall undercroft and the lower half of the Kitchen Tower are genuine. So is the ground stage of the Well Tower, with its well and pit prison. However, the 'keep' (which is no larger than the other towers) and its attached gate tower had to be rebuilt from their footings. Burges found evidence of mining tunnels, indicating a deliberate slighting at some point in the Middle Ages. If this occurred as a result of Gilbert's truce with Llywelyn the Last in 1271, then the castle had a short life indeed.

Having taken due note of how much is genuinely old, it is best to forget it and enjoy the spectacle. The big conical roofs of the towers are the most doubtful feature of the whole restoration. They would be more plausible in France than Britain, but their effect is striking. A ramp ascends to the gateway, which is overlooked by a wooden gallery or hoarding (a reconstruction of a common medieval feature). Both the drawbridge and the portcullis can be raised from the chamber above the gate passage. The drawbridge is a turning bridge, its inner part descending into a pit within the gate passage when the outer part is raised. This is a faithful reconstruction of the original arrangement. The concentration of arrow slits in the curved stretch of curtain between the Well and Kitchen towers is unusual. Above them, Burges roofed the wall-walk and placed hinged shutters between the merlons. A covered stairway leads from the courtyard to the hall. Internally the castle is all Victorian medieval-ism, seen on a grander scale at Cardiff Castle. The hall is suitably baronial, and the rebuilt keep contains a galleried drawing room. Most of the decoration was done according to Burges' designs by others, following his death in 1881.

> *Access:* Open daily (Cadw).
> *Reference:* Guidebook by D. McLees.
> *Relations:* Gruffudd ap Rhys' Castell Morgraig, and Gilbert de Clare's Caerphilly. William Burges created the state rooms in Cardiff Castle.

CASTELL MORGRAIG lies concealed in woods above the A469, two miles south of Caerphilly. It is interesting as a native Welsh castle built by Gruffudd ap Rhys, last prince of Senghenydd. Gruffudd took advantage of Simon de Montfort's revolt to build this castle on his frontier. The castle occupies a ridge overlooking the narrow coastal strip of the lordship of Glamorgan. It provoked a heavy-handed response from the young lord of Glamorgan, Gilbert de Clare. In 1266 he invaded Senghenydd, captured Gruffudd and led him off to captivity in Ireland. Gilbert left his adversary's castle unfinished, erecting the great castle of Caerphilly in its place. Hence Castell Morgraig, like a number of other castles erected by ill-fated Welsh princes, had a very short life. Excavations have shown that it was never occupied.

Castell Morgraig was an unusually strong native Welsh castle, consisting of a pentagonal courtyard with a deeply-projecting tower at each angle. The largest tower was a square keep. The other four were U-shaped, like some of the towers built by Llywelyn the Last, but here comprehensively flanking the curtain. A simple gateway pierced the curtain on the west, though it was adequately flanked by the two adjacent angle towers. Excavations in 1903 uncovered the remains, but since then neglect and decay have ensued. Some of the curtain stands to a reasonable height, but the towers are reduced to rubble footings and the keep has disappeared.

> *Access:* On private land.
> *Reference: Transactions of the Cardiff Naturalists' Society* (XXXVIII).
> *Relations:* Nearby Caerphilly. Gruffudd ap Rhys may also have built Castell Coch. Compare the similar layout of Holt Castle.

CASTELL TAL-Y-FAN, one of several castles near Cowbridge, occupies a hilltop between Ystradowen and Welsh St Donat's. It belonged to the St Quintin family. The triangular Norman enclosure preserves some rubble footings of a curtain, one piece still standing on the east side. There is also the curved segment of a flanking tower, and next to it two ruinous walls from a domestic building, probably the hall. They may have stood by 1245, when the castle was captured by the Welsh. Afterwards it disappears from history.

> *Access:* On private land.

Reference: Glamorgan County History (III).
Relations: St Quintin's Castle was founded by the St Quintin family.

COITY CASTLE, two miles north-east of Bridgend, is one of several castles in the vicinity of that town. They mark the early frontier of Norman settlement in Glamorgan. Tradition has it that Payn de Turbeville, one of Robert Fitz Hamon's adventurers, was sent westwards to conquer lands of his own. A native lord gave him Coity in return for marrying his daughter. Payn then supported the Welsh against further Norman inroads, though evidently not for long. The circular ringwork is no doubt Payn's, but the earliest masonry is late Norman. It may be attributed to Gilbert de Turbeville, who also married a Welsh heiress around 1200. He built a curtain on the ringwork, with a square keep commanding the entrance.

The existing castle is quite rare in Wales for its different periods of construction. Extensive rebuilding took place sometime in the fourteenth century, probably by Sir Roger Berkerolles who inherited the castle by marrying the Turbeville heiress. He may have been prompted by fears of a French invasion in the 1370s. Sir Roger remodelled the inner bailey on the ringwork and created an outer bailey to its west, so Coity is one of the few major post-Edwardian castles of Wales. It displays a preference for square towers instead of round for greater domestic convenience. Militarily the record is silent until 1404, when Sir Laurence Berkerolles resisted Owain Glyndwr in a long siege which attracted the attention of parliament. The House of Commons demanded that a relieving force be sent, but the winter weather prevented it from reaching Coity. The castle was still under siege a year later – we do not know if it ever fell. After Laurence's death in 1411 Sir William Gamage besieged the castle during an inheritance dispute. The Gamages occupied the castle until the Elizabethan period.

Coity Castle is a battered but extensive ruin which dominates the village. Square turrets flank each end of the west front. A ruinous gateway in the centre leads into the oblong outer bailey, added by Sir Roger Berkerolles. Much of the surrounding wall still stands but it is not of great military strength, showing the defensive limitations of a castle built after the Edwardian age. On the south side are the foundations of a large barn with a central porch, and beyond is the base of an oblong tower.

For most of its circumference the ringwork ditch is still deep, but the portion facing the outer bailey has been filled in. The inner bailey is entered through a long gate passage flanked by the stumps of square towers. Sir Roger is responsible for this arrangement, but the larger tower to the left is the old Turbeville keep. It is very ruinous, with only one wall rising high. The tall central column and the remains of a ground-floor vault belong to Sir Roger's remodelling. A projecting turret still stands to full height, but this is another Berkerolles addition with inserted Tudor windows.

Most of the inner curtain still stands to parapet level. The Norman curtain was built in straight sections around the edge of the ringwork. Sir Roger Berkerolles raised it to its present height and rebuilt one stretch, but in places the older walled-up parapet can be seen below the corbels of its successor. The North Gate, which survives virtually intact, may be an addition by Sir William Gamage. It is a square tower of three storeys, its outer archway framed within a square recess for the drawbridge. Projecting entirely outside the line of the curtain, this gatehouse provided a convenient exit to Coity's fine medieval church.

On the south side of the courtyard are Sir Roger Berkerolles' residential buildings, which follow the curve of the Norman curtain. They are now badly ruined. Beyond some foundations of the kitchen is the hall undercroft, retaining the springers of a stone vault upon its walls. An unusual feature is the stone corridor in front. It leads to a large spiral stair which ascended to the hall. Beyond is the site of the chapel. The hall itself has vanished, except for the curtain side. Here a damaged fireplace discharges into a tall Tudor chimney. Reached from a corner of the hall is the Ovoid Tower. Its round plan and deep projection suggest that this tower was an earlier, Turbeville addition to the castle. However, Sir Roger thoroughly remodelled it to house a suite of latrines serving his apartments. Such latrine towers are typical of the later Middle Ages.

> *Access:* Always open (Cadw).
> *Reference:* Guidebook by J. R. Kenyon (includes Newcastle and Ogmore). *Glamorgan: The Early Castles.*
> *Relations:* Norman tower keeps at Fonmon, Ogmore and Penllyn. Crickhowell Castle was another Turbeville foundation.

COWBRIDGE TOWN WALL Cowbridge grew up in the thirteenth century under the patronage of the de Clare lords of Glamorgan. Though small, it was prosperous enough to be walled in stone about 1300. The medieval town straddled a crossroads on the main route west from Cardiff. Just half a mile long, the wall enclosed an oblong area with gates at the four road intersections. It must have looked rather humble when compared with the major walled towns of Wales. Much of the circuit has vanished but the south-western quadrant survives, along with one gate. The South Gate, overlooked by the medieval parish church, is an oblong structure with archways to front and rear. It has lost its upper chamber. From here the wall stretches west to a round corner turret, then north to the main road where the West Gate stood. Cowbridge is a rare instance of a walled town with no castle on its perimeter. The de Clare stronghold of St Quintin's Castle is a mile away.

> *Access:* Freely accessible (LA).
> *Reference:* GAHW *Glamorgan and Gwent.*
> *Relations:* Town walls in South Wales at Chepstow, Kidwelly, Pembroke and Tenby.

DINAS POWYS CASTLES—The commanding hill above the little town of Dinas Powys was first occupied in the Dark Ages, as excavations have revealed. There are steep falls from the summit except on the south. In the sixth century this side was cut off by a bank and ditch to create a hillfort. However, most of the earthworks belong to a Norman castle. A ringwork crowns the summit, and facing the southern approach is an impressive line of three consecutive ramparts separated by ditches. The inner rampart, which is the slightest of the three, is the Dark Age one. These earthworks are attributed to Roger de Somery, who arrived with Robert Fitz Hamon around 1091.

Later on the Somerys moved to a more accessible site lower down the hill, half a mile to the south-east. The transfer probably took place in Norman times because a square, keep-like tower once stood at the north corner of the present stone enclosure. The plain curtain probably dates from the early thirteenth century. It encloses an oblong area but the hillside location was hardly ideal, resulting in a sloping courtyard. No towers guarded the vulnerable corners, and the entrance is a broken archway through the south-east curtain. Much of the curtain survives to full height, though very overgrown and likely to collapse if it is allowed to decay further.

Access: Both castle sites are freely accessible (uphill walk).

Reference: Dinas Powys by L. Alcock. *Glamorgan: The Early Castles.*

Relations: Castell Dinas Emrys is another castle site with Dark Age origins. The Somerys built Dudley Castle in Staffordshire.

EWENNY PRIORY, just south of Bridgend, is a rare medieval fortified monastery. Founded in 1141 by Maurice de Londres, lord of nearby Ogmore, the priory housed Benedictine monks until the Dissolution. Dominated by a central tower and lacking only its north transept, the church is a fine example of a Norman priory church. It occupies the north-east corner of a large precinct, still surrounded by much of its defensive curtain. This began as a typical monastic precinct wall. However, towards the end of the thirteenth century it was heightened and given flanking towers. The circumstances which led this small community to erect such an ambitious circuit of fortifications is unknown. Although some Welsh monasteries suffered in the wars, no raids on Ewenny are recorded. The curtain must have been too long to patrol effectively and there was no accompanying ditch, making it a less formidable barrier than it might have been. In addition to the church and cloister, the precinct would have contained the barns and workshops necessary for the monks' survival. The area now forms the garden of the Mansion House. This was built on the site of the cloister by the Carne family, who acquired the site when the priory was dissolved in 1536.

Owing to the extension of the churchyard, the north-east corner of the circuit has been destroyed. The curtain now begins at a truncated square tower with a vaulted ground floor. Beyond a barn is the handsome North Gate. Projecting buttresses with pyramid spurs flank the wide entrance gateway. This arch was closed by a portcullis (its grooves survive), while murder holes can be seen further back in the gate passage. Above is a roofless chamber with a lancet window. The curtain – here complete except for its parapet – changes course at the round north-west angle tower, which is pierced by cross-slits. No tower guarded the south-west corner. Opposite the North Gate is the South Gate, preserving the round-headed archways and vault of the original Norman gatehouse. It was given its polygonal flanking tower when the wall was fortified. Most of the south wall has vanished but the oblong south-east corner tower remains, its upper floor converted into a dovecote. The more ruinous east curtain leads back towards the churchyard.

Access: Much of the precinct wall can be followed externally (Cadw).
Reference: Priory guidebook. GAHW *Glamorgan and Gwent.*
Relations: The fortified cathedral close at St David's. For Maurice de Londres see Ogmore.

FONMON CASTLE   was held from Norman times until the seventeenth century by the St John family. Its present appearance is due to a thorough remodelling by Thomas Jones in the 1760s, but Fonmon began as a medieval castle. The core of this is an oblong keep, now barely recognisable as such, built in the late twelfth century. It is the wing to the left of the entrance porch, but its subdivided interior is now Georgian and is notable for the splendid library on the top floor. In the thirteenth century the keep became the north side of a small square courtyard. The west range has long disappeared, but the other two survive beneath their Georgian veneer. The only original feature is the curious double tower at the south-east corner. This is semi-circular to the east but has a square projection to the south. North of the keep a long extension was added in the seventeenth century. The castle stands five miles west of Barry and about a mile from Penmark Castle.

Access: Private.
Reference: Fonmon Castle by P. Moore. BOW *Glamorgan.*
Relations: Norman tower keeps at Coity, Kenfig, Ogmore and Penllyn. Compare the smaller inhabited castles at Penhow, Picton and Upton.

KENFIG CASTLE   overlooks the meandering River Kenfig, three miles north-west of Porthcawl. Hidden among the sand dunes known as Kenfig Burrows are the rubble footings of a square Norman keep. This keep was probably built by William, earl of Gloucester and lord of Glamorgan. It is known to have been attacked in the Welsh rising of 1183. The Pipe Rolls record wood being brought here two years later, perhaps to repair the damage, the lordship being temporarily in royal hands following William's death. Excavations from 1924 demonstrated that the 'motte' on which the keep appears to stand had in fact been piled up against its ground floor, an illusion probably intended to keep siege engines at bay. They also showed that the thin south wall of the keep was a later rebuilding, perhaps a result of further Welsh attacks in 1232 and 1295.

In its thirteenth-century form this was a substantial castle, with a curtain closely surrounding the keep. The buried foundations of a hall are visible in the outer bailey. Llywelyn Bren stormed the castle and its accompanying town during his rebellion of 1316. By 1400 the encroaching sand dunes had forced the inhabitants to evacuate the site.

Access: On a nature reserve (LA).
Reference: Glamorgan: The Early Castles.
Relations: Earl William also built Newcastle and (perhaps) the shell keep at Cardiff. Compare the false 'motte' around the keep at Skenfrith.

LLANDAFF PALACE   Now a suburb of Cardiff, Llandaff has been a religious centre since the Dark Ages. Close to the cathedral is the ruined Bishop's Palace. Though called a palace in the tradition of medieval bishops' residences, this is a castle of the Edwardian period. The gatehouse resembles those on the northern dam at Caerphilly Castle. It is likely that the same unknown master mason was responsible. That would put the building of the palace in the episcopate of William de Braose, who had been enthroned as bishop during the consecration of the newly-rebuilt cathedral in 1266. William contributed to the fabric of the cathedral by adding the Lady Chapel. According to tradition the palace was damaged by Owain Glyndwr and afterwards abandoned by the bishops, who seldom visited their cathedral at that time.

The palace overlooks the original course of the River Taff. Though truncated, the gatehouse is the best-preserved part of the palace. Despite its similarity to the Caerphilly gatehouses, it is not a copy. The spur bases are much lower here and the flanking towers are basically square with canted corners. Note the portcullis groove in the outer arch. A doorway on the right of the gate passage leads into the guard chamber. The vaulted room in the left tower, entered from the courtyard, stood over a prison. At the back of the gatehouse a spiral stair ascends to the ruinous upper floor, which originally formed a single chamber. It was probably the constable's lodging, modestly echoing the Edwardian keep-gatehouse theme. One more storey must at least have been intended.

A garden now occupies the courtyard. The palace is quadrilateral, its west side longer than the others. On the west the curtain stands complete to the wall-walk, but the east curtain is more ruinous, while the north and south sides are bounded by garden walls on the older foundations. A small, circular tower projects at the south-east corner, but the South-West Tower is square for greater domestic convenience. The hall was oddly positioned at the north-east angle of the enclosure. Only the east wall (i.e. the curtain) survives, its large window openings a concession to comfort at the expense of security. Why the hall should be situated at this vulnerable point is unclear, unless the bishop wanted to keep watch over his cathedral.

> *Access:* Freely accessible.
> *Reference:* Guidebook by C. N. Johns.
> *Relations:* Compare the gatehouses on the dam at Caerphilly. Episcopal castles at Llanddew and Llawhaden.

LLANDOUGH CASTLE   The forecourt of a brick Georgian house incorporates some mutilated portions of a late medieval fortified manor house – a rare sight in Wales. Adjoining the present house is a square tower house with a projecting turret. Only one small window is original, the tower having been thoroughly remodelled when the new house was built. It stood at the north-west corner of a quadrangle. A smaller tower at the south-west corner was converted into a gatehouse in Jacobean times. The wall which bounded the east side of the courtyard survives, its blocked windows and latrine shafts marking the site of the hall. The castle is attributed to

John de Van, who inherited Llandough from the Walshe family in 1427. It stands beside the River Thaw, a mile south of Cowbridge.

> *Access:* Visible from the road.
> *Reference:* BOW *Glamorgan.*
> *Relations:* Tower houses at Beaupre, Candleston and Weobley.

LLANGYNWYD CASTLE occupies a Norman ringwork on a wooded promontory, two miles south of Maesteg. It complemented Neath in guarding the western approach to the lordship of Glamorgan. Llywelyn the Last sacked the earth-and-timber castle in 1262. Gilbert de Clare seems to have begun a rebuilding in stone when he inherited the lordship the following year, so Llangynwyd was the first castle of the redoubtable 'Red Earl'. Unfortunately it is far too ruined to tell us much. The curtain is a buried mound of rubble, with just a fragment of one flanking tower discernible. The strongpoint was an Edwardian gatehouse, foreshadowing the main gatehouse at Caerphilly which Gilbert built a few years later. The lower parts of its rounded flanking towers still remain but are buried in the rubble of the collapsed superstructure. Like Gilbert's later castle of Morlais, Llangynwyd was sacked during the Welsh uprising of 1295 and seems to have lain abandoned ever since.

> *Access:* On private land.
> *Reference: Glamorgan: The Early Castles.*
> *Relations:* Gilbert de Clare's castles of Caerphilly, Castell Coch and Morlais.

LLANILID CASTLE, two miles east of Pencoed, is a good example of a 'raised' ringwork, consisting of a low, circular mound with a tree-clad rampart around the summit. The surrounding ditch is crossed by an entrance causeway facing the old parish church. This Norman castle was probably raised by the St Quintin family, who held the manor until 1245. No stone walls ever replaced the wooden palisades, and the Siwards moved to a moated site nearby.

> *Access:* Freely accessible.
> *Reference: Glamorgan: The Early Castles.*
> *Relations:* Ringworks at Coity, Dinas Powys and Ogmore.

LLANTRISANT CASTLE was probably raised by Richard de Clare, earl of Gloucester and lord of Glamorgan, after he seized the district of Meisgyn from Senghenydd in 1245. It emerges from obscurity early in the fourteenth century. The castle was damaged by Llywelyn Bren in 1316, and again by the barons who rose up against Hugh le Despenser five years later. In 1326 Hugh and Edward II were brought here following their capture by Queen Isabella's supporters. Hugh was sent off to execution at Hereford while Edward went on to his abdication and murder. The castle occupies a commanding position in this hilltop town, to the east of the parish church. Little remains and it continues to suffer from neglect. It consists of a small, ditched bailey which preserves fragments of its retaining wall. The high piece of masonry formed part of the circumference of a round keep, probably the Raven Tower mentioned by John Leland. A doorway high up led onto the curtain.

Access: Exterior visible.
Reference: Archaeologia Cambrensis (CX).
Relations: Richard de Clare's castles at Neath.

LOUGHOR CASTLE, between Swansea and Llanelli, is one of a string of castles which guarded river crossings along the coastal plains of South Wales. It overlooks the estuary of the River Loughor, commanding the approach to the Gower peninsula. The Roman fort of Leucarum stood here. A ringwork was raised in one corner of the fort by Henry de Beaumont, earl of Warwick, after his invasion of Gower. This was later built up into the present oval motte. The castle was destroyed by the Welsh in 1151, and again during Llywelyn the Great's campaign of 1215. Today the Roman fort has vanished and the shell keep which stood on the summit of the motte is buried in the turf. However, a tower which flanked the entrance to the keep remains in a ruinous condition. This rather modest tower may have been built by John Iweyn. He was steward to the last Braose lord of Gower, and received this manor in 1302. Its square shape is unusual for that time. Enough remains to show that the two upper floors of the tower were residential, with fireplaces and latrines. One corner of the tower lies fallen but still intact on the ground.

Access: Freely accessible (Cadw).
Reference: Archaeologia Cambrensis (CXLII). *Glamorgan: The Early Castles.*
Relations: Castles in Roman fortifications at Cardiff, Caerwent and Tomen-y-Mur. Weobley was built by another of William de Braose's stewards.

MORLAIS CASTLE, a northern outpost of the lordship of Glamorgan, was raised by Gilbert de Clare, the 'Red Earl' of Gloucester and Hertford. He began building on this hilltop site once his great castle of Caerphilly was complete, perhaps following Rhys ap Maredudd's rebellion in 1287. History repeated itself because, as at Caerphilly, the construction of Morlais led Gilbert into a dispute with one of his neighbours. This time, however, the neighbour was not a Welsh prince but one of Gilbert's baronial peers: Humphrey de Bohun, earl of Hereford and lord of Brecon. In 1289 Humphrey complained to the king that Gilbert was building the castle on territory which he also claimed. Some of Gilbert's henchmen raided the lordship of Brecon and Humphrey retaliated. Edward I, having subjugated Welsh Wales, seized the opportunity to assert his authority over the Marcher lords. Twice Gilbert refused to answer a royal summons but he was eventually forced to submit to the king, suffering a heavy fine and the temporary seizure of his Welsh estates.

It is likely that the castle was left incomplete as a condition of the settlement. It was captured during the Welsh uprising of 1295, and Gilbert died soon after. There is no further record of the castle. This wild upland was desolate in medieval times – Morlais is virtually the only castle in northern Glamorgan. Conditions changed with the Industrial Revolution, and the castle is now just a couple of miles north of Merthyr Tydfil.

Its elevated position, commanding a view of the Brecon Beacons, made for a castle quite unlike Gilbert de Clare's lake-bound, concentric fortress at Caerphilly. The castle follows an elongated plan, bounded on the west by the steep drop to the Taff Gorge and elsewhere by a rock-cut ditch. There is a triangular inner ward with the foundations of a circular keep at the acute northern apex, and a larger outer ward to the south. Rounded mural towers projected on the east and south but – in contrast to Caerphilly – the entrances were just simple gateways through the curtain. How much was actually built is impossible to tell. Some portions of wall still stood a couple of centuries ago, but now there is little more than buried foundations, with mounds of rubble marking the sites of towers. A large pit just outside the cross-wall dividing the two baileys is a cistern – it would have been necessary to dig hundreds of feet to reach the water table. Only one fragment shows the quality of Gilbert's intentions. The stony mound at the south-east angle of the outer ward denotes a round tower which was as large as the keep. Beneath the debris its ground floor is intact, with a vault carried on a central column like a monastic chapter house.

Access: Freely accessible (uphill walk).
Reference: Bulletin of the Board of Celtic Studies (XXX). GAHW *Glamorgan and Gwent.*
Relations: Gilbert de Clare's castles of Caerphilly, Llangynwyd and Castell Coch. Hilltop castles such as Castell Dinas, Cefnllys and Castell Dinas Bran.

NEATH CASTLE   Richard de Granville raised the first castle within the old Roman fort of Nidum. Nothing remains of it, though Neath Abbey – which he founded in 1130 – is still an extensive ruin close by. Later the castle was transferred to the present site on the east bank of the River Neath, its dependent borough remaining tiny until the Industrial Revolution. This stronghold of the lords of Glamorgan had a stormy history with periodic attacks by the Welsh. Richard de Clare rebuilt the castle in stone after Llywelyn the Great's raid of 1231, and this served to thwart another attack under Llywelyn the Last in 1258. The gatehouse is attributed to Edward II's unpopular favourite, Hugh le Despenser the Younger. It may have been built after the scare of 1321 when Hugh's baronial enemies invaded Glamorgan, capturing Neath along with his other castles. Hugh was finally overthrown and executed in 1326.

Hugh's gatehouse forms the most substantial part of the ruins. Now drearily overlooking a supermarket car park, it is a typical if modest Edwardian gatehouse. The twin-towered outer front is intact except for its parapet. A wide machicolation slot overhangs the gate arch. However, this is just a facade because the courtyard front of the gatehouse has fallen. It stood at the west end of Richard de Clare's small, D-shaped enclosure. This was once crammed with buildings, leaving just a tiny yard in the centre. The circuit of the curtain is complete but little stands to any great height. At the east end are the collapsed remains of a U-shaped keep. It projected deeply to the east, while on the north side there is the base of a latrine block.

Access: Exterior only (LA).
Reference: Morgannwg (XVII). GAHW *Glamorgan and Gwent.*

Relations: Richard de Clare's castle at Llantrisant, and Hugh le Despenser's additions at Caerphilly and Dinefwr. Compare the U-shaped keeps at Roch and Ewloe.

NEWCASTLE crowns a hill overlooking Bridgend. Robert Fitz Hamon, the Norman conqueror of Glamorgan, granted the church of *Novo Castello* to Tewkesbury Abbey in 1106. The rebuilt church stands just beyond the castle gate. Why this particular castle should be called Newcastle is difficult to tell – perhaps it was to distinguish it from nearby Coity Castle, which may have been raised a few years earlier. At that time Newcastle, Coity and Ogmore guarded the western boundary of the new lordship of Glamorgan, though the Normans soon pushed further on. Nothing quite that old survives here. Instead we have a late Norman walled enclosure, quite ruinous but preserving a remarkable Norman entrance gateway. Its style places it in the last years of William, earl of Gloucester and lord of Glamorgan. He died in 1183, and expenditure in the Pipe Rolls over the next two years shows that work continued on the castle while it was temporarily in Henry II's custody. The quality of the gateway has convinced some scholars that it is Henry's work.

The splendid gateway is the finest piece of Norman architecture in any Welsh castle. Its outer arch is carried on slender columns with carved capitals. This frames a segmental inner arch adorned with regular bands of 'billet' moulding. Ashlar masonry surrounds the gateway, but elsewhere the stone robber has been busy. The curtain encloses a courtyard which is straight on the east, where the ground drops steeply to the Ogmore river, but polygonal elsewhere.

Although the gateway is a simple entrance through the curtain, it is immediately flanked by a square tower. Steps ascend to a first-floor entrance (the courtyard-level doorway is a later insertion), so the tower recalls the keeps flanking the gateways at Coity and Ogmore. However, there is another, slightly larger tower on the west side of the castle. Only its ground floor survives, but it is enough to show that this tower must also have been entered higher up. So were there two keeps? In England at this time the single keep characteristic of Norman castles was giving way to a series of flankers along the curtain. The two towers at Newcastle flanked the more vulnerable sections of curtain. Neither tower was large enough to provide lordly accommodation, and from the first there was a hall in the courtyard. Its foundations survive against the east curtain.

In 1217 Newcastle was granted to the Turbevilles, and thereafter was subordinate to their castle at Coity. Nevertheless it was still occupied in Elizabethan times, as shown by the windows inserted in the gate tower and the footings of a new residential building beside the older hall.

Access: Apply to key-keeper (Cadw).
Reference: Guidebook by J. R. Kenyon (includes Coity and Ogmore). *Glamorgan: The Early Castles.*
Relations: Nearby Coity and Ogmore castles. Earl William's work at Cardiff and Kenfig.

OGMORE CASTLE stands two miles south-west of Bridgend. It is pleasantly situated overlooking the Ogmore river, which is still forded here by massive stepping stones. We know that William de Londres had a castle here by 1116, because in that year he was forced to abandon it when the Welsh appeared in force. The earthworks comprise an oval ringwork, surrounded by a deep ditch, and a small bailey to the west. William's son Maurice is credited with the oblong keep – perhaps the oldest Norman keep in Glamorgan. Like its neighbour at Coity the keep is placed frontally to command the entrance. Originally it was entered at first-floor level, in common with most Norman tower keeps. At that time there was just a hall above the ground floor, the walls rising higher to shield the roof from attack by fire. Later in the century, however, windows were inserted in the roof space to form a solar above the hall. Today only the west wall of the keep stands to its full height, the rest having collapsed, but two windows and the fireplace are original.

Opposite the keep are the footings of a square building in the middle of the ringwork. Steps descend to an undercroft, which is all that is preserved, but the plan is unique and its purpose obscure. The most convincing theory is that it was built in late Norman times as a strong house for treasure.

A timber palisade continued to surround the ringwork until c. 1200, when Thomas de Londres replaced it with a stone wall. This wall is built in straight sections without mural towers, except for a rounded latrine turret where it joins the keep. Beside the keep is a vaulted gateway which was probably built up into a tower. Apart from these features the curtain is in a very ruinous condition. A large hall on the north side, overlooking the river, has been reduced to foundations. Wing walls cross the ditch towards the bailey, but there is no indication that the bailey itself was ever walled in stone.

Thomas' heiress married into the Chaworth family of Kidwelly, whose lands passed to the earl of Lancaster in 1298. Thus in its later history Ogmore belonged to powerful, absentee landlords. Nevertheless the castle remained the manorial centre. Having sustained damage during Owain Glyndwr's revolt, the duchy of Lancaster built a new court house in the bailey in 1454. Its gabled ruin remains.

Access: Always open (Cadw).
Reference: Guidebook by J. R. Kenyon (includes Coity and Newcastle). *Glamorgan: The Early Castles.*
Relations: The Norman keeps at Coity, Fonmon and Penllyn. Maurice de Londres founded nearby Ewenny Priory.

OYSTERMOUTH CASTLE stands on a hill overlooking Swansea Bay. Its name is a corruption of the Welsh Ystum Llwynarth. This picturesque castle, though nominally a ruin, lacks little more than its roofs and floors. The intricate domestic buildings, which accumulated over more than a hundred years, are exceptionally well preserved.

A castle was first established here by William de Londres, lord of Ogmore, in the wake of Henry de Beaumont's invasion of Gower. The Welsh sacked it in 1116. Supporters of Llywelyn the Great took the castle again during the Magna Carta war, and

Llywelyn the Last attacked in 1258. Rhys ap Maredudd, prince of Deheubarth, captured the castle after a two-week siege during his revolt of 1287. The core of the present castle is a hall of c.1200. It is attributed to William de Braose, lord of Brecon. He acquired the lordship of Gower in 1203 but fled into exile four years later. His descendants added the solar and the adjoining north wing in the mid-thirteenth century.

At this stage Oystermouth formed an extensive manor house, presumably within the earth-and-timber defences of a Norman ringwork. This suggests that the Braose lords of Gower used the castle as a country retreat in times of peace. It is only three miles from their chief castle at Swansea. However, the length of the siege in 1287 suggests that the stone defences existed by that time. If so they were built by another William de Braose (d.1290), who entertained Edward I here. The splendid chapel takes us into the time of John de Mowbray. He inherited the lordship in 1321 but, unlike his Braose predecessors, was mainly an absentee landlord.

The castle is entered through a gatehouse at the southern apex of the castle. Today it looks like a projecting gate tower, but the concave recesses on either side show that William de Braose at least intended to provide round flanking towers. They retain the beam holes for wooden floors, but if the towers were ever built they were later pulled down. The entrance arch leads into a long gate passage, with an upper chamber from which the portcullis was operated.

From the gatehouse two high stretches of curtain connect with the domestic buildings at the back of the small courtyard. Against these walls are ruinous ranges dating from the Mowbray period. One housed a large kitchen with three fireplaces sunk into the curtain; the other probably accommodated the garrison. The east curtain ends at John de Mowbray's chapel block, which is the tallest and most handsome of the castle buildings. Massively buttressed, its three storeys begin with an undercroft which served as another kitchen. Above is a residential chamber, perhaps for the priest. On top is the fine chapel with tall windows and a piscina. The flowing tracery is a delight, though most of it was restored in 1845. A large east window faces the outside world, high enough to be safe from assault.

To the left of the chapel is the original hall, the oldest part of the castle. It is solid enough to be regarded as a hall-keep. However, later thirteenth-century alterations have softened its character, and the present vaulted porch is a replacement for the original blocked doorway. Immediately behind the hall, and equally large, is the solar, with tall lancet windows. This apartment stood over an undercroft, and owing to the sloping ground there is a vaulted cellar beneath. A door in one corner leads to the north wing, which is an early example of extra private accommodation for family or guests. A mural passage from the hall leads directly into this wing, curving around the spiral staircase. In this way guests could reach their apartments without disturbing the privacy of the solar.

Returning to the courtyard, a narrow corridor separates the hall from a second guest range to its west. This is probably another addition by John de Mowbray. The west wing contains two storeys of apartments above a row of vaulted store rooms. Thus Oystermouth in its final form contained an unusually extensive medieval house, its many rooms well served with fireplaces and latrines. Owing to the piecemeal accumulation of these buildings, the north front of the castle forms a startling group of domestic fronts which are graded back from the north wing, through the great rectangular projection of the hall and solar, to the chapel. The steep fall on this side was considered adequate protection against attack.

> *Access:* Open daily in summer (LA).
> *Reference:* GAHW *Glamorgan and Gwent.* BOW *Glamorgan.*
> *Relations:* The Gower castles of the Braose family at Pennard and Swansea. Compare the residential buildings at Weobley, Carew and Chepstow, and the chapels at Kidwelly and Manorbier.

PENLLYN CASTLE, four miles south-east of Bridgend, was probably built by Robert Norris, Earl Robert of Gloucester's sheriff. Lord of Penllyn by 1135, he seems to have erected one of the first Norman keeps in Glamorgan. It was an oblong tower, like contemporary Ogmore. The two surviving walls stand on the edge of a low cliff above the River Thaw. Near the base are six courses of 'herringbone' masonry, a feature of early Norman work in which the stones are set in alternate diagonal layers. Above are traces of a blocked first-floor entrance. The keep now forms one corner of a derelict building. This began as a Tudor manor house of the Turbeville family, but was converted to a stable when the adjacent mansion replaced it in the 1790s.

> *Access:* Private.
> *Reference: Glamorgan: The Early Castles.*
> *Relations:* The early keeps at Ogmore and Chepstow.

PENMARK CASTLE Behind the medieval parish church are the neglected remains of a castle of the Umfravilles, a family better known on the Scottish border. The site is an oblong enclosure on the edge of a steep drop to the River Waycock. Sometime in the thirteenth century a stone curtain was built on the line of the earlier earthworks. One length survives on the west and there are footings elsewhere. A semi-circular tower survives at the north-west angle, with a latrine block added alongside. Other angle towers are suggested by grassy mounds. The remains are quite featureless, though they would be more telling if they were stripped of their ivy. Within the courtyard are the ruins of a much later barn. Penmark lies four miles west of Barry.

> *Access:* Visible from the churchyard.
> *Reference: Mediaeval Military Architecture* by G. T. Clark.
> *Relations:* The Umfraville castles of Cockermouth and Prudhoe in northern England.

PENNARD CASTLE, though very ruinous, occupies an exhilarating position overlooking Oxwich Bay. This was one of the castles of the Gower lordship, probably replacing the nearby ringwork of Penmaen. For nearly two centuries the castle was a ringwork with wooden palisades, but although the defences were of timber a

1 Beaumaris Castle

2 Caernarfon Castle

Caerphilly Castle

6 Cardiff Castle

5 Carew Castle

6 Carreg Cennen Castle

Chepstow Castle

8 Chirk Castle

Conwy Castle

10 Criccieth Castle

11 Harlech Castle

12 Kidwelly Castle

13 Pembroke Castle

14 Powis Castle

15 Raglan Castle

16 Rhuddlan Castle

stone hall was built in the Norman period. This has been found by excavation, and the shifting sands sometimes reveal a portion of it.

Stone defences were finally built around 1300 by William, the last Braose lord of Gower. Everywhere the Marcher barons were emulating their king with Edwardian castles to consolidate their power, but William de Braose was a notorious spendthrift who was forced to sell manors to maintain his lavish style. Pennard has the appearance of a castle built on a tight budget. A low curtain survives along the north side of the enclosure, with a small, semi-circular tower guarding the north-west angle. On the south the curtain has collapsed down the steep slope. Guarding the eastern approach is a rather small and squat gatehouse. Its outer front, with twin flanking turrets, still stands but the inner part has collapsed. The southern flanking tower, though less complete than its northern twin, is higher than the rest. Within the gate arch can be seen the portcullis groove. This sandy, windswept site was abandoned by 1400 at the latest.

Access: Freely accessible.
Reference: Glamorgan: The Early Castles. GAHW *Glamorgan and Gwent.*
Relations: The Braose castles of Oystermouth and Swansea.

PENRICE CASTLES

A castle was first established at Penrice by Henry de Beaumont, following his invasion of Gower in 1099. His overgrown ringwork, known as Mounty Brough, can be seen in the village. A rampart guards the vulnerable approach from the church. The present Penrice Castle stands half a mile north, on a promontory in Penrice Park. Overlooking a house built in the 1770s, it is an example of a ruin deliberately retained as a picturesque landscape feature. The castle is the work of the Penrice or Penres family. Robert de Penres erected the small, circular keep before 1250. Later he or his son, another Robert, built a curtain around the promontory, with a hall and solar adjoining the keep and a gatehouse nearby. The roughly triangular layout of the castle is dictated by the terrain. Despite its position on a country estate, the castle is now woefully neglected and overgrown. It is extensive enough to deserve better treatment, even if one critic has uncharitably described it as a weak castle.

All the main buildings were concentrated on the north-west front, facing the only level approach. The gatehouse and the keep, at either end of this front, are the best-preserved parts of the castle. Although the gatehouse has the usual twin flanking towers, they are square with rounded corners. At the rear is a square, three-storey gate tower, its corners also rounded off. The whole is a rather curious version of the Edwardian gatehouse.

There is a long gap in the curtain which led towards the keep. The ruinous wall appearing halfway along formed the courtyard side of the hall. It is curious that the hall occupied this vulnerable front, instead of a safer position on one of the less accessible sides. At the far end of the hall is a solar block which doubles up as a projecting tower, again with rounded corners like the gatehouse towers. The solar masks the earlier round keep. As originally built the keep contained a single chamber over an unlit basement, but the walls rose higher to shield the roof from projectiles. Later, as often happened, this roof space was converted into a third storey. Both the keep and the solar stand more or less intact apart from their parapets. Towards the courtyard part of the circumference of the keep is covered by a concentric annexe with arrow slits. It resembles the forebuilding of a Norman keep, but it did not contain the entrance. Originally the first-floor doorway would have been reached by a flight of steps, but once the solar had been added the keep was entered directly from it.

The curtain surrounding the promontory is quite plain except for three solid turrets on the south wall and a single round tower. Against the east curtain are the gable ends of a large barn. By 1367 the castle was suffering from neglect. Edward III ordered its repair in anticipation of a French invasion. Ten years later another Robert de Penres was dispossessed for murdering a woman, though he kept his life owing to the doubtful evidence. His son bought back the estate, but on the failure of the line in 1410 Penrice passed to the Mansels of nearby Oxwich.

> *Access:* The castle is private but can be seen from a public footpath. Mounty Bank is visible in the village.
>
> *Reference: Archaeologia Cambrensis* (CX). *Glamorgan: The Early Castles* for Mounty Brough.
>
> *Relations:* Round keeps such as Dinefwr, Pembroke, Skenfrith and Tretower. Compare the other Gower castles of Oystermouth, Pennard, Swansea and Weobley.

ST DONAT'S CASTLE is one of the few stately home castles of Wales, preserving much of its original fabric despite extensive later alterations. It occupies a promontory overlooking the Bristol Channel, within spacious grounds two miles west of Llantwit Major. The castle is one of the small but distinguished group of Welsh concentric castles, though much of the inner curtain has been supplanted by a Tudor mansion. An unusual feature of the castle is the amount of medieval architecture transported here in the twentieth century by a fabulously wealthy American owner.

There is still something to be seen of the original Norman castle, built by the de Hawey family. The surviving portions of the inner curtain date from around 1200, though the only original feature is a blocked window in the Mansel Tower. Sir Peter de Stradling, a Swiss knight in the service of Edward I, is credited with the remodelling of St Donat's. He married the Hawey heiress about 1297 but died soon afterwards, so construction probably continued under her second husband, John de Pembridge. The concentric theme was no doubt inspired by Caerphilly, though the irregular plan here was dictated by the older inner curtain. Another contrast is the apparent paucity of flanking towers. A curved bay in the Gun Room (next to the hall) is evidence that at least one round tower was added to the inner curtain. Perhaps there were others before the Tudor demolition.

The outer curtain survives virtually intact except on the west, where it has been breached to make way for the modern dining hall. It is quite plain apart from the distinctive corbelled parapet. One square tower guards the northern angle, though it does not project externally. Apart from that there is just a square gate tower, its height more impressive when viewed from the bottom of the ditch. A modern portcullis is operated from the chamber above the gateway. Much of the narrow outer courtyard has been filled by later buildings. To foil a direct attack, the outer gatehouse is not quite in line with the inner gateway. The latter is flanked on one side by the oblong Mansel Tower. Hence St Donat's, like several other late Norman castles in Glamorgan, had a tower guarding the entrance. It is rather small to be called a keep. The surviving stretches of inner curtain on either side of the gate are largely concealed by later additions.

During the later Middle Ages the Stradlings steadily increased their wealth and influence. They suffered a blow in 1449 when the young heir Henry was captured by a pirate in the Bristol Channel. He was only released upon payment of a large ransom. According to a colourful but highly improbable legend, Henry later exacted a bloody revenge when the same pirate was shipwrecked on the coast below the castle.

None of the existing residential buildings are as old as the curtain walls. The earliest structure is the hall, which stands against the south curtain. Though modest in size, it retains its original roof adorned with Tudor roses. Towards the courtyard are the twin projections of the porch, with an oriel window lighting the room above, and a large bay window. The hall dates from around 1500. At that time the castle was held by Sir Rhys ap Thomas, a favourite of Henry VII, as guardian of the young heir Edward Stradling.

When Sir Edward came of age, he built an ambitious Tudor mansion in the inner courtyard. He retained his guardian's hall but demolished much of the inner curtain to make way for new ranges on the north and west sides, creating a more regular quadrangle. The courtyard facades still retain their Tudor character though the interiors have been modernised. Note the three Italian Renaissance roundels depicting Roman emperors – part of a set otherwise to be seen at Hampton Court. Before the mansion was built, the inner curtain was no doubt roughly parallel to the outer. Although its destruction shows that defence had become a lower priority, the mansion was still protected by the outer curtain. Furthermore, there was a conscious attempt to blend in with the older fortifications. The Tudor ranges are heavily embattled, while at the north-west corner rises the tall and menacingly-named Gibbet Tower.

The last Stradling was killed in a duel in 1738. To add insult to injury, the castle passed to the victor! St Donat's had already been considerably restored before 1925, when it was purchased by a magnate of a different kind: the American press baron William Randolph Hearst. Hearst used the castle as a summer retreat and expanded the accommodation to his own grandiose designs. It must be admitted that his additions considerably enrich the castle, though the plundering of old material from elsewhere attracted criticism even at the time. On the south, occupying the space between the inner and outer curtains, stands the Bradenstoke Hall. Its tall, traceried windows and the magnificent timber roof (both fourteenth century) were ripped out of Bradenstoke Priory in Wiltshire. Beside it is the keep-like Lady Anne Tower, with mock machicolations. Hearst was no less an architectural scavenger in building the vast dining hall on the west side of the castle, overlooking the sea. Its wooden Tudor vault comes from Boston Church in Lincolnshire. Throughout the castle are magnificent fireplaces taken from England and France. All this, however, is quite modest compared with the vast collection of imported treasures which make up Hearst Castle in California.

Access: The castle now serves as Atlantic College. It is open to visitors during the summer vacation.
Reference: Guidebook by E. Blackburn and R. Williams. BOW *Glamorgan. Archaeological Journal* (CL).
Relations: Concentric castles in South Wales at Caerphilly and Kidwelly. Cardiff, Picton, Powis and Chirk are other stately home castles.

ST FAGAN'S CASTLE   A castle was first raised here by Peter le Surs, one of the Normans who followed Robert Fitz Hamon into Glamorgan around 1091. Situated on a narrow ridge overlooking the River Ely, the D-shaped plan of the present courtyard may follow the line of a Norman ringwork. What stands is a simple curtain without flanking towers. Even the battlements are restored and the present entrance is a wide Victorian archway. The narrow gateway behind the Tudor house can only have been a postern. This small enclosure may date from around 1200, but its builder is obscure.

Half of the small courtyard is now occupied by an Elizabethan mansion, built by Sir Nicholas Herbert after 1586. Whitewashed and gabled, its exterior is little altered though the interior reflects Victorian tastes following a long period of neglect. The castle played no part in the battle of St Fagan's (1648), when the Royalist rebels of South Wales were crushed by parliamentary troops. Four miles west of Cardiff city centre, the castle now forms part of the Museum of Welsh Life, a vast open-air display of vernacular buildings re-erected from all over Wales.

Access: The castle and museum are open daily.
Reference: Transactions of the Cardiff Naturalists' Society (IX).
Relations: Tudorised castles at St Donat's, Laugharne, Carew and Powis.

ST GEORGE'S CASTLE   Castle Farm, in the village of St George's-super-Ely outside Cardiff, incorporates a fine medieval hall house. Its upper floor is now a single chamber, but the room was once divided into a hall and a solar. This is a relic of an unfortified manor house, built by the Malefant family in the fifteenth century. However, the thick wall at the back, overlooking the River Ely, is a remnant of an earlier castle of the Sullys.

Access: Exterior visible.
Reference: BOW *Glamorgan.*
Relations: Halls at Beaupre, Caerphilly, St Donat's and Weobley.

ST QUINTIN'S CASTLE   is named after the St Quintin family, who occupied this site in Norman times. However, the existing castle is a monument to the last de Clare lord of Glamorgan. Young Gilbert de Clare, son of the redoubtable 'Red Earl', came into possession of his estates in 1307, aged seventeen. Seven years later he was struck down by the Scots at Bannockburn. An inventory into his possessions records that this castle had recently been begun. Hugh le Despenser the Younger may have continued building. It was seized by his baronial enemies when they invaded Glamorgan in 1321. Afterwards the castle disappears from history.

The castle stands at Llanblethian, a mile south-west of the little walled town of Cowbridge. Virtually all that stands is the impressive Edwardian gatehouse facing the road. Like the two gatehouses on his father's northern dam at Caerphilly, its flanking towers are semi-octagonal. The gate passage was closed by two portcullises, and the vaulted guard chambers in the flanking towers are pierced by cross-slits. A spiral staircase at the back leads to the two upper floors, which probably contained the constable's apartments in keep-gatehouse fashion.

Little else survives; the castle may never have been completed. A stretch of wall connects the gatehouse to fragments of an octagonal tower which guarded the east corner of a quadrilateral enclosure. Just behind the gatehouse a mound of rubble preserves a bit of wall with a mural staircase. This is a relic of a square keep from the older castle of the St Quintins.

Access: Freely accessible (Cadw).
Reference: BOW *Glamorgan.*
Relations: The last Gilbert de Clare also built Llangybi.

SWANSEA CASTLE　　was the centre of the Marcher lordship of Gower. Henry de Beaumont, earl of Warwick, founded the castle after his invasion of 1099. It was burnt as early as 1116 by the Welsh prince Gruffudd ap Rhys, and its history is punctuated by several more Welsh attacks. These culminated in a sacking by Rhys ap Maredudd, last prince of Deheubarth, during his revolt of 1287. By that time Swansea had developed into a port under the patronage of the Braose lords of Gower. Its town wall has vanished in the course of urban development and the castle is just a portion of its former self. Nevertheless it is a handsome relic – the only historic building in a city centre much rebuilt after war bombing. Facing Castle Square, close to the docks and the River Tawe, the remains are overlooked by a modern tower block.

Virtually all that survives of the castle is the main residential range, containing the hall and solar. It dates from c. 1300 and is probably the work of the last William de Braose. The hall survives as an empty shell overlying a row of vaulted undercrofts. Tall windows pierce the hall on the side which doubled up as the curtain, while cross-slits light the undercrofts. Beyond the hall, the solar projects at an angle. At the other end of the hall the ruins terminate in a slender, semi-circular turret. The once-fine interior of the hall is scarred by the later industrial uses which preserved it.

The whole range is given unity by a row of arches immediately below the embattled parapet. These arches do not project from the face of the wall so they are not machicolations. They are really just a decorative feature, though they served to carry rain water off the roof. Similar parapet arcades are to be seen on Bishop Henry de Gower's halls at St David's and Lamphey in Pembrokeshire. Because of this the arcade is traditionally attributed to that bishop, but he never held Swansea. John de

Mowbray inherited the Gower lordship in 1321 and may well have employed the bishop's architect.

Beyond the solar is another, much mutilated fragment of the castle. This is the stump of a square chamber block. It was later converted into a debtors' prison and the interior is divided into eighteenth-century cells. Conditions were so notorious that the prison was finally closed by order of parliament in 1858. Beyond is the built-over site of the Norman motte, which carried a shell keep.

> *Access:* Exterior only (Cadw).
> *Reference: Swansea Castle and the Medieval Town* by E. Evans. GAHW *Glamorgan and Gwent.*
> *Relations:* For the Braose lords see Oystermouth and Pennard. Compare the castle halls at Caerphilly, Oystermouth, St Donat's and Weobley.

WEOBLEY CASTLE   is attractively situated overlooking the marshes of the north Gower coast, a mile west of Llanrhidian. Although there is no documentary reference to the castle until 1397, the whole complex appears to date from the early fourteenth century. It was begun by David de la Bere, steward to Lord William de Braose of Gower. Building probably continued under his successor, Adam. The castle remains as they left it, despite damage inflicted by Owain Glyndwr in 1403. The only later alterations are due to Sir Rhys ap Thomas. He became a local magnate after helping Henry VII to gain the throne, and a number of castles in south-west Wales show his additions.

Weobley is best described as a manor house with certain defensive features, and as such is rare in Wales. It consists of a group of residential buildings irregularly arranged around a small courtyard. All the main rooms stood at first-floor level above undercrofts. A tower house occupies one corner and there are other projecting towers. Nevertheless the castle was first and foremost a residence, attesting the growing sense of security after the Edwardian conquest of Wales. It offered remarkably extensive accommodation for a relatively minor lord. Today Weobley is a castle of two halves. The well-preserved northern apartments, which are partly roofed, contrast with the very ruinous south side of the castle.

The castle is entered on the west through an archway which was only defended by a pair of wooden gates, emphasising the rather half-hearted attitude towards defence. It leads through the ruined west range into the courtyard. To the left is the undercroft of the solar. Its stone vault (the only one in the castle) is a later insertion, probably by Rhys ap Thomas.

On the north side of the courtyard is the hall. Its facade is largely obscured by Rhys' porch. The undercroft beneath the hall housed the kitchen, an unusual and rather hazardous arrangement because even here there is no stone vault, so the risk of fire must have been great. At hall level one handsome window is permitted to pierce the outer wall, but the hall must always have been rather dark. The adjoining solar, which has been re-roofed, preserves another fine window overlooking the courtyard. A mural passage originally connected with the chamber over the gateway.

Rhys ap Thomas' porch, and the chamber alongside, are other roofed portions.

They were occupied by tenant farmers long after the rest of the castle had been abandoned. Beyond is the east wing, which is divided into three storeys. This guest suite was meant to be one of a pair, but the southern half of the east range was never built above the foundations. A plain piece of curtain closes the gap.

Only low ruins remain of the south range, which had a chapel on the vanished upper floor. At the south-west corner is the stump of a keep or tower house, probably the oldest of the castle buildings. Only its latrine turret still rises high. No doubt the keep was intended as a refuge for the de la Beres in times of danger, though its square plan – conservative for the Edwardian period – again demonstrates the secondary nature of the defences.

The defensive arrangements are better appreciated from outside. A corbelled parapet extending all the way around gives Weobley its castellated appearance, with cross-slits in the few surviving battlements. The solar flanks the gateway while the hall forms a broad, tower-like projection on the north front, with a round stair turret in one corner. At the angle of the guest chamber is a diagonally-set flanking tower with canted corners. This tower housed latrines, so again its function was primarily domestic. Foundations remain of a larger square tower which would have flanked the other end of the unfinished east range.

Access: Open daily (Cadw).
Reference: Guide by D. M. Robinson.
Relations: Well-preserved domestic buildings at Caerphilly, Oystermouth and Chepstow. Compare Rhys ap Thomas' additions at St Donat's, Kidwelly and Carew.

OTHER SITES Mottes such as *Felin Isaf* (near Clawdd-Coch) and *Ystradowen* attest the Norman invasion. The motte of *Talybont* now overlooks the M4 motorway, near Hendy. *Twyn Castell* at Gelligaer and *Tomen-y-Clawdd* (near Pontypridd) are native Welsh efforts. These are all quite modest mounds compared with the great motte at Cardiff. More numerous are the Norman ringworks, though some of them are of the 'raised' variety consisting of a low mound with a rampart around the top:

Beganston Castle (near Michaelston)
Bishopston Old Castle
Bonvilston Castle
Cae Castell (near Pontardawe)
Caerau Castle
Cil Ifor Ring (near Llanrhidian)
Gelli Garn (near Coychurch)

Gwern-y-Domen (near Caerphilly)
Llantrithyd Castle
Morganstown Castle (near
  Tongwynlais)
Penmaen Castle
St Nicholas Gaer

Cardiff's suburbs contain the sites of two other de Clare castles. *Whitchurch* had a round keep attributed to Gilbert de Clare, and excavations at *Rumney* revealed a small stone castle. Some of the lesser castles of the Vale of Glamorgan are marked by masonry fragments. The ringwork of *Llanquian* (near Cowbridge) has the base of a square keep on its perimeter. A suburban garden in *Peterston* retains one wall of an oblong tower from a castle captured by Owain Glyndwr. At *Marcross* a stretch of curtain survives among farm buildings. *Castleton*, a Tudor farmhouse near St Athan, incorporates what may be a truncated tower house. Near Bonvilston are the moated sites of *Liege* and *Worleton* castles, the latter a fortified manor house of the bishops of Llandaff.

Some inland castles were raised by the native Welsh of Senghenydd. *Trecastle*, on a rock near Pontyclun, is represented by some walling in a barn. Drystone footings on a low mound are all that remain of *Penlle'r Castell* (near Ammanford). *Plas Baglan*, on a promontory at Baglan, is reduced to the buried foundations of an oblong keep. The forbidding hilltop of *Castell Nos*, near Aberdare, is surrounded by a rock-cut ditch.

Ruined *Oxwich Castle* (Cadw) in Gower is sometimes regarded as an unusually late fortified house owing to Sir Edward Mansel's grand residential range, with its three projecting towers. However, castellated features are common in Elizabethan mansions, especially in Wales where castles still exerted a strong influence.

Merioneth

Meirionnydd formed part of the Welsh principality of Gwynedd. The mottes at Bala and Tomen-y-Mur are probably relics of a brief Norman occupation under Hugh d'Avranches. However, several others can be attributed to the Welsh, notably the stone mound of Castell Prysor. Deudraeth was the first native stone castle in the area but it has vanished. In 1221 Llywelyn the Great began Castell-y-Bere to consolidate his power. There is also Castell Carndochan, which may be the work of Llywelyn the Last. Both castles are very ruined, but splendidly situated in the native Welsh manner. They are overshadowed by Edward I's mighty concentric castle on the rock at Harlech, a symbol of the English conquest of Gwynedd in 1283. It has one of the best Edwardian gatehouses and a particularly stirring history.

CASTELL CARNDOCHAN   lies six miles south-west of Bala. It is reached from Llanuwchllyn by a minor road which follows the Afon Lliw. A mile and a half along, the castle occupies a steep spur above the bridge, but nothing stands high enough to make out from below. In fact the walls are little more than piles of rubble. It is a pity that it is so neglected, because this is evidently one of the thirteenth-century castles of the Welsh princes. In the absence of historical records excavations might reveal a great deal.

The remains show a small courtyard with two primitive semi-circular towers along the curtain. On the south-west are the footings of a U-shaped keep, which projects entirely outside the enclosure. It is an addition, and built of finer masonry than the rest. U-shaped keeps at Castell-y-Bere and Ewloe are attributed to Llywelyn the Last, and it is likely that he also built this keep. Perhaps the older curtain should be attributed to Llywelyn the Great, being built in conjunction with Castell-y-Bere to control Meirionnydd. The end of this castle is just as obscure as its beginning.

There is no mention of it even after the Edwardian conquest of 1283, so perhaps the castle had already been abandoned.

Access: On private land.
Reference: Journal of the Merioneth Historical and Record Society (II).
Relations: Llywelyn the Last's work at Castell-y-Bere, Criccieth, Ewloe and Dolforwyn.

CASTELL PRYSOR A conical mound beside the Afon Prysor, four miles east of Trawsfynydd, does not look out of place in this mountainous landscape. It is in fact a motte, and one of unique Snowdonian construction, because excavations have shown it to be a pile of stones held together by a clay revetment. This remarkable structure is historically obscure. We can only assume that it was built by one of the twelfth-century princes of Gwynedd. It may have remained a retreat of the two Llywelyns because Edward I, touring his new conquests, sent a letter from here in 1283.

Access: Visible from the road.
Reference: Archaeologia Cambrensis (C).
Relations: Welsh mottes at Tomen-y-Faerdre and Tomen-y-Rhodwydd.

CASTELL-Y-BERE is one of the castles built to control Gwynedd by Llywelyn the Great. The *Chronicle of the Princes* tells us that Llywelyn seized the cantref of Meirionnydd from his illegitimate son, Gruffudd, and began building a castle there in 1221. This is the only documentary reference to Llywelyn's castle building and probably refers to Castell-y-Bere. The site, seven miles inland from Tywyn, is a narrow spur overlooking the Dysynni valley, in the shadow of Cader Idris. It is remote today, involving an ascent up minor roads from Abergynolwyn. At the time it was built, however, the castle commanded the main road (or rather track) through the mountains.

The castle is unfortunately very ruinous, with little masonry rising to any great height, but the whole layout has been laid bare by excavation. It is well worth the detour for its breathtaking position. The enclosure, built on a slope, is roughly triangular, and is interesting for the variety of towers. At the southern apex, on the highest point of the rock, is the stump of a small oblong keep, once similar to Llywelyn's keep at Dolwyddelan. The curtain descends to the entrance which, as first built, was a simple gateway. However, it is closely flanked on one side by the keep and on the other by a circular tower. They show that Llywelyn's builders were catching up with the latest developments in military architecture.

From here the curtain twists eastwards, with the foundations of small lodgings against it. In the courtyard a large cistern is cut into the rock to catch rain water – it was never excavated deeply enough to be a well. At the north end of the courtyard steps ascend to a long, U-shaped tower. Only the lower part survives, but architectural fragments discovered during excavation suggest that the upper floor contained a chapel. The Chapel Tower flanks the straight south-east curtain which crowns the rock at a higher level than the rest, and returns to the keep.

Beyond is a later phase of masonry attributed to Llywelyn the Last. Across the

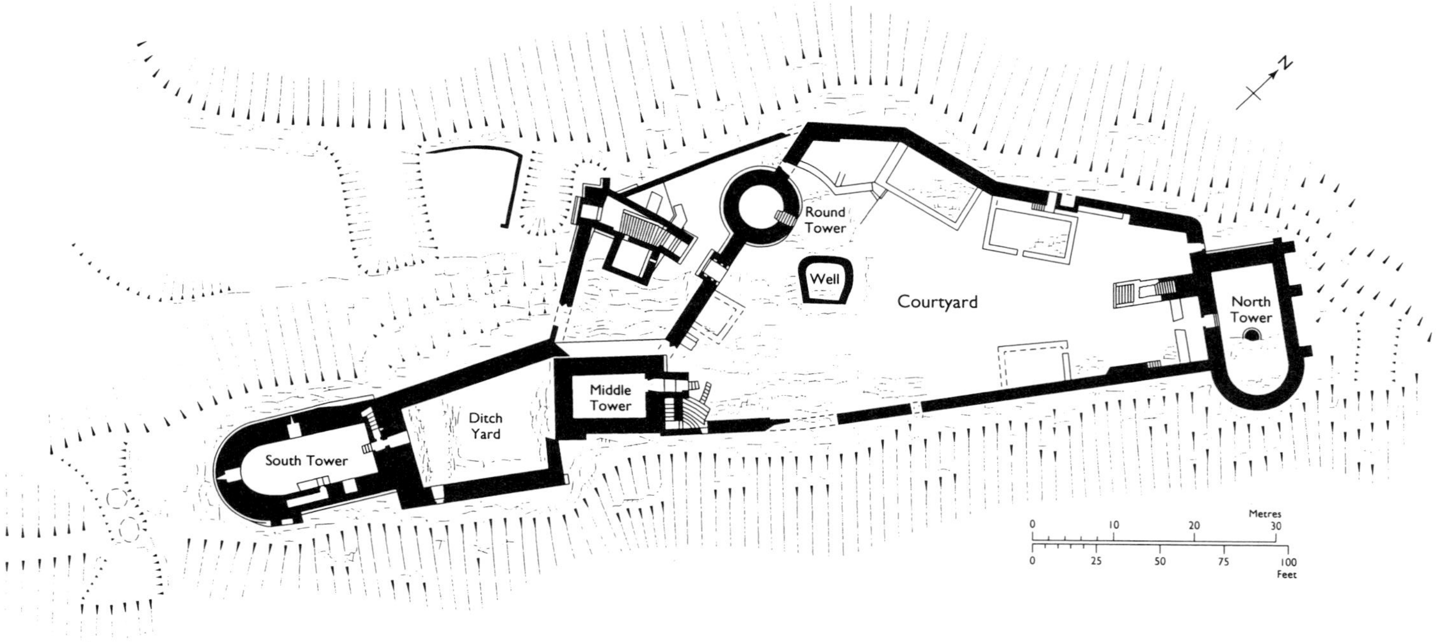

North Tower

Courtyard

Well

Round
Tower

Middle
Tower

Ditch
Yard

South Tower

N

Metres
0 10 20 30
0 25 50 75 100
Feet

CASTELL Y BERE

broad ditch behind the oblong keep is another U-shaped tower, built more massively than the Chapel Tower and commanding the main approach to the castle. This tower may have been intended as a new keep, securely isolated from the rest of the enclosure. It resembles Llywelyn's keep at Ewloe. Llywelyn also strengthened the entrance to his grandfather's castle. From the original gateway a broad flight of steps descends past the base of a square tower to an outer screen wall. This barbican is rare for a native castle.

Castell-y-Bere was besieged and captured by William de Valence in April 1283. Dafydd ap Gruffudd had tried to make a last stand here. He escaped to Dolbadarn prior to its fall, subsequently being betrayed and handed over to the English. Edward I initially retained the castle and spent £265 here in the years 1286–90. Perhaps some of this was necessitated by siege damage. The only tangible relics of his expenditure are the thick wing walls which connect Llywelyn the Last's U-shaped keep to the original oblong keep. However, the castle proved too remote to be supplied in times of siege. Burnt during Madog ap Llywelyn's uprising in 1294, it was never restored.

Access: Always open (Cadw).
Reference: Guide by R Avent. *Archaeologia Cambrensis* (CXXIII). *HKW* (I).
Relations: Llywelyn the Last's U-shaped keeps at Castell Carndochan and Ewloe. Other castles of the two Llywelyns at Criccieth, Dolbadarn, Dolwyddelan and Dolforwyn.

HARLECH CASTLE is one of the great Edwardian strongholds of Wales. Standing on a mighty rock above Tremadog Bay, and overlooked by the peaks of Snowdonia, Harlech is the most awesomely sited of the four new castles which Edward I built to surround Gwynedd. It also has the most dramatic history. The castle was begun in May 1283 at the instigation of Sir Otto de Grandison, a Savoy nobleman who led the central contingent of the English invasion army. Like the other royal castles it was designed by Otto's compatriot James of St George, Master of the King's Works in Wales. Levelling the summit and ditching the site seem to have occupied the first two years, but from 1285 a rapid building campaign employed up to 950 workmen. The castle was virtually complete by the end of 1289, the Pipe Rolls recording a total expenditure of £8,184. This does not include the initial laying out, which must have claimed a share of the £9,400 spent at various sites in 1283–84. James was rewarded with the constableship of the castle, so for three years he no doubt lived in the great gatehouse which he had designed.

Although no previous castle stood here, the rock of Harlech figures in Welsh mythology as a seat of the ancient kings of Britain. James of St George created a compact Edwardian castle on the summit. The gatehouse is the dominant feature of a square enclosure which is defended by a strong curtain and circular corner towers. It is a formative example of the quadrangular plan which would become the standard for later English castles. Furthermore it is closely surrounded by an outer curtain, so Harlech is one of that distinguished group of concentric castles. We are fortunate that Harlech, like the other Edwardian castles of Gwynedd, survives unaltered and virtually intact. Although it has lost most of its battlements, and the

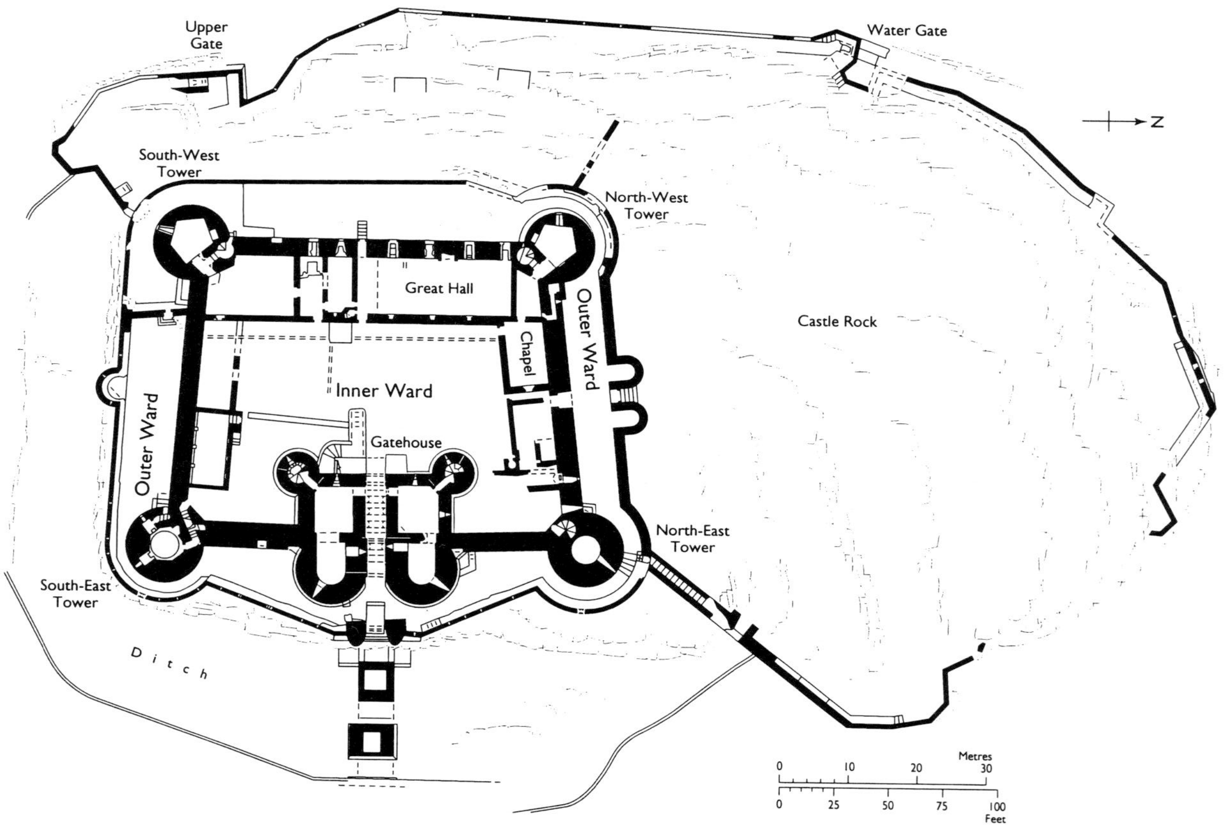

HARLECH CASTLE

Water Gate

Castle Rock

North-West Tower

Outer Ward

Chapel

Great Hall

Inner Ward

Gatehouse

North-East Tower

Upper Gate

South-West Tower

Outer Ward

South-East Tower

Ditch

N

Metres
0   10   20   30
0   25   50   75   100
Feet

towers are open to the sky, the walls rise to their full height and the wall-walk is still complete.

In common with the other Edwardian castles, a small borough of English settlers was founded at Harlech. The magnificent east front of the castle, with the gatehouse in the centre, glowers over the little town. This is the only level approach, and the east curtain is thicker than the others (thirteen feet) to withstand the buffeting of siege engines. The first obstacle is a wide ditch hewn out of the rock. Then, in front of the main gatehouse, a gate arch with round flanking turrets pierces the outer curtain. Today a wooden staircase ascends to the entrance. Originally there must have been a ramp, as at Conwy, but in 1322 the entrance was made still more secure by building two gate towers in the ditch in front. Drawbridges crossed the gaps in between, but the towers have been reduced to their footings.

The main gatehouse is the best-preserved example of a fully-developed Edwardian gatehouse, with twin rounded towers flanking the entrance. Between the towers, the impression of uncompromising security is dispelled by a disarmingly large chapel window at first-floor level. Below it, an archway leads into a long gate passage, which retains the grooves for three portcullises and the drawbar holes for two pairs of gates. There are also arrow slits from the porters' lodges on either side. What is surprising is the absence of stone vaulting even above the gate passage. The general lack of vaults aggravated the decay which plagued all of Edward's rain-soaked castles, as the Black Prince's survey of 1343 reveals.

As at Beaumaris the gatehouse has a large courtyard projection, which permitted suitably grand accommodation on the upper floors as well as lengthening the gate passage. The courtyard facade is flat, its angles marked by slender stair turrets which rise higher than the rest. Harlech's gatehouse is one of those described as a keep-gatehouse, but this side was only nominally defensive. It is true that the third portcullis was at the courtyard end, but the main reason for this would have been to trap besiegers in the gate passage. Once inside, attackers could climb the grand staircase and force their way through the little doorway at the top. Furthermore, the courtyard facade of the gatehouse has two rows of three windows lighting the apartments within. These windows were covered by iron grilles, but the gatehouse could at best have offered temporary resistance if besiegers got this far. Harlech relied upon its outer defences.

On the floor above the gate passage the gatehouse contained a hall and solar, separated by a cross-wall. There were further chambers in the flanking towers and a small chapel between them – its east window is the one overlooking the outer gateway. The constable or his deputy would have occupied this floor in order to control the portcullises, which must have disturbed his hall and chapel. The suite on the top floor was identical, but uncluttered by winding gear. It has been suggested that this floor was occupied by the king's justiciar when he was visiting.

The inner ward lies in the shadow of the curtain, which is so high that the corner towers rise little higher. These towers, though round externally, contain polygonal rooms. Both eastern towers comprised two residential chambers above miserable basement prisons for the recalcitrant Welsh. The western towers are divided into four storeys, and these two have watch turrets rising above the main parapet. The wall-walk of the curtain is continuous, by-passing the towers to aid mobility under siege – a feature common to most of the Edwardian castles. Note that, in the haste to raise a defensible circuit, the curtain was first built to about three-quarters of its final thickness. To the right of the gatehouse a diagonal offset marks a section where the thickening was never applied.

Only fragments remain of the inner ward buildings which the garrison of thirty men occupied. The main range, against the west curtain, has been reduced to foundations. It contained the hall and a large kitchen. On this inaccessible side a row of windows is allowed to pierce the curtain quite low down. The end walls of an austere chapel stand against the north curtain, and beside it a postern leads into the outer ward. On the south stood a timber-framed hall, taken from a manor house of the Welsh princes and re-erected here for symbolic reasons. It was probably intended for royal visits, which proved extremely rare.

Owing to the confines of the site, the outer curtain is as utilitarian as James of St George's outer curtain at Beaumaris is lavish. The outer ward is exceptionally narrow, particularly where the wall curves outwards to accommodate the corner towers of the inner curtain. This admirably served the principles of concentric planning, which demanded two tiers of arrow fire upon attackers and an uncomfortably narrow space for them to operate in front of the inner wall. Opposite the north gate through the inner curtain is a second gateway with rounded turrets, leading out onto the northern face of the castle rock. The only other feature on the outer curtain is a corbelled turret on the south side.

From the south-west corner of the outer curtain a wing wall descends the precipitous face of the castle rock. At one point the accompanying path is interrupted by a gateway and drawbridge pit, then the wall continues down to a second gateway nearly two hundred feet below. The sea is nearly a mile away now, beyond the marshes of Morfa Harlech, but when the castle was built it lapped the rock. Ships could have supplied the castle through this Water Gate, at least in times of siege (it would have been intolerable to carry heavy supplies up the 137 steps in peacetime). The castle was thus able to hold out in 1294 when Madog ap Llywelyn blockaded it. Perhaps the vulnerability of the Water Gate was exposed on that occasion. After Madog's revolt had been crushed the wing wall was extended to enclose the gentler north slope of the rock, rejoining the outer curtain at its north-east corner.

Harlech's later history is dominated by four great sieges. On each occasion the castle held out so tenaciously in difficult conditions that it has been dubbed 'the castle of lost causes'. The first two sieges took place during Owain Glyndwr's revolt. Owain besieged Harlech in 1404. The siege was a long one, and the garrison imprisoned the constable when he contemplated surrender. However, their fate was sealed with the arrival of a French fleet, which thwarted the customary expectation of relief by sea. For four years Harlech was the capital of an independent principality. Owain was recognised as prince of Wales and a Welsh parliament assembled here.

Nevertheless the young Prince Henry was slowly reclaiming his inheritance. He appeared in front of Harlech sometime in 1408, and this time it was Owain's turn to be isolated. The castle endured the terrifying din of a cannon bombardment – some of the stone cannon balls are now inside the gatehouse. It has been suggested that the outer curtain was reduced in height by this bombardment, but if so the damage was surprisingly uniform. Certainly the castle is not pock-marked with direct hits, which seems to demonstrate how ineffective early cannon were. One of Henry's guns exploded in action. Owain escaped the blockade to rekindle his flagging rebellion elsewhere, but his family fell into captivity when the castle finally succumbed early the following year.

The next two causes were English wars which the Welsh embraced with surprising enthusiasm. After Edward IV had seized the throne there were pockets of support for the deposed Henry VI, and none more determined than Harlech Castle under its Welsh constable, Dafydd ap Ievan. In 1468 William and Richard Herbert were despatched to conduct the most dramatic siege of the Wars of the Roses. The Men of Harlech, who are immortalised in the song, only surrendered when compelled by starvation. Edward IV was reluctant to ratify the honourable terms which the brothers had negotiated, until they threatened to put Dafydd back!

In the Civil War Harlech once again lived up to its reputation. Under William Owen the decaying castle held out against parliament for nine months until March 1647 – a staggeringly late date, considering that the war elsewhere had ended the previous summer. Major-General Thomas Mytton's forces were hampered by their inability to bring artillery to this remote place, which may explain why this symbol of Royalist resistance was not slighted afterwards.

Access: Open daily (Cadw).
Reference: Guidebook by A. J. Taylor. *HKW* (I).
Relations: Edward I's castles of Caernarfon, Harlech and Beaumaris. Beaumaris is concentric, along with the castles of Edward's first invasion at Aberystwyth and Rhuddlan. Aberystwyth also endured two long sieges during Owain Glyndwr's revolt.

TOMEN-Y-BALA   A large, conical motte rises off Bala High Street. The motte has been landscaped and a hedge borders the path spiralling up to the summit. Presumably there was a bailey, but it has been built over. The motte is believed to be Norman, raised like Tomen-y-Mur in the years 1088–94 when Hugh d'Avranches occupied Meirionnydd, but it then became the seat of Welsh lords of Penllyn. The *Chronicle of the Princes* tells us that Llywelyn the Great destroyed the castle of Bala when he invaded in 1202. That is the last we hear of it.

Access: Apply to key-keeper (LA).
Reference: GAHW *Gwynedd.*
Relations: The mottes of Castell Prysor and Tomen-y-Mur.

TOMEN-Y-MUR   is reached by a minor road leading east from the A470, three miles north of Trawsfynydd. The name means 'Mound on the Wall', so called because this motte was raised within a Roman fort. Excavations have shown that the Roman governor Agricola established the fort when he overran North Wales in AD 78. This fort was later rebuilt in stone, but only its surrounding ditch can be seen. The conical motte at the west end of the fort is an impressive feature. Although

Tomen-y-Mur figures in Welsh legend as the seat of the princes of Ardudwy, the motte was probably raised by Hugh d'Avranches, earl of Chester, when he invaded Gwynedd around 1088. It was burnt by the Welsh in 1113, but temporarily recovered when Henry I invaded the following year. The hummocky summit of the mound suggests that a stone keep was later built on it by one of the princes of Gwynedd. It offers a fine view over the Llyn Trawsfynydd.

    Access: The site can be reached by a public footpath.

    Reference: GAHW *Gwynedd.*

    Relations: Earl Hugh's mottes at Abergwyngregyn and Castell Aberlleiniog. Compare the mottes raised on Roman fortifications at Cardiff, Caerleon and Caerwent.

OTHER SITES Several mottes are the work of Welsh lords. A mound near *Cymer* Abbey, with a Georgian summer house on top, is the first native castle for which there is documentary evidence. The *Chronicle of the Princes* relates that it was raised in 1116 and burnt in a feud a few months later. *Castell Cynfal* (near Tywyn) was also sacked soon after its construction. Another motte on the *Rug* country estate, outside Corwen, is a heightened burial mound, while *Domen Las* at Pennal was raised in a Roman fort, like Tomen-y-Mur. *Owain Glyndwr's Mount* (near Glyndyfrdwy) was later a seat of the great Welsh rebel.

    Deudraeth Castle, built by one of the feuding grandsons of Owain Gwynedd, was one of the first stone castles in Gwynedd. Like contemporary Castell Garn Fadrun it was probably a rude drystone construction. The site is a rock within the Italianate show village of Portmeirion, but the remains were swept away by an irate landowner in the nineteenth century to discourage visitors.

Monmouthshire

Much of the Welsh district of Gwent was colonised by the Normans within a few years of their conquest of England. William Fitz Osbern, earl of Hereford, invaded from his new castles of Monmouth and Chepstow before his death in 1071. Castle building in Gwent starts spectacularly with William's hall-keep on the cliff at Chepstow. This is not only the oldest stone castle in Wales, but probably in England too. It provided the model for later Norman hall-keeps at Monmouth and Grosmont. Together with the tower keeps at Penhow and Usk, and the stone curtains of Abergavenny and White castles, Monmouthshire has (for Wales) an unusual amount of Norman masonry. In addition, there are the usual motte-and-bailey castles. The motte of Twmbarlwm crowns an ancient hillfort, while those at Caerleon and Caerwent were raised over Roman fortifications.

    Nevertheless the great period of castle building in Monmouthshire, like the rest of Wales, is the thirteenth century. It begins with William Marshal's cross-wall at Chepstow, which is equipped with early round flanking towers. William's five sons went on to expand Chepstow into a mighty castle of four consecutive baileys on its narrow ridge, entered through a gatehouse of the new, twin-towered type. The Marshals also erected round-towered curtains at Usk and Caerleon. Elsewhere other barons were building in the new style: Grosmont and Skenfrith are the work of the king's justiciar, Hubert de Burgh, while Humphrey de Bohun raised the impressive castle of Caldicot. Both Skenfrith and Caldicot are dominated by circular keeps, and there are fragments of another at Castell Meredydd.

The strengthening of White Castle may be attributed to Edward I before he became king. This leads us into the Edwardian period. Llangybi has a large but unfinished castle of the de Clares, while Abergavenny received a substantial new tower. Roger Bigod added the domestic buildings of Chepstow Castle, as well as erecting Chepstow's town wall. A unique monument of the era is the Monnow Bridge gate at Monmouth. Lesser Edwardian remains can be seen at Cas Troggy and Pencoed.

Newport – notable for its water gate – was the only new castle of the fourteenth century. However, Caldicot was given its great gatehouse by Richard II's uncle and Grosmont was remodelled by the duke of Lancaster. Finally, Monmouthshire has the one great fifteenth-century castle of Wales. Raglan Castle, with its machicolated towers and moated, hexagonal keep, is a monument to the ambitions of William ap Thomas and William Herbert. It remains splendid despite its slighting in the Civil War.

ABERGAVENNY CASTLE occupies a strong position on a promontory overlooking the old town. Hamelin de Ballon raised the original motte-and-bailey before 1100. Like some other Norman lords in Gwent, he founded a priory nearby. In 1175 the last of the Ballons was killed in a battle against his Welsh neighbour, Sitsyllt. As a consequence the lordship of Abergavenny passed to William de Braose, lord of Brecon, who perpetrated an act of vengeance which was notorious even by the standards of the time. William summoned Sitsyllt to the castle under the pretext of delivering a royal proclamation. While they were feasting in the hall, he and his entourage were slaughtered. Those sons of Sitsyllt who survived the 'Abergavenny Massacre' launched a surprise attack on the castle in 1182. They overran the bailey but were repulsed at the keep.

William de Braose probably walled the bailey. In 1207 he rebelled against King John and had to flee into exile. His son temporarily recovered the castle during the Magna Carta war. Abergavenny fell in 1233 during the rebellion of Richard Marshal, earl of Pembroke, but it resisted Llywelyn the Last in 1263. Henry, Lord Hastings, added the Solar Tower after he inherited the lordship in 1273. His later medieval successors favoured Abergavenny – the priory church of St Mary contains a splendid series of their effigies. In 1402 the townsfolk stormed the castle when the constable attempted to hang three burgesses. The following year Owain Glyndwr burnt the town, despite the defensive wall (now vanished) which surrounded it. He failed to take the castle, but William Beauchamp afterwards strengthened it to forestall any future attack. The ruinous state of the castle can be blamed on a visit by

Charles I in 1645. In a rare departure from his usual tenacity, he ordered the slighting of the castle to prevent its use by the Roundheads.

Today the castle is very much a ruin. The layout was dictated by the Norman earthworks, and the most substantial remains occupy the north side of the bailey. William Beauchamp added the gatehouse, which projects deeply in front of the curtain. Its side walls remain but the vault has fallen. A stretch of William de Braose's curtain stands alongside, with the foundations of the hall behind. It leads to the Solar Tower. This is the most prominent part of the ruins, though the courtyard front has collapsed. Square with canted corners, the tower rises from a square base. Large windows lit the three upper floors, but they have been robbed into ragged holes. The tower contained Lord Hastings' solar and other private apartments. It forms part of a curious double tower guarding the north-west angle of the enclosure. The other part is a shallow round bastion.

Footings survive of the cross-wall which divided the castle into two baileys. An eighteenth-century print shows the ruins of a square keep on Hamelin's low motte, at the apex of the promontory. This keep may already have stood when the Welsh attacked in 1182, but nothing is left of it. A neo-Gothic hunting lodge now stands on its summit. It contains the local museum. On the south side of the bailey the curtain only survives as a retaining wall, with the base of a square tower. Close by, steps descend to a vaulted cellar.

Access: Open daily (LA).
Reference: Guidebook by A. L. Ralphs. GAHW *Glamorgan and Gwent.*
Relations: For William de Braose see Brecon, Castell Dinas, Hay and Oystermouth.

CAERLEON CASTLE Caerleon originated as the Roman Isca, where the Second Legion was based. Some interesting portions of the vast Roman fortress are visible, notably the amphitheatre and the baths. According to Welsh legend Caerleon was King Arthur's capital. However, unlike the other legionary fortresses at York and Chester, Caerleon did not develop into a city after the departure of the Romans. The ensuing settlement has never been much more than a village. Its medieval castle stood just outside the fortress area, beside the River Usk.

The castle is mentioned in the Domesday Book (1086). It had recently been founded by the Norman adventurer Turstin Fitz Rolf, and the conical motte is no doubt his. There was a period of Welsh occupation during the Anarchy, but Caerleon was important enough to be taken over by Henry II. He was building here from 1171. Giraldus Cambrensis mentions a 'gigantic tower', presumably on the motte. However, the Welsh of Gwent again captured the castle in 1173. They held it until William Marshal drove out Morgan ap Hywel in 1217. His son, William Marshal the Younger, erected a curtain with round corner towers. Thus strengthened, the castle resisted Llywelyn the Great in 1231. When the Marshal line came to an end in 1245, Caerleon was taken over by the de Clare lords of Glamorgan.

With the rebuilding of Newport Castle in the fourteenth century, Caerleon was neglected. A garden was laid out on the site in Victorian times, the motte being retained as a landscape feature. Its summit can be glimpsed over the garden wall. One of the round towers stands almost complete, behind the Hanbury Arms inn.

Access: On private land, but the tower is visible.
Reference: Archaeologia Cambrensis (6th series, XIII).
Relations: Compare the younger William Marshal's work at Chepstow, Cilgerran and Pembroke.

CAERWENT CASTLE   Caerwent, two miles north of Caldicot, was the Roman town of Venta. Its defensive wall forms an oblong enclosure over a mile long. The south side of the circuit, with its fourth-century flanking bastions, is one of the most impressive Roman fortifications left in Britain. It shows that Roman towns were just as strongly defended as those of the Middle Ages. However, the town did not survive the departure of the Romans and there is now just a village inside. At the south-east corner the Roman wall is buried by a Norman motte. This motte may have been one of those raised during William Fitz Osbern's invasion of Gwent. The Normans sometimes built their castles within abandoned Roman forts, but Caerwent's town enclosure would have been much too large for a small Norman garrison to defend. A bailey was probably formed in this corner, but no trace survives.

Access: Freely accessible (Cadw).
Reference: Site guidebook by R. J. Brewster.
Relations: Mottes in Roman forts at Caerleon, Cardiff and Tomen-y-Mur.

CALDICOT CASTLE   is a splendid stronghold associated with some of the foremost Marcher barons. Though nominally a ruin, the surrounding curtain lacks little more than some of its battlements, while the keep and the main gatehouse are intact due to Victorian restoration. The first castle may have been raised by William Fitz Osbern, earl of Hereford, when he overran Gwent in the years 1067–71. By the time of the Domesday Book it was held by the sheriff of Gloucester. The later stone walls and towers overlie the Norman motte-and-bailey. In 1158 Caldicot began its long association with the Bohuns earls of Hereford, most of whom bore the name Humphrey.

The present stone castle was raised towards the middle of the thirteenth century, probably by Humphrey 'the Good' who acquired the lordship of Brecon in 1241. Its oldest part is the circular keep, built of ashlar masonry and perfectly preserved from its plinth to its embattled parapet. The keep sits on top of the motte at the north-west corner. After centuries as an empty shell, the keep was given a new roof and floors by the antiquary J. R. Cobb, who purchased the castle in 1885. Like most round keeps, the entrance is at first-floor level, reached by a flight of steps. It leads into a living room with four narrow windows and a fireplace. A spiral stair ascends to a similar chamber above. The top floor was originally just a shield to protect a conical roof from combustible missiles. From the entrance another stair curves down in the thickness of the wall to the plain ground-floor room. A tiny prison occupies the base of a projecting semi-circular turret. It is curious that the turret is otherwise solid all the way up.

Evidently the keep was built first, because the stretch of curtain descending the motte blocks an arrow slit. The west curtain is an impressive composition, with three flanking towers including the keep. At the foot of the motte, the U-shaped Bohun Tower contains a gateway in its side wall, perhaps modelled on William Marshal's inner gate at Pembroke Castle. This was the original entrance to the castle. Another rounded tower flanks the south-west corner of the circuit. Elsewhere the curtain is less comprehensively flanked. The long south wall extends past the later main gatehouse to a stretch which is pierced by three traceried windows. They mark the site of the hall and show a relaxation of security in the early fourteenth century. Alongside is a U-shaped tower near the eastern apex of the castle. Though less stoutly built, this tower is larger than the keep and contained the Bohuns' solar.

Except for the later Woodstock Tower, the curtain along the north side of the bailey is quite plain. Fireplaces on the courtyard face show that retainers' lodgings once stood against it. With the destruction of all the interior buildings, the bailey is now laid out as a garden.

The main gatehouse and the Woodstock Tower opposite are both later additions to the castle, though their ashlar facing matches the keep. They were built by Thomas of Woodstock, youngest son of Edward III and duke of Gloucester, who married the 10-year-old Bohun heiress in 1376. His name is inscribed on an archway in the Woodstock Tower. This handsome tower is square with canted outer corners. Three storeys of apartments overlie a narrow gate passage through the tower. The machicolated crown is typical of later medieval castle building.

Much grander is Thomas' main gatehouse on the south front, which vies with the keep as the dominant feature of the castle. Like the Edwardian gatehouses of the previous century, it has a long gate passage once protected by two portcullises and two sets of gates. On the other hand, while the exterior is quite severe, no towers flank the gateway. The gatehouse forms a rectangular block protruding only a little beyond the curtain. Machicolated latrine turrets at each end rise a little higher than the main parapet. The courtyard facade is quite domestic in character and there was no attempt to make the gatehouse a self-contained fortification. All this typifies the less formidable character of later medieval castle gatehouses. A hall occupies the single upper floor. This was probably the castellan's residence in the Edwardian tradition. J. R. Cobb restored the gatehouse from ruin as a residence for himself. His timber-framed gable ends, while attractive, seem rather incongruous.

After leading the baronial opposition to his nephew, Richard II, Thomas was taken to Calais as a prisoner and murdered there in 1398. Caldicot passed to the Stafford dukes of Buckingham. A turreted gateway at the eastern apex of the castle – giving four entrances in all – probably dates from their occupation. This portion is more ruinous than the rest. It has been suggested that the breach here represents a deliberate slighting by the Yorkists after Humphrey Stafford was killed in 1460. If so, the episode closed off an unusually peaceful history in this securely English corner of Wales. By 1613 the castle was in ruins.

Access: Open daily except in winter (LA).

Reference: The Architecture and History of Caldicot Castle by O. Morgan and T. Wakeman. GAHW *Glamorgan and Gwent.*
Relations: The Bohuns' hall at Brecon. Compare the round keeps of Skenfrith, Usk, Bronllys, Tretower and Pembroke.

CASTELL MEREDYDD, or Castell Machen, is the only native Welsh castle in Gwent. Morgan ap Hywel, lord of Gwynllwg, built it after he lost Caerleon to William Marshal in 1217. His castle occupies two rocky outcrops on a cliff between Upper and Lower Machen. The eastern knoll preserves a fragment of a small round keep, with a latrine shaft overlooking the cliff. There was a hall on the larger knoll to the west. The two rocks are separated by a ditch from a large bailey to the north. Some footings of a curtain here are attributed to Gilbert Marshal, earl of Pembroke, who seized the castle in 1236 but was ordered to return it to Morgan by Henry III. Gilbert de Clare finally took it when he overran Senghenydd in 1266.

> *Access:* Visible from the road.
> *Reference: Castles of the Welsh Princes* by P. R. Davis.
> *Relations:* Native round keeps at Dinefwr, Dryslwyn and Dolbadarn.

CAS TROGGY was built by Roger Bigod, earl of Norfolk and lord of Chepstow. It is recorded as newly built in 1305. Roger died the following year and may have left the castle incomplete, since there is no further record of it. Cas (i.e. Castell) Troggy lies concealed in woodland two miles south-east of Llantrisant. It was intended as a small quadrangle. Three sides have vanished, if they were ever built, but the ashlar south curtain stands to an appreciable height above a tall plinth. On the inner face is the imprint of a fireplace which probably heated the hall. At either end are the rubble stumps of corner towers with octagonal ground-floor rooms. One is larger than the other and probably formed a keep.

> *Access:* On private land.
> *Reference: A History of Monmouthshire* by J. A. Bradney.
> *Relations:* Roger Bigod's additions at Chepstow.

CHEPSTOW CASTLE AND TOWN WALL Chepstow Castle, perched on a cliff above the River Wye, is one of Wales' finest castles. Although nominally a ruin, most of this castle is extremely well preserved, despite its adaptation for artillery defence after the Civil War. With its four walled baileys on a narrow ridge Chepstow is the supreme example of a castle employing successive lines of defence, and the central keep is probably the oldest stone castle building not just in Wales but the whole of Britain.

The Domesday Book relates that the castle was raised by William Fitz Osbern. In 1067 William I created him palatine earl of Hereford with the task of 'defending' the Welsh border – in the aggressive way that the Normans interpreted defence. Fitz Osbern swiftly conquered Gwent from his new castles on the Wye at Chepstow and

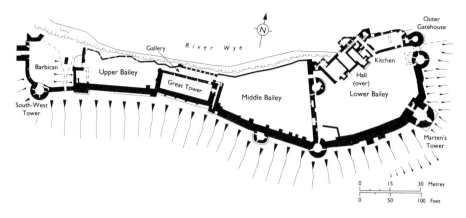

CHEPSTOW CASTLE

Monmouth. The early Norman character of the keep supports the view that it was at least begun by him. This hall-keep resembles those built in northern France before the Norman Conquest. It is perhaps surprising that the first essay in stone castle building should be on the periphery of Norman rule, though this is also true of the early stone castles at Ludlow and Richmond in England.

Even if William Fitz Osbern began the keep, it was probably still unfinished when he was killed in Flanders in 1071. His son, Roger de Breteuil, had only a few years to complete it before his banishment for taking part in a rebellion against William I. There followed forty years of royal guardianship which are considered much less likely for significant building here. Nevertheless, the Normans did not overrun South Wales until the 1090s, and before that time Chepstow was the key stronghold of the region. The keep was surely built before 1115, when Henry I awarded the lordship of Chepstow to the de Clares.

For over a century Chepstow was held by the earls of Pembroke. As at Pembroke, no masonry can be attributed to the de Clares, but William Marshal strengthened the castle after he married the Clare heiress in 1189. His contribution here is not as spectacular as his work at Pembroke, but the cross-wall closing off the inner eastern bailey has two flanking towers which are probably the oldest circular towers in Wales. His five sons – William the Younger, Richard, Gilbert, Walter and Anselm – successively held the earldom between 1219 and 1245. Anselm only lasted for eleven days, but the others may all have contributed to the expansion of this ambitious Marcher castle to its present extent. All four baileys are their work, except for the elder William's cross-wall. Mural towers are used sparingly and the entrances are simple gateways, except for the strong gatehouse at the east end of the castle. It is an early example of the twin-towered type, built either by Gilbert or Walter.

In 1245 the Marshal lands were divided, Chepstow passing to the Bigod earls of Norfolk. There was further building under Roger Bigod in the Edwardian period, and the rare survival of non-royal building accounts allows us to follow the works. Roger's main additions were a new suite of domestic apartments and the mighty Marten's Tower, both in the outer eastern bailey, as well as the heightening of the keep. His munificence extended to rebuilding the splendid abbey church of Tintern further up the Wye.

Upon Roger's death in 1306 the castle reverted to the Crown as a means of discharging his debts. The younger Hugh le Despenser augmented his personal empire in South Wales by purchasing Chepstow. He and Edward II took refuge temporarily during their flight in 1326, though the castle soon surrendered to Queen Isabella's forces. In the later Middle Ages Chepstow was another neglected holding of absentee landlords. Its strategic importance was recognised during Owain Glyndwr's revolt, the substantial garrison installed at that time successfully deterring the Welsh from attacking. In Tudor times the castle enjoyed a new lease of life as a seat of the Herbert earls of Worcester, whose chief residence was Raglan Castle.

Chepstow's only real military activity took place during the Civil War. After a token resistance against the Roundheads in 1645, the castle put up a sterner fight during the Royalist uprising of 1648. Oliver Cromwell commenced siege operations before moving west to Pembroke. A prolonged bombardment resulted in the breach of the curtain, which so unnerved the garrison that they ran out to surrender. Instead of the usual slighting, Chepstow Castle entered its last phase, serving as a state fortress and prison until its abandonment in 1690. It was probably soon after the siege of 1648 that the long south curtain was thickened to withstand artillery.

The long ridge on which the castle stands has the Norman keep at its narrowest point, with a pair of baileys on either side. Owing to the sheer drop there is only a low retaining wall along the north side of the castle, except where the domestic buildings are securely placed at the east end. By contrast, the long south front presents an impressive display of military strength.

It is worth examining the south front from outside first. West of the keep an embattled, oblong tower marks the end of the inner western bailey, with a circular tower projecting boldly from the small outer enclosure beyond. The Norman character of the keep is evident in the shallow 'pilaster' buttresses which project at intervals. A portion of early Norman curtain extends to the east, showing that William Fitz Osbern or his son created a walled courtyard in front of the keep. It ends at a semi-circular tower added by one of the Marshal brothers. The next tower is one of those on the elder William Marshal's cross-wall. It appears that the last stretch of curtain is entirely a rebuilding of the Commonwealth period, so it is probably here that the breach was made during the siege of 1648. Marten's Tower, one of Roger Bigod's additions, dominates the east end of the castle. Perfectly preserved, this U-shaped tower rises from a square base with pyramid spurs. Note the flanking turrets which are slightly higher than the tower itself.

A tall stretch of curtain links Marten's Tower to the main gatehouse on the edge of the cliff. The gatehouse, with its rounded towers flanking the entrance, anticipates on a smaller scale the great gatehouses of Edwardian times. A machicolation arch hangs high above the outer gateway. Within the gate passage are the grooves for two portcullises and a pair of old wooden gates. A miserable prison occupies the base of the northern flanking tower. The gate passage was once longer but the inner part of the gatehouse has disappeared.

Immediately beyond the gate passage we are confronted with Roger Bigod's domestic buildings, which follow the curve of the cliff above the river. The accounts reveal that they were built in 1278–85, in time for a visit by Edward I. They form an unusually complete example of a medieval lord's residence. It is odd to find the main domestic buildings in the outer courtyard of a castle, but this compact enclosure is the largest of Chepstow's four baileys and the others would have been very cramped. A curious feature (also found in the great episcopal palaces of the period) is the presence of two halls – a great hall for public use on the west, and a private eastern hall with an attached solar.

A vaulted porch leads into the western hall. There are the standard three doorways at the service end of this hall, leading into the buttery, the pantry, and a staircase in between. Owing to the slope the western hall is at a higher level, its buttery and pantry overlying those of the eastern hall. A passage between the two halls leads to a straight staircase at the rear. This descends to a vaulted undercroft beneath the western hall. Provisions brought by boat could be hoisted straight into this storage cellar from an opening overlooking the cliff.

Marten's Tower was rising in the years 1287–93. It contains three residential storeys above a ground-floor cellar. An ornate little chapel occupies one of the flanking turrets at parapet level. Although the rooms were residential, the windows in the curved outer wall are narrow slits, while the larger ones facing the courtyard are Tudor insertions. The entrance from the courtyard and the doorways leading to the curtain wall-walks were all protected by portcullises. This tower was in effect a new and dynamically placed keep, superseding the old hall-keep further back. Though possibly intended by Roger Bigod as a last resort, it no doubt formed the constable's residence. Commanding the most vulnerable approach to the castle, the tower was linked to the gatehouse by a short stretch of wall-walk. The tower takes its name from Henry Marten, one of the regicides who signed Charles I's death warrant. He endured twenty years of imprisonment here.

The cross-wall dividing the two eastern baileys is the elder William Marshal's work. It is mutilated by brick patches and inserted fireplaces, recalling a vanished Tudor range. Its two ruinous flanking towers are among the earliest examples of round mural towers. A gateway beside one of the towers leads into the inner eastern bailey. Although the south curtain here is part Norman and part Marshal work, it was thickened in the seventeenth century. Note how the original parapet has been replaced by larger merlons for defence by cannon. These are cut through the entire thickness of the medieval wall.

Ahead is William Fitz Osbern's hall-keep. The east facade preserves its original, round-headed doorway, placed high up and once reached by a flight of steps. Internally the keep, a hundred feet long, forms an impressive shell. Its north wall, facing the cliff, is much thinner than the other walls and the only one allowed the luxury of frequent windows. Several Norman slits lit the undercroft, and beneath it a sloping basement reflects the drop in ground level from west to east. Above the undercroft was the hall, the domestic hub of the castle until Roger Bigod built his new halls in the outer bailey. Arched recesses along its south and west walls show a rudimentary early Norman attempt at decoration, with a blocked fireplace in the centre. The north wall is much richer owing to a series of large windows inserted by the Marshals.

Originally the keep only rose to the level of this hall. The top storey is another thirteenth-century addition, but its building history is complex. One of the Marshal brothers added a solar above the west end of the hall, its east wall once supported on two arches. Only the springers of these arches survive but they are enough to demonstrate the high quality of carving. For fifty years the western third of the keep rose a stage higher than the rest. Then, in the 1290s, Roger Bigod heightened the remainder. His windows are quite different in style to the Marshal windows. It shows that the keep still formed an important residence despite Roger's new suite of domestic buildings. Today only two sides of the top storey remain. The others were probably taken down during the Commonwealth period to provide stone for the thickened curtain.

The narrow ledge between the keep and the cliff is filled by a walled passage known as the Gallery. It is another addition of the Marshal brothers. We now enter the west part of the castle, which is narrower than the eastern baileys. In contrast to the rounded forms of the other mural towers, the angle tower of the inner western bailey is oblong, containing a single lofty chamber above an undercroft. Now isolated, this room probably formed part of a residential range linking up with the Norman keep.

Beside the oblong tower another gateway leads into the outer western bailey. A modern bridge crosses the deep ditch between them. Immediately beyond rises a circular flanking tower. The curtain of this small enclosure was not reinforced in the seventeenth century and so preserves its original appearance, with a row of arrow slits at courtyard level and an embattled parapet. Again the entrance was originally a simple archway – Roger Bigod added the present gate tower in front.

Chepstow is one of the small group of Welsh towns preserving its medieval town wall, here known as the Port Wall. The town grew up in Norman times under the protection of the castle. Its parish church of St Mary incorporates the truncated Norman nave of a priory, perhaps founded by William Fitz Osbern. Chepstow occupies a bend in the River Wye – its alternative name of Striguil derives from the Welsh for 'bend'. The river was considered adequate protection on the north and east, so the town wall ran in an arc defending the landward approaches only. Even so it was three quarters of a mile long, the wall being built further out than the small population required in order to occupy higher ground. It has been suggested that Roger Bigod built the wall (no doubt with hefty contributions from the townsfolk) in the 1270s, before commencing his works on the castle. If so, then the town wall is a decade earlier than the classic Edwardian town walls of Caernarfon and Conwy. It foreshadows these walls with its open-backed, semi-circular flanking towers, originally ten in number.

A square turret marks the beginning of the town wall, below the west end of the castle. The first stretch, with two semi-circular towers, is obscured by houses. We reach the Town Gate, a square tower originally forming the only entrance through the town wall. Newly rebuilt in 1487, the heraldic panel above the outer gateway dates from another remodelling in 1524. The present archways, windows and battlements are Victorian.

Beyond the Town Gate the wall is complete except for one narrow breach. The five flanking towers along this stretch rise slightly higher than the wall, but steps maintain the continuity of the wall-walk. This contrasts with Caernarfon and Conwy, where the wall-walks continued across the tower gaps as wooden bridges. It should be admitted that the town wall is not very high, but it would have appeared more formidable when the ditch lay in front. Unfortunately the wall no longer continues as far as the river. The eastern portion, along with the last three flanking towers, was swept away to make room for the railway.

Access: The castle is open daily and the town wall is freely accessible (both Cadw).
Reference: Guidebook by J. K. Knight.
Relations: Castles of the Marshals at Caerleon, Usk, Pembroke and Cilgerran. Compare the hall-keeps at Grosmont and Monmouth, and the early twin-towered gatehouses of Montgomery and Criccieth. There are contemporary town walls at Tenby, Caernarfon and Conwy.

GROSMONT CASTLE, on a hill overlooking the River Monnow and the English border, is close to Skenfrith and White castles. These three formed a triangle of defence guarding the open country of northern Gwent. During the Anarchy, when the Welsh exploited the divisions of their Norman conquerors, King Stephen acquired this territory by an exchange of lands, and the three castles shared a common ownership from then on. The large, D-shaped mound on which the later ruin stands may well be Stephen's work, since it contrasts with the conical mottes more typical of the earlier Norman invaders. The castle is first mentioned in 1162. From that time onwards Grosmont frequently appears in Henry II's Pipe Rolls, though the minor expenditure is consistent with repairs to an earth-and-timber castle.

The hall on the east side of the mound resembles the early Norman hall of Chepstow. As King Stephen is not credited with any stone castle building, and Henry II's small expenditure cannot account for it, it is usually attributed to Hubert de Burgh, a Norfolk knight who received the three castles in 1201. The hall is substantial enough to be regarded, like that at Chepstow, as a hall-keep. It is an oblong block of two storeys, most of it standing to full height. A number of slit windows lit the undercroft, but the larger windows in the hall above have been robbed of their worked stone. The fireplace was probably central, indicating that one end of the hall was partitioned off to form a solar. Originally the only entrance was at first-floor level, reached by steps from the courtyard. Both of the ground-floor doorways are later insertions.

It is likely that the hall was complete by 1205. In that year Hubert was captured by the French following his gallant defence of Chinon on the Loire. During his imprisonment King John gave the three castles to William de Braose, though he was soon driven into exile. Hubert de Burgh returned to become chief justiciar, and following another heroic defence – of Dover Castle against the invading Dauphin Louis – he again received the three castles in 1219.

Over the next thirteen years Hubert raised the stone defences of Grosmont and Skenfrith. They reflect the great advance of military architecture in the early thirteenth century. At Grosmont he erected a curtain on the mound, except on the side already occupied by his hall. This curtain is built in straight sections, with semi-circular towers at the angles. Owing to the confines of the site Grosmont is a compact castle and its towers are closely spaced (the outer bailey was never walled in stone). The South Tower, adjoining the hall-keep, formed the gatehouse, but only a fragment stands high. Hubert's South-West Tower was remodelled later. The West Tower is the best preserved of the original four, while the northern tower has perished. Hubert may also have begun the fine parish church in the village below.

Hubert's relationship with the resentful Henry III was often tempestuous. In 1232 he fell victim to court intrigue and was deprived of his office and his castles. The following year he escaped captivity to join Richard Marshal's revolt. Ironically, the royal army was camped outside Grosmont Castle when Richard and Hubert scattered it in a night attack, forcing the king into an ignominious retreat. Henry III later granted Monmouth and the three castles to his younger son, Edmund 'Crouchback', thus beginning a long tenure by the earls and dukes of Lancaster. Edmund's grandson, Henry of Grosmont, was born in the castle. He won renown in the Hundred Years' War and was made first duke of Lancaster in 1351. Perhaps an affection for his birthplace caused him to remodel Grosmont. Hubert de Burgh's castle was probably a severely military piece of work, like Skenfrith, but Henry's alterations have mellowed it.

The ruinous barbican in front of the gatehouse is Henry's addition. He also reconstructed the South-West Tower. This is now the most impressive feature of the castle, with three storeys of comfortable apartments above the storage basement. Its courtyard front, with a tall archway, dates entirely from that time. Henry demolished the northern tower to make way for a rectangular block containing extra accommodation. Though largely collapsed, it retains a charming octagonal chimney. Delicate trefoiled openings are capped by a stone crown.

Grosmont saw action during Owain Glyndwr's revolt. His supporters were defeated in a skirmish outside the village in 1404. An attack upon the castle the following year was thwarted by a relieving force. After that the castle sank into ruins.

Access: Always open (Cadw).
Reference: Guidebook by J. K. Knight. *The Three Castles* by J. K. Knight. *HKW* (II).
Relations: Skenfrith and White castles. Hubert de Burgh also built Hadleigh Castle in Essex. Compare the Norman hall-keeps of Chepstow, Monmouth and Manorbier.

LLANGYBI CASTLES The present house known as Llangibby Castle nestles between its two medieval predecessors. To the east is the ditched motte of an obscure earthwork castle, perhaps raised by the native Welsh. Its flat summit was later put to use as a bowling green. Overlooking the house to the west, on a wooded hill, are the sparse ruins of an unusually large Edwardian stronghold. Its builder is still a matter of debate. Gilbert de Clare, the 'Red Earl', gave Llangybi to his brother Bogo, who died in 1294. Gilbert also died the following year. His son came of age in 1307, and this last Gilbert de Clare is considered a more likely candidate than Bogo. The choice of location is odd, considering that the Clares also held Usk Castle just three miles further up the Usk valley. Perhaps Gilbert wanted to emulate his castle-building father. However, he was killed at Bannockburn in 1314. Edward II's favourite Hugh le Despenser forced the de Clare heiress to hand over Llangybi and other lands, but there is no later mention of the castle.

A large, roughly oblong courtyard filled the summit of the hill. It was surrounded by a curtain which is fragmentary except on the north side, where a long stretch survives to the wall-walk. Midway along is a semi-circular flanking tower, originally one of several on the perimeter. However, it is the west side of the castle which holds the chief interest, because here stand the sadly truncated remains of an unusual keep and one of the largest Edwardian gatehouses.

It appears that the keep began as a circular tower flanking the north-west corner of the enclosure. Subsequently the oblong body of the keep was built onto it, resulting in a curious structure with the original tower at one end and round angle turrets at the other. Little more than the ground floor of this keep now stands, but the springers of the vault can still be seen. The absence of any other domestic buildings suggests that the keep was meant to house Gilbert de Clare's private apartments.

The gatehouse, at the south-west corner of the enclosure, was almost as large as Edward I's gatehouses at Beaumaris. Again only the ground floor stands, and the rounded fronts of its twin towers have collapsed. A long gate passage, once defended by several doors and portcullises, is flanked by guard chambers. At the rear corners are the stumps of circular stair turrets. No doubt this keep-gatehouse was intended to have a large hall at first-floor level, but it is doubtful if the building ever rose that high. In view of the young Gilbert's untimely death it seems likely that Llangybi was one of several ambitious de Clare castles left incomplete. It was briefly brought out of its slumber by a Royalist garrison, who made a stand here during the abortive uprising of 1648.

Access: On private land.

Reference: Archaeologia Cambrensis (CV).

Relations: St Quintin's Castle was also built by the last Gilbert de Clare. Compare the keep-gatehouses at Caerphilly, Kidwelly, Harlech and Beaumaris.

MONMOUTH CASTLE AND TOWN DEFENCES

Monmouth originated under William Fitz Osbern. He was made palatine earl of Hereford in 1067, overrunning most of Gwent before his death in Flanders in 1071. Monmouth and Chepstow castles were the key strongholds from which he launched this invasion. His son, Roger de Breteuil, was forced into exile after taking part in a rebellion against William the Conqueror in 1075. The lordship was then divided, and by the time of the Domesday Book William Fitz Baderon was lord of Monmouth. His descendants, who called themselves 'de Monmouth', held it until 1256. Henry III then granted Monmouth – along with the three castles of Grosmont, Skenfrith and White – to his younger son, Edmund 'Crouchback'. Northern Gwent thus became part of the vast estates of the earls and dukes of Lancaster. The future Henry V was born in the gatehouse in 1387. When his father, Henry of Bolingbroke, seized the throne in 1399, Monmouth became a royal castle.

This secure English stronghold saw little action against the Welsh. Monmouth was captured by the rebels Richard Marshal (1233) and Simon de Montfort (1264). It was not attacked during Owain Glyndwr's rising, though his supporters won a skirmish nearby and pursued the fleeing English to the town gates. Monmouth changed hands three times in the Civil War, finally surrendering to a large Roundhead army in October 1645. The castle was slighted two years later.

Monmouth Castle is now just a fragment of its former self. It occupied a large ringwork on the west side of the old town, overlooking the River Monnow. The houses of Agincourt Square mark the line of the castle ditch. From here a lane leads to the site of the gatehouse, which was rebuilt under Henry VI to commemorate his father's birthplace. The castle bailey is laid out as a regimental parade ground. To the right, Great Castle House was built as a town residence of the marquis of Worcester in 1673. It stands on the site of a circular keep, destroyed during the slighting. This is unfortunate because it was described as being of 'great height and strength', so it may have been on a par with Pembroke's round keep.

On the west side of the enclosure are the only remains of the medieval castle. Here stand the original Norman keep and the later great hall. The keep is a hall-keep, modelled on William Fitz Osbern's great keep at Chepstow, but smaller and not quite as old. Built by one of the de Monmouths around the middle of the twelfth century, it is now a ruin. Its west wall collapsed in 1647, not during the slighting but as a result of undermining in the siege two years earlier. The north-east corner has also perished, a Victorian house now encroaching upon the site. The Norman character of the keep is still evident in the 'pilaster' corner buttresses and several tiny windows. However, it was remodelled by Henry of Grosmont, who became first duke of Lancaster in 1351. He inserted several Gothic windows, one of which remains complete, with the stumps of flowing tracery in its head. Henry also inserted the present entrance doorway, still at first-floor level like its Norman predecessor. The remodelling suggests that the Norman hall had become the dukes' solar.

Edmund Crouchback added his new hall at right-angles to the Norman keep. It stayed in use as a court house and was the only castle building still habitable by the time of a survey in 1550. Three sides stand, though the windows are blocked. The back wall is the only surviving fragment of the curtain which once surrounded the ringwork.

Monmouth town grew up under the patronage of its Norman lords. It occupies the high ground between the rivers Monnow and Wye. Like several castle towns of Gwent, it had a Norman priory which partly survives in St Mary's Church. Between the castle and the Wye Bridge was a stone town wall, which can be dated to murage grants in 1297 and 1315. The only relic is a turret of the Dixton Gate, on Old Dixton Road. On the south the defences remained of earth and timber, but beyond them the bend of the Monnow enclosed a lower town. Monnow Street descends to the three-arched Monnow Bridge across the river, with its unique bridge gate. Even this is not the end of Monmouth's outer defences, because the suburb of Over Monnow across the river preserves much of its ditch, the Clawydd Ddu. So Monmouth had three lines of defence guarding the approach from Wales.

A number of towns once had bridge gates, but most of them were destroyed in later centuries to ease the flow of traffic. Just two survive in Britain, and this is the only one where the gate actually stands on the bridge. The bridge was built in 1272, but the gate tower was probably added a few decades later. It rises from one of the bridge piers, which explains its narrow plan with rounded ends. Three machicolations overhang the outer archway. Though it was fortunate to escape destruction in the nineteenth century, the demands of traffic resulted in the widening of the main gateway and the insertion of pedestrian entrances on either side. Before that the Monnow Bridge was not quite so wide, and the latrine projection in the portcullis chamber would have discharged straight into the river. The tiled roof which gives the building its picturesque silhouette is Victorian.

> *Access:* The castle ruins (Cadw) and bridge gate (LA) can only be viewed externally.
> *Reference:* Castle guidebook by A. J. Taylor. *Archaeologia Cambrensis* (CXLII) for the Monnow Bridge. *HKW* (II).
> *Relations:* See the hall-keeps at Chepstow and Grosmont – the latter was also remodelled by Henry of Grosmont. The other surviving bridge gate is at Warkworth (Northumberland).

NEWPORT CASTLE   The first castle stood near the Norman church of St Woolos (now Newport Cathedral). It existed by 1172 and endured several sieges, more from English rebels than the Welsh. The last of these took place in 1321, when Hugh de Audley briefly seized Newport during the baronial rising against Hugh le Despenser the Younger. De Audley assumed full possession on Despenser's downfall in 1326. It is not known when the move to the present site beside the River Usk took place. The handsome east front, which is the only part of the castle to survive, dates from the fourteenth century. The boldly-projecting corner towers with their tall pyramid spurs are typical of Edwardian castle architecture in South Wales. Hugh de Audley may therefore have been the builder during his twenty-year tenure, though the castle is usually attributed to his successor Ralph, earl of Stafford.

Both corner towers are octagonal above their square bases. The apartments within are square except for angle fireplaces. Between them is the remarkable Water Gate, a square tower with shallow flanking turrets. Its outer archway opens straight onto the river so that boats could have sailed in at high tide to unload their cargoes in the gate passage. From there, supplies were stored in a cellar below courtyard level.

This was always the show front, and it still lacks little more than its battlements. The other three sides of the irregular courtyard, which have disappeared, were bounded by a plain curtain without flanking towers. Even the landward entrance was just a simple gateway, so Newport was a strangely river-oriented castle. Perhaps building continued on a humbler scale than originally intended. The castle may not have been finished, because masons were hurrying to make it defensible against Owain Glyndwr in 1405.

A remodelling took place around 1430 under Humphrey Stafford, later created duke of Buckingham. The effort was again concentrated on the east front, mellowing its Edwardian severity. Humphrey rebuilt the upper part of the Water Gate. Over the gateway is his presence chamber, a lofty room with an elaborate ribbed vault. The large Gothic window overlooking the Usk shows a more relaxed attitude to defence, while the wide archway facing the courtyard led into the vanished audience chamber. A chapel on the top floor has largely been destroyed. When it existed, the Water Gate would have been the dominant feature of the castle. Humphrey also remodelled the residential buildings which stood against the east curtain. His hall is marked by two pointed windows in the curtain between the Water Gate and the North Tower. He remodelled the South Tower to house his private apartments, with larger windows inserted in its three storeys. A mural passage (its inner face has collapsed) connected the tower with the Water Gate, thus by-passing the kitchen which stood against this section of curtain.

Humphrey was a victim of the Wars of the Roses, falling at the battle of Northampton in 1460. The next two dukes of Buckingham both lost their heads and the castle fell into decay. It is fortunate that the east front has survived so well in this urban landscape, hemmed in as the site now is by the railway and a busy roundabout.

> *Access:* Exterior only (Cadw).
> *Reference:* GAHW *Glamorgan and Gwent.*
> *Relations:* Compare fifteenth-century Raglan Castle. Not to be confused with Newport in Pembrokeshire.

PENCOED CASTLE   Six miles east of Newport, beyond the village of Llanmartin, stands a Tudor mansion built by Sir Thomas Morgan in the 1490s. A handsome gatehouse leads into the courtyard, but the main residential range is sadly derelict. There is nothing defensive about this complex but it occupies the ditched site of an older castle. The only stone relic is a round corner tower – now very ruinous – to the right of the gatehouse. This tower presumably formed part of a walled enclosure, but everything else has vanished. The history of the castle is obscure. It may have been built by Richard de la More, who was here in 1270.

> *Access:* Visible from the road.
> *Reference:* *Pencoed Castle* by O. Morgan and T. Wakeman.
> *Relations:* Tudorised castles at St Donat's, St Fagan's, Carew and Laugharne.

PENHOW CASTLE,   midway between Newport and Chepstow, provides a welcome contrast in a county full of impressive but bare castle ruins. This is the only inhabited castle in Monmouthshire and its homely scale reflects the modest pretensions of the gentry who built it. Ironically, although the Seymours of Penhow remained tenants of the lords of Chepstow, another branch of the family rose to prominence elsewhere, becoming dukes of Somerset and providing Henry VIII with one of his ill-fated wives.

The name Seymour is a corruption of St Maur. This family is recorded in Gwent in Norman times but the first one definitely associated with Penhow is William de St Maur. A document of c. 1235 shows him conspiring with his overlord, Gilbert Marshal, to deprive a Welsh lord of a neighbouring manor. William may have built the small keep, though its oblong plan is rather antiquated for the thirteenth century. Three storeys high, the keep was originally entered only at first-floor level. The present ground-floor doorway and the corbelled parapet are later medieval work. After centuries as a roofless shell the tower was refurbished in the 1970s.

William de St Maur may also have built the curtain around the small courtyard. It was a tower-less wall built in short, straight sections. Most of it has been absorbed by the later buildings on three sides of the courtyard. Only on the east does it remain complete, including its battlements.

Beside the keep a gabled annexe forms a quaint gatehouse. The original entrance arrangements are unclear, the present gateway being Tudor. Because the keep rises straight ahead two right-angled turns are necessary to reach the courtyard – a contrivance surely due to lack of space rather than defensive calculation. The rest of the south range forms the hall. This has displaced the curtain and shows a disregard for defence in the later Middle Ages, though the rock-cut ditch remains in front. Built by one of the Seymours in the fourteenth century, the hall block was remodelled by Sir Thomas Bowles, who was knighted for his role in the siege of Berwick in 1482. His hall lies at first-floor level. Its screen is a modern reconstruction incorporating portions of old woodwork. The ground-floor chamber served as a separate hall for Sir Thomas' retainers.

This medieval manor house was superseded in the seventeenth century by a new house north of the keep. Its north front, with three rows of large windows, contrasts with the severe stretch of curtain alongside. It is remarkable that so many different periods of occupation are concentrated in such a small space. An outer courtyard lay beyond the ditch, oddly containing the parish church.

> *Access:* Open regularly in summer.
> *Reference: Penhow Castle* by O. Morgan and T. Wakeman. Guidebook.
> *Relations:* Smaller inhabited castles at Fonmon, Picton and Upton. Compare the square keep at Usk.

RAGLAN CASTLE   is a magnificent ruin. There was an older castle on the site, the present keep and inner courtyard following the line of a Norman motte-and-bailey. The castle visible today is the last great stronghold of Wales – indeed the only major new castle of the fifteenth century. It is a monument to the Herbert family, who rose to prominence during the Wars of the Roses. Raglan remained an aristocratic seat until it was ruined by the Civil War.

The castle was begun by William ap Thomas, an obscure Welsh knight who made good through a lucrative marriage and a profitable spell in the French wars. Returning to hold various offices in South Wales, his rough justice was no doubt typical of the Welsh Marches. Although he acquired Raglan through his wife, it was only in 1432 that he obtained outright possession. It is likely that he began Raglan Castle after that date. The most notable feature of his building campaign is the moated keep, which dominates the castle while standing apart. Its hexagonal plan – rare in Britain – shows the influence of his French campaigns, and the castle may have been financed by French booty.

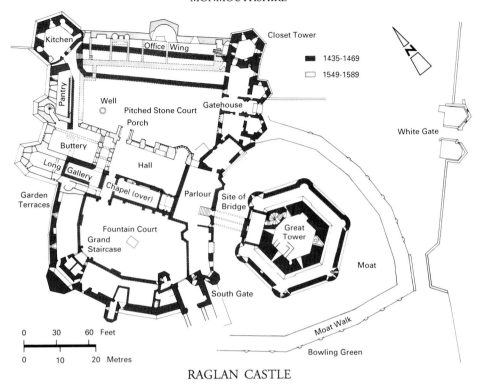

Kitchen

Office Wing

Closet Tower

■ 1435-1469
□ 1549-1589

Pantry

Well

Pitched Stone Court

Gatehouse

Porch

White Gate

Buttery

Long Gallery

Hall

Chapel (over)

Parlour

Site of Bridge

Garden
Terraces

Fountain Court

Grand
Staircase

Great
Tower

Moat

South Gate

Moat Walk

0   30   60 Feet

0   10   20 Metres

Bowling Green

RAGLAN CASTLE

Much of the inner courtyard can also be attributed to William ap Thomas before his death in 1445. There was a lengthy pause before his son, William Herbert, continued building. He completed the inner courtyard and built an outer one beyond, with several polygonal towers paying homage to his father's keep. This construction took place during a career which led him briefly to great power and influence as a supporter of the Yorkist faction. William Herbert was instrumental in putting Edward IV on the throne, supplying the Welsh army which won Edward's crucial victory at Mortimer's Cross in 1461. After crushing the last vestiges of Lancastrian resistance at Harlech Castle in 1468, William was made earl of Pembroke. However, the following year he was beheaded after the battle of Edgecote, when Edward IV was temporarily overthrown by the earl of Warwick.

William's son and namesake regained the title. He may have completed the castle, but the next great building campaign is due to William Somerset, earl of Worcester (d.1584). His additions blend with the fifteenth-century work. Here as elsewhere in Wales, Tudor builders showed deference to castle architecture. Outwardly they maintained the defensive character of the castle, while bringing the interior up to date with Elizabethan standards of comfort.

Unfortunately this splendour was not to last. The first marquis of Worcester was a staunch Catholic, reputedly donating a million pounds to the king's cause during the Civil War. Hence Raglan was the last outpost of Royalist resistance in South Wales. Charles I stayed here for several weeks in 1645. After the fall of Oxford, the parliamentary commander Sir Thomas Fairfax arrived to direct siege operations. With the full might of parliament against it, the castle creditably withstood ten weeks of bombardment before surrendering in August 1646. The keep was slighted and the rest of the castle became a quarry. Fortunately, a plan to rebuild it as a residence in the nineteenth century did not come to fruition.

Its Civil War performance has given Raglan the reputation of a great stronghold, but even some unfortified English mansions endured long sieges during that conflict. The real strength of such places lay in the artillery-proof earthworks which were hurriedly thrown up around them. One such angle bastion can still be seen to the north-east of the castle. Raglan was built in an era of castellated mansions, when defensive features were increasingly just for show, so it must be asked to what extent the castle was a genuine fortification. By the standards of the thirteenth century, when castles were an instrument of warfare, perhaps it was not. Later medieval castles were not intended to withstand prolonged sieges, despite the limitations of early cannon. Castles played little part in the Wars of the Roses, even though William Herbert found Harlech a tough nut to crack.

Nevertheless the castle was capable of holding out in the petty wars which a Marcher baron might still expect. Because of this, Raglan is stronger than its English contemporaries. Most of the external windows are quite small, and the main gatehouse was well defended by a series of obstacles. In addition to the traditional arrow slits, the small round holes visible in the lower walls of the castle are early gun ports. Admittedly their range was extremely limited and some of them were awkwardly sited – two are behind the kitchen fireplaces and others occupy a cesspit! The keep, surrounded by a concentric wall and isolated in its own moat, is the most formidable part. Like other late tower houses in England, this was the work of a powerful lord who needed a safe refuge, if only from his potentially mutinous retainers. At the same time Raglan is a very handsome castle, built in the finest ashlar masonry, though brick was used internally for vaults. Unfortunately, although the outer walls and towers are largely intact, the palatial buildings which stood against them have perished. Only the central hall range survives.

The keep is dynamically positioned in front of the castle. Ahead is the main gatehouse, with its polygonal flanking towers. These towers, and the adjacent Closet Tower, are the best-preserved parts of the castle, rising complete to their machicolated parapets. Machicolations are the crowning glory of late medieval castles. Another row of machicolations overhung the outer gateway, but the front wall of the gatehouse has fallen, marring an otherwise splendid front. The gate passage, once amply defended by a drawbridge, two portcullises and two sets of gates, leads into the outer courtyard.

No doubt the range behind the gatehouse formed the castellan's residence in the Edwardian tradition. Raglan's two courtyards followed the late medieval trend in separating the lord's retainers from his private household. The outer courtyard is known from its cobbled surface as the Pitched Stone Court. Both the north and west ranges were rebuilt further out by the earl of Worcester to increase the size of the courtyard. Hence the north corner towers, both hexagonal, are the only other original portions of the outer courtyard. We have already observed the machicolated

Closet Tower, which has a prison in the basement. The larger Kitchen Tower has lost its machicolations but preserves two kitchen fireplaces at ground level.

Unlike older castles with their consecutive lines of defence, the two courtyards are not divided by a defensive wall. Instead the hall range runs down the middle. The great hall was first built by William ap Thomas. However, its outer courtyard facade is a reconstruction by the earl of Worcester, with Elizabethan windows, a three-storey porch, and a projecting bay at the dais or high table end. Though a shell, and deprived of its once-magnificent furnishings, the great hall survives complete. Beyond a stone passage is the buttery, lengthened by Worcester.

The positioning of a hall across the middle of the castle allowed large windows on either side without any external loss of security. However, William Herbert blocked the windows facing the inner courtyard when he added a chapel on this side. The earl of Worcester built a long gallery above it, which extended all the way to the surviving tower on the west front of the castle. This tower is entirely Worcester's, but its polygonal front deliberately matches the older towers of the castle.

Beyond the great hall is the Fountain Court, its eponymous fountain now vanished. The residential ranges which stood against the curtain have also disappeared. A hint of their sophistication is shown by the remains of a grand staircase in one corner, with part of its stone handrail still in place. Both towers on the south front contained latrine blocks. At the end nearest the keep is the South Gate. This square gate tower formed the original entrance to William ap Thomas' castle. Fragments survive of the elaborate 'fan' vault which once covered the gate passage.

William Herbert's private apartments lay on the east side of the inner courtyard, centred upon the traditional solar. Here much of the curtain has perished, but the wing linking up with the gatehouse breaks free of military restraint, sporting some ostentatious windows even at ground level. This is the weak part of the castle perimeter, evidently considered secure enough because it is overshadowed by the keep.

At last we face William ap Thomas' hexagonal keep, known from the colour of its ashlar as the Yellow Tower of Gwent. It is reached from the former solar by a rebuilt bridge across the wet moat. Originally there was a gap at the far end of the bridge, crossed by a drawbridge which was raised by two wooden beams. The postern beside it was also closed by a drawbridge, this one with a single beam above it. Note the recesses which housed these beams when the drawbridges were raised. William Herbert did away with the drawbridges and added a forebuilding in front of the keep. He built a second bridge over the first, allowing direct access to the keep from both floors of the solar block. Both the forebuilding and this remarkable double bridge have perished. That the keep was still intended to be a strong defence is shown by the concentric wall which William Herbert added around it, with rounded turrets at the six angles. Although much reduced now, this wall would have blocked the gun ports at the base of his father's keep.

Despite its ruinous condition the keep is still a powerful structure. Two sides were brought down by undermining at the slighting, but the other four rise through four storeys. There is said to have been a fifth, and it is likely that the keep had a machicolated crown. The main entrance led into the first-floor hall, from which a wide spiral stair descends to the kitchen below. In addition to the gun ports there are handsome cross-slits here. The two upper floors of the tower contained private chambers lit by larger windows.

Access: Open daily (Cadw).

Reference: Guidebook by J. R. Kenyon. *Archaeological Journal* (CXXXII).

Relations: Fifteenth-century work at Newport, Tretower Court, Powis and Hawarden. Ashby-de-la-Zouche, Caister and Tattershall are contemporary English castles. Compare the older concentric keeps at Tretower and Ewloe.

SKENFRITH CASTLE   stands on the Welsh bank of the River Monnow, midway between Monmouth and Grosmont. Along with Grosmont and White castles, it guarded the open country of northern Gwent. These three formed part of a single lordship throughout the Middle Ages and were probably all founded by King Stephen. From 1186 Henry II spent £65 here, no doubt on earth-and-timber defences. However, unlike the other two castles, Skenfrith shows no evidence of its Norman roots. There appears to be a motte, but excavations have shown that this mound was in fact piled up against the later keep to keep siege engines at bay.

The present castle is the creation of Hubert de Burgh, earl of Kent and king's justiciar. He first held the three castles in 1201–05, losing them while a prisoner in France. Hubert regained them in 1219 as a reward for his exploits during the Dauphin Louis' invasion, when he successfully defended Dover Castle and defeated the French at sea. He thus earned a reputation as a great soldier, though he was chiefly an administrator and diplomat. Hubert restored order in England during the minority of Henry III. It is also in these years that he rebuilt Skenfrith and Grosmont castles in stone. A disastrous campaign against Llywelyn the Great led to his fall from power in 1232. Stripped of his offices and forced to surrender his castles, he joined Richard Marshal's revolt. Hubert was reinstated two years later, to be toppled again (this time for marrying off his daughter without the king's permission) in 1239. He died a few years later.

Skenfrith and Grosmont followed the new trend in castle architecture, both having a strong curtain flanked by round towers, but in some respects they are quite different. Grosmont's compact enclosure was dictated by the older mound on which it stands. At Skenfrith a new layout was adopted, the curtain (once fronted by a wide ditch) enclosing a large but irregular quadrangle. The longest wall lies beside the river, with a postern midway along. A round tower guarded each of the four angles. Lacking fireplaces and pierced only by arrow slits, these towers did not combine defence with accommodation as many towers of the next generation would. Although the castle is a ruin, the curtain survives complete except for its battlements, and only the west corner tower has perished. The gap in the north-west curtain marks the site of the gatehouse, about which nothing is known. The south-west curtain, facing the village, also has an intermediate tower. This solid, semicircular tower is an early addition, either by Hubert during his second building campaign or by one of its subsequent royal owners.

Grosmont was built onto an older hall-keep, but Skenfrith was originally a keep-

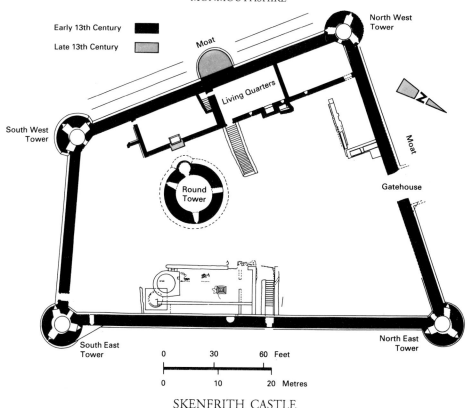

SKENFRITH CASTLE

less castle, its defence conducted entirely from the surrounding wall. Excavations have shown that the circular keep which dominates the rest was built after the court-yard had been laid out, probably during Hubert's last tenure in 1234–39. The keep stands within the bailey but rises high enough to command the approach from the village. It is a good example of the round keeps which were popular in thirteenth-century Wales. Rising from a bold plinth, its circumference is interrupted only by a semi-circular turret containing the spiral stair. The main apartment, and the only one with a fireplace, occupied the highest of its three storeys. A gaping hole marks the two entrances into the keep. Immediately below the usual first-floor doorway, originally reached by a wooden stair, there is a ground-floor opening which is surely a later insertion.

The limited accommodation in the keep was augmented from the outset by a long residential range against the south-west curtain. Its footings have been exposed. Fireplaces show that the basement rooms were meant to be lived in, though they no doubt underlay the usual hall and solar.

Hubert de Burgh seems to have left the castle unfinished on his second downfall in 1239. The keep was only being roofed in 1244, when the castle was in royal hands. Henry III successively granted the three castles to his sons, Edward and Edmund. One of them probably added the solid tower. Unlike Grosmont, Skenfrith

141

was not remodelled by the House of Lancaster. It probably fell into decay quite early, and so retains its original austerity.

Access: Always open (Cadw / NT).
Reference: Guidebook by O. E. Craster. *The Three Castles* by J. K. Knight. *Archaeologia Cambrensis* (CXVI).
Relations: Grosmont and White castles. Compare the round keeps at Caldicot, Usk, Tretower, Bronllys and (just across the Herefordshire border) Longtown.

TWMBARLWM is magnificently sited on a commanding hill about two miles north of Risca. A steep ascent leads to the summit. It is surrounded by a bank and ditch of Iron Age date, left incomplete in places owing to the steep drop. A conical motte rises within the hillfort enclosure, surrounded by a rock-cut ditch with sheer sides. Historically the castle is quite obscure, but it seems likely that the motte was raised by one of the Norman lords of Glamorgan. This inconvenient site was probably not occupied for long.

Access: Freely accessible (LA – uphill walk).
Reference: GAHW *Glamorgan and Gwent.*
Relations: Hillfort castles such as Dinas Powys, Castell Dinas and Castell Garn Fadrun.

USK CASTLE is another of the striking ruins of Monmouthshire. Ivy still clings to the masonry here, the ruins having become the setting for a garden. Majestically crowning a hill overlooking the little town and its priory church, the origins of the castle are unclear. It existed by 1138, when it was captured by the Welsh. The earthworks consist of a roughly oblong enclosure on the summit of the hill, with an outer bailey on the slope to the south.

Usk became a possession of Richard de Clare, earl of Pembroke. Better known as 'Strongbow', he led the Normans into Ireland in 1170. The castle was captured by the Welsh during his absence. In 1189, when the dying Henry II was faced with the rebellion of his sons, an obscure knight called William Marshal unhorsed Prince Richard in a battle in France. On becoming king, Richard recognised William's loyalty to his father by marrying him to the young Clare heiress and giving him the earldom. William proved to be a capable soldier. In addition to his Welsh campaigns, he saved England from a French invasion after King John died. He was the builder of the great keep at Pembroke.

The oldest part of the castle is a square keep commanding the approach from the outer bailey. This is probably Richard de Clare's work. Like the other Norman tower keeps of Wales, it is quite a modest structure and its walls are just four feet thick. Later medieval windows have been cut through, but two Norman slits in round-arched recesses can be seen high up.

William Marshal is credited with the rest of the inner bailey defences. If so Usk is the earliest example of a castle flanked all round by circular towers. Perhaps building continued after William's death in 1219 under his son, William Marshal the Younger. In addition to the older keep at the east corner, towers stood at the other three angles and in the middle of the two longer sides. However, the twin-towered gatehouse had not yet made its debut. The entrance is a simple gateway near the Norman keep.

Unfortunately the curtain is now very ruinous and three of the mural towers have vanished. The scale of the work is only attested by the so-called Garrison Tower in the middle of the south-west curtain. This tower rises complete to its embattled parapet. Owing to the fall in ground level it is still more impressive outside. Its four storeys were meant be lived in, which is unusual for a mural tower of the early thirteenth century. Although it was no larger than the others, this tower may therefore be regarded as a new keep, supplanting the Norman tower. The castle was probably complete when William's brother Richard rebelled in 1233. Henry III laid siege to the castle but was forced to abandon the attempt.

The semi-circular North Tower was rebuilt by Gilbert de Clare, the 'Red Earl' of Gloucester, as a strong house for treasure. It was described as new in 1289. When the last de Clare lord was killed in 1314 the castle passed to his sister, Elizabeth de Burgh. She erected new residential buildings against the north-west curtain. Beyond the foundations of a chapel are the buttressed walls of the hall, probably served by a kitchen in the vanished west corner tower. The solar projects from the curtain as a ruinous square tower. Elizabeth fell victim to Hugh le Despenser's territorial ambitions. He seized the castle and threw her into the prison.

Later in the century Usk passed to the Mortimer earls of March. The outer curtain is attributed to them, and its construction was timely. Usk was attacked by Owain Glyndwr's brother Tudur in 1405, but he was killed and his army routed by a relieving force at the battle of Pwll Melyn. Much of the outer curtain has perished, but a circular angle tower survives as a dovecote. The square outer gate tower is incorporated in the present seventeenth-century house.

> *Access:* There are occasional open days. Otherwise visitors are welcome by appointment.
> *Reference: Archaeologia Cambrensis* (XCIX). GAHW *Glamorgan and Gwent.*
> *Relations:* The Marshal castles of Caerleon, Chepstow, Cilgerran and Pembroke. Compare the Norman keeps at Hay, Coity and Ogmore.

WHITE CASTLE, five miles east of Abergavenny, is the most impressive of the three castles which guarded the relatively easy approach to England through northern Gwent. Like Grosmont and Skenfrith, it was probably founded by King Stephen c. 1138, when the Welsh were taking advantage of the Anarchy in England to turn the tide of the Norman advance. Stephen united the surrounding territory into one royal lordship. As at Grosmont, the main castle occupies an oval mound which is much larger than the standard Norman motte. Originally it was called Llantilio Castle (Llantilio Crossenny lies two miles to the south-east). The castle acquired its present name from the limewash which once covered the walls.

Grosmont and Skenfrith were rebuilt in stone by Hubert de Burgh after 1219, but White Castle has a different building history. As a stone castle it began earlier, under Henry II. This is his only masonry work in the Welsh Marches, though the £129 spent here in 1184–86 is a trifling amount compared with some of his English

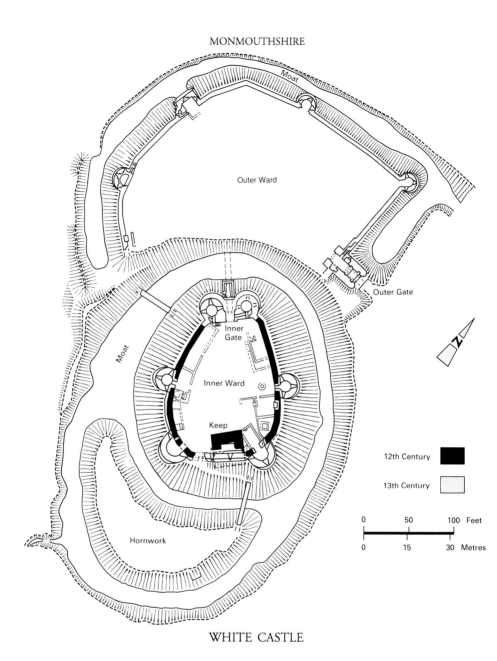

Outer Ward

Outer Gate

Moat

Inner Gate

Inner Ward

Keep

Moat

Hornwork

12th Century

13th Century

0	50	100	Feet
0	15	30	Metres

WHITE CASTLE

castles. No doubt it accounts for the curtain which surrounds the summit of the mound.

In 1254 Henry III granted Monmouth and the three castles to his heir, Prince Edward. During the crisis of the 1260s, when civil war raged in England and Llywelyn the Last overran the lordship of Brecon, White Castle was strengthened. Rounded flanking towers were added to the Norman curtain, and an outer curtain was built in front. It is likely that all this was an early work of the future Edward I, whose later castles in North Wales are so celebrated. Edward was active in the wars against Llywelyn during this period. However, Henry transferred the three castles to his younger son, Edmund 'Crouchback', in 1267. In that year Henry was forced to recognise Llywelyn as prince of Wales, so some of the work may be Edmund's. Created earl of Lancaster, Edmund founded a dynasty which would ultimately seize the throne in 1399. The Welsh threat ended with his brother's conquest of Gwynedd. Unlike Grosmont, the castle was never occupied by the House of Lancaster, and it was abandoned by the Tudor era.

Although a ruin, the castle lacks little more than its battlements. The inner curtain forms an impressive composition above the steep slope of the Norman mound. Its towers are reflected in the water of a surrounding moat, which may come as a surprise on this hilltop site. The castle consists of an inner bailey on the Norman mound, an outer bailey to the north and a smaller earthwork to the south. Prince Edward's outer bailey is entered through a long gate passage which was originally surmounted by a guard chamber. This gatehouse is commanded by the inner curtain. The outer curtain has four open-backed flanking towers. Three of them are semi-circular, but the other is a square-fronted residential tower with a curved latrine projection.

Ahead rise the twin round towers of the inner gatehouse. The towers are a matching pair, but the outer front of the left tower was rebuilt in the nineteenth century. A modern bridge crosses the wet moat, over the remains of the old drawbridge pit. It leads to the vaulted gate passage, which was defended by a portcullis and gates. This gate passage is relatively short because, unlike the fully developed gatehouses of the Edwardian period, there is no inner portion housing the constable's hall. This was not a keep-gatehouse with the inevitable concessions to domestic comfort that such a function would entail – it was purely defensive. The same is true of the other four towers which Edward added to the Norman curtain. These towers are pierced only by arrow slits, well positioned to cover the moat and the adjacent stretches of curtain. Each has an unlit middle storey, perhaps used by the garrison to store arrows.

The uncompromisingly military nature of the additions supports the notion of a castle built in an emergency. By the 1260s mural towers were usually residential as well as defensive, and this would be true of Edward I's later Welsh castles. White Castle never seems to have had a lord in residence for long, so the modest hall and solar against the east curtain (now reduced to foundations) probably housed the constable. A chapel occupied the South-East Tower, though even here only arrow slits pierce the walls.

Prince Edward turned the castle around by building his gatehouse and outer bailey to the north. The castle was originally entered from the south, via the small moated enclosure in front. Like other Norman castles in South Wales, the gateway was flanked by a small, square keep. Only some foundations of the keep can now be seen, Prince Edward having filled the gap with a new stretch of curtain. Its disappearance is intriguing. The keep was not in a bad state of decay, because its roof had only been repaired a few years earlier. One theory is that it was deliberately demolished to create a keep-less castle in the fashion of the time, but such an action seems rather dogmatic given the hurried nature of Edward's building campaign.

Access: Open daily in summer (Cadw).
Reference: Guidebook by O. E. Craster. *The Three Castles* by J. K. Knight.
Relations: Grosmont and Skenfrith. Compare Edward I's later castles at Flint, Rhuddlan, Aberystwyth, Caernarfon, Conwy, Harlech and Beaumaris.

OTHER SITES   The moated castle site at *Dingestow* was attacked by the Welsh in 1182 while still under construction. *Llanvair Discoed* had a small Edwardian castle built by Ralph Monthermer. Only fragments remain in the garden of the present house. Nearby *Dinham* once possessed a square Norman keep. Excavations near the motte at *Llanhilleth* revealed the bases of two towers from a successor castle. One of them, circular with a central column, was reminiscent of Morlais. *Kemeys House* (near Llantrisant) incorporates a small tower house, and there is a motte-and-bailey castle nearby. *Llangwm* preserves a Norman ringwork.

Monmouthshire has a number of other motte-and-bailey castles:

Ballan Mount (near Caldicot)
Gwern Castle (near Pandy)
Langstone Court (near Newport)
Llanfair Kilgeddin Motte (near Bettws Newydd)
Newcastle
Penrhos Motte

Pen-y-Clawdd Court (near Llanvihangel Crucorney)
Trecastle (near Pen-y-Clawdd)
Trelleck Tump
Twyn Tudor Motte (near Pontllanfraith)

Montgomeryshire

Montgomeryshire equates roughly with the Welsh principality of Powys. Numerous motte-and-bailey castles attest the Norman invasion which began under Roger de Montgomery, palatine earl of Shrewsbury. The best – Hen Domen, Gro Tump and Rhos Ddiarbed – were probably raised by Roger himself. However, Powys survived the onslaught and its princes responded with mottes of their own, such as Mathrafal. Caught in the vice between England and Gwynedd, the princes of Powys were slow to invest in stone castles. Powis Castle is their one masonry effort but that belongs to the Edwardian period. Its ridge-top layout emulates Henry III's earlier castle at Montgomery, now very ruinous but possessing what may be the earliest round-towered gatehouse in Britain. Dolforwyn Castle, even more ruined, is a symbol of Llywelyn the Last's ill-fated defiance to Edward I.

DOLFORWYN CASTLE is a monument to Llywelyn the Last. It was under construction in 1273, when Llywelyn received an order from the king's officials to cease work on this unlicensed stronghold. His letter to Edward I (who was absent on crusade) shows Llywelyn's determination to be an independent ruler. He wrote, 'We are sure that the writ was not issued with your knowledge . . . for you know well that the rights of our principality are entirely separate from the rights of your kingdom'. Dolforwyn is provocatively near the royal castle of Montgomery, just four miles away. In fact the castle was intended more to threaten Powys, demonstrating to its beleaguered prince that he was surrounded by his powerful neighbour. Llywelyn invaded Powys the following year, when he discovered that the prince had joined Dafydd ap Gruffudd's plot to overthrow him. The castle must barely have been complete when Edward I captured it during his invasion of 1277. It was granted to Roger Mortimer. Though still habitable in 1322, the castle seems to have fallen into ruins soon after.

Like most of the native Welsh castles, Dolforwyn has a splendid setting. It crowns a ridge above a minor road about a mile west of Abermule. Obscured by trees from below, the castle is surprisingly difficult to find. Only a few knobs of stonework still rise to any appreciable height, but the lower courses have been uncovered after intensive excavations in the 1980s. They reveal a castle which, though strongly situated, was by no means formidable by the standards of the Edwardian period. It consists of an oblong courtyard surrounded by a curtain. One circular tower projects shallowly on the east, and is closely surrounded by a concentric wall. A rectangular keep occupies the west side of the courtyard. Its shape seems remarkably antiquated for the time, though Llywelyn also built oblong towers at Criccieth. The surviving ground level of the keep is divided into two unequal parts by a cross-wall. An external staircase led to the vanished floor above. The curtain continues beyond the keep to form a small inner enclosure.

Originally the entrance to the castle was from the north. Most of this side was occupied by a large hall, which has a rock-cut cellar beneath its northern half owing to the drop in ground level. There are footings of further domestic buildings on the south, so the courtyard was just a narrow space between them.

Access: Freely accessible (Cadw – uphill walk).
Reference: Archaeologia Cambrensis (CXXXVIII and CXLIV).
Relations: Llywelyn the Last's work at Ewloe, Criccieth, Castell Carndochan and Castell-y-Bere.

GRO TUMP This is a splendid motte-and-bailey castle, overlooking a bend in the River Severn to the north-east of Newtown. The ditched motte is surrounded by three baileys of different sizes. That to the north is bounded by the steep drop to the river, the eastern bailey is just a wide platform skirting the motte, while a large outer bailey extends to the west. There is no historical record of this castle but it is attributed to Roger de Montgomery, earl of Shrewsbury, during his push up the Severn valley in the 1080s.

Access: On private land.

Reference: RCAHMW *Montgomeryshire.*
Relations: Roger's motte-and-bailey castles of Hen Domen and Rhos Ddiarbed.

HEN DOMEN is a motte-and-bailey earthwork overlooking the River Severn, a mile north-west of Montgomery. The name ('Old Mound') is applied to two castle sites in Montgomeryshire. This one is really Old Montgomery, the original castle of Roger de Montgomery, palatine earl of Shrewsbury. The castle was probably raised around 1072 after Roger began his advance into Powys. It is mentioned in the Domesday Book and survived a sacking by the prince of Powys in 1095. The site is compact but powerful, with a high motte and two ramparts separated by the bailey ditch. After the rebellion of Roger's son in 1102 the castle was granted to Baldwin de Boulers, whose descendants held it for a century. Although the site is just an overgrown earthwork now, intensive excavations have revealed how the interior was crammed with timber buildings which were frequently rebuilt. The finds demonstrate that the site continued to be occupied long after Henry III founded the new castle and town of Montgomery in 1223.

Access: Freely accessible.
Reference: Timber Castles by R. Higham & P. Barker. GAHW *Clwyd and Powys.*
Relations: Its successor, Montgomery. Gro Tump and Rhos Ddiarbed are other castles of Roger de Montgomery.

MATHRAFAL CASTLE Its prominent, tree-clad motte stands isolated between the B4389 and the River Banwy, six miles north-west of Welshpool. The motte occupies one corner of a large, square enclosure, its ditch now rather faint. According to later tradition Mathrafal was the Dark Age 'capital' of Powys, and the motte was probably raised by one of the twelfth-century princes. However, there is documentary evidence that King John erected a castle here during his invasion of North Wales in 1212. Excavations have shown that the ditched enclosure dates from his time. It is large enough to have served as a secure camp for the royal army. Llywelyn the Great destroyed the castle following John's withdrawal.

Access: Visible from the road.
Reference: RCAHMW *Montgomeryshire.*
Relations: The princes' stone castle of Powis.

MONTGOMERY CASTLE AND TOWN DEFENCES Montgomery takes its name from the Norman invader Roger de Montgomery, but his castle was the nearby motte-and-bailey of Hen Domen. The name was passed on when the young Henry III founded a new castle on a stronger site in 1223, to act as a bulwark against Llywelyn the Great. Over £2,000 was spent here in the next five years, but the castle was still unfinished when Henry awarded it to his justiciar, Hubert de Burgh, in 1228. This put the onus on Hubert to defend it during the ensuing war with the Welsh. Llywelyn twice failed to capture the castle, but he was successful elsewhere.

As a result of his failures in the war Hubert fell from favour in 1232, and the king resumed possession. Henry III returned to Montgomery in 1267 to sign the humiliating Treaty of Montgomery, which recognised Llywelyn the Last as prince of Wales.

Edward I augmented the domestic buildings of the castle. However, with his conquest of Gwynedd it lost its strategic role and was granted to the powerful Marcher dynasty of Mortimer. Roger Mortimer, earl of March, restored the castle in the 1340s, and it was garrisoned against Owain Glyndwr. After a period of decay, the Herberts of Powis Castle built a timber-framed mansion inside the walls in the 1620s. In 1644 the Royalists besieging the castle were routed by a relieving force at the battle of Montgomery. Despite its Roundhead garrison, the castle was slighted in 1649 owing to the Royalist sympathies of the Herberts. The slighting was a severe one, and later stone-robbing reduced the castle to just a few fragments.

It is a pity that the castle is so ruinous, but excavations in 1963–73 have removed the debris and exposed the lower parts of the walls. This is a good example of a castle employing successive lines of defences, because its dramatic position on a long ridge resulted in a progression of three narrow courtyards. The southernmost was only defended in earth and timber. Originally the next bailey was the same, but Henry III had the curtain rebuilt in stone in 1251–53. This wall still stands on the east side, with four shallow rounded bastions along its length. Elsewhere the outer curtain and its twin-towered gatehouse have been reduced to foundations. This is where the Herbert mansion stood.

A wide, rock-cut ditch cuts off the inner ward, which occupies a knoll at the highest part of the ridge. Its narrow south front is entirely occupied by the stump of the gatehouse. This gatehouse is probably the earliest example in Britain of the type with a pair of round-fronted towers closely flanking the entrance. The long gate passage would become typical, though this one is open to the sky since all the superstructure has fallen. Although solid at the surviving bases, the flanking towers were hollow further up. A survey of 1592 mentions a wooden chapel which was supported on posts against the courtyard face of the gatehouse.

A thick curtain surrounds the ward, though the only chunks rising to any height now are a stretch beside the gatehouse and part of the U-shaped Well Tower. Projecting from the west side of the castle, the Well Tower is large enough to be considered a keep. U-shaped keeps were a feature of some native Welsh castles, but in its present form this tower dates from Roger Mortimer's restoration of the 1340s. It must have housed the main apartments because the courtyard was too small to accommodate a lord's suite. Foundations here mark the site of the kitchen and retainers' lodgings. These stood against the curtain and reduced the open space to a tiny yard in the centre. A smaller U-shaped tower projected at the northern apex of the curtain, but this seems to have collapsed early on.

The castle commands the town of Montgomery, which was also founded by Henry III. It lies on lower ground to the east. The scale of Henry's intentions is evident in the defensive perimeter, which stretched for well over a mile. Much of the surrounding earthwork still survives. It begins below the castle rock, a long stretch of ditch and rampart climbing southwards to the highest point of the circuit, where they turn eastwards. Little survives on the south, but the ditch reappears beyond

Back Lane and continues along the east side of the town. It is also prominent at the northern apex, near Cottage Inn. Here is the base of a round bastion, evidence that at least a start was made in walling this long circuit in stone; Edward I contributed £80 for the purpose in 1279–80. St Nicholas' Church is an early Gothic structure which was rising at the same time as the castle. Despite these defences Llywelyn the Great sacked the town during one of his raids, and Owain Glyndwr did likewise.

> *Access:* The castle is always open (Cadw). Much of the town rampart can be followed.
> *Reference:* Guidebook by J. D. Lloyd and J. K. Knight. *Archaeologia Cambrensis* (CXLI). *HKW* (II).
> *Relations:* Compare the similar layout of Powis Castle. See Henry III's castle at Deganwy, and Llywelyn the Great's gatehouse at Criccieth.

POWIS CASTLE, known in Welsh from its red sandstone as Castell Coch, is similar in conception to Montgomery Castle. The latter no doubt inspired its strong setting on a ridge and the elongated layout of two walled courtyards. The inner ward is crammed on the highest point of the rock, with a twin-towered gatehouse occupying the whole of the narrow entrance front. However, whereas Montgomery is now extremely ruinous, Powis Castle is very different. Apart from Chirk it is the only castle in North Wales to have become a stately home. Admittedly the transformation has been as injurious to the medieval fabric as a slighting would have been, but a lot of original masonry does survive. This is really the castle of Welshpool, though the town lies a mile to the north-east. The castle is surrounded by lush parkland, and the steep slope of the ridge has become a terraced garden. Indeed, the 'Hanging Gardens of Powis' are one of the great attractions here.

The castle also differs from Montgomery in its native Welsh origin. Known in medieval times as the castle of Pool, the present name recalls its occupation by the princes of Powys. They had earlier castles nearby: the motte known as Domen Castell, near Welshpool railway station, and another (Lady's Mount) in the castle grounds. A square tower embedded in the south-east corner of the present castle is regarded by some scholars as a late Norman keep. However, Llywelyn the Last was still building square towers just before the Edwardian conquest, and the princes of Powys had no previous experience of stone castle building. Seeking to throw off his enforced allegiance to Gwynedd, Prince Gruffudd ap Gwenwynwyn joined Dafydd ap Gruffudd's plot against Llywelyn in 1274. Llywelyn invaded Powys and drove the prince into exile, destroying whichever castle at Welshpool was then in use. It likely that Gruffudd began the present castle when he was reinstated by Edward I after the invasion of 1277. As well as the keep, he may be responsible for the hall which is embodied in the present north range.

Gruffudd may have enjoyed his revenge, but he merely became an English puppet. In the settlement of 1283 Gruffudd retained his lands but lost his princely title, in effect becoming just another Marcher baron. Gruffudd's son Owain adopted the Anglo-Norman surname de la Pole. His daughter Hawys married John de Charlton, after which the Welsh blood in the lords of Powys was well and truly diluted. During these years the castle was built up into a powerful Edwardian fortress. How much was built by Owain and how much by John is impossible to say. It was strong enough in 1312 to resist a siege from Hawys' uncle, who claimed the estate on the grounds that women were not entitled to inherit according to Welsh law.

The approach to the castle from the west is through an outer gateway of 1668, replacing a medieval predecessor. It leads into the outer ward. The north side of this courtyard is bounded by a row of lodgings, Tudor in origin but much altered. They lie against a thick stretch of Edwardian curtain with a strong, U-shaped tower projecting from the middle. On the south the curtain has been supplanted by the garden terraces.

Steps ascend to the main gatehouse, which is typically Edwardian. It is the most impressive and original part of the fabric, despite the Elizabethan windows and mock battlements (the walled-up originals can be detected just below). The fat, rounded flanking towers almost meet, so much so that they are cut back at the base to make room for the entrance gateway. A narrow gate passage, retaining two portcullis grooves, bends slightly in the course of its length. Beyond is the tiny courtyard, surrounded by high buildings. To the left is the original hall, left unrecognisable by later alterations. The courtyard would have been a little wider before the building of the Renaissance loggia on the right. This is one of the additions made by Sir Edward Herbert, who purchased the castle in 1587. It supports a Long Gallery which retains its original panelling and a magnificent plaster ceiling.

Sir Edward converted the old castle into an Elizabethan mansion. It survived the Civil War intact despite being stormed one night in 1644 by Sir Thomas Myddelton, who lost his own Chirk Castle to the Royalists while he was away! The Herberts have remained here ever since except for two short interruptions arising from their loyalty to the exiled Stuarts. Successive generations have transformed the interiors, so the main apartments offer surprising contrasts in style and throw little light on their medieval origins. Nevertheless the bulging south front of the castle is still the original curtain, pierced by rows of Tudor windows, and the lavish State Bedroom of the Restoration period occupies the original keep in the south-east corner. Externally, this keep is only evident from the rougher masonry of its lower part. It is no longer recognisable as a tower because the rest of the south range is as high.

The more conspicuous tower projecting from the east front was added sometime in the fifteenth century, when the Greys of Ruthin held the castle. This was a new gate tower, providing a more direct entrance to the castle from the town. It has an elaborate vault over the gate passage. In 1828 the architect Sir Robert Smirke heightened the East Tower, making it the dominant feature of the castle skyline.

Access: Open regularly except in winter (NT).
Reference: NT guidebook. BOW *Powys. Montgomeryshire Collections* (LXXXI).
Relations: Compare Montgomery's similar layout. Chirk, Cardiff, St Donat's and Picton are other inhabited Welsh castles.

RHOS DDIARBED CASTLE   is a classic example of a motte-and-bailey stronghold, occupying a level site two miles north of Llandinam. The high motte is surrounded by a ditch, and the oval bailey has its own ditch and rampart. A gap in the rampart at the point furthest away from the motte marks the entrance. Beyond is an outer bailey, now occupied by a farmhouse. This is probably the Llandinam Castle raised, according to the *Chronicle of the Princes*, by the prince of Powys in 1162. However, its layout is very similar to Hen Domen. It seems more likely that he only restored the earthworks of a castle first established by Roger de Montgomery during his invasion of Powys in the 1080s.

> *Access:* On private land.
> *Reference:* RCAHMW *Montgomeryshire* (under Llandinam).
> *Relations:* Roger de Montgomery's motte-and-baileys of Hen Domen and Gro Tump.

OTHER SITES There are few castle sites in the elevated western half of the county, but eastern Montgomeryshire is dotted with motte-and-baileys, particularly in the Severn valley. They reflect both the Norman invasion and resistance by the native Welsh of Powys:

Bronfelin Motte (near Caersws)
Castle Caereinion
Domen Castell (Llanfechain)
Domen Castell (Welshpool)
Hen Domen (another one – near Deytheur)
Hyssington Castle
Kerry Moat
Llyssin Motte (near Llanerfyl)
Luggy Moat (near Berriew)
Manafon Motte

Munlyn Motte (near Forden)
Neuadd Goch Motte (near Mochdre)
Rhyd-yr-Onen Moat (near Llangurig)
Simon's Castle (near Church Stoke)
Tafolwern Castle (near Llanbrynmair)
Tomen Cefn Coch (near LLanrhaeadre)
Tomen Moel Frochas (near Penygarnedd)
Tomen-yr-Allt (near Llanfyllin)

Cefn Bryntalch (near Abermule) and *Pen-y-Castell* (near Trefeglwys) are ringworks. The ditched enclosure known as *Hubert's Folly*, overlooking Sarn, is an unfinished castle of Henry III's justiciar, Hubert de Burgh. *Newtown* preserves the earthwork platform of a castle raised by Roger Mortimer of Chirk around 1280. *Carreghofa Castle* had a stormy history, frequently changing hands between Normans and Welsh. This quarried site, near Llanymynech, preserves nothing of the stone defences built for Richard I. *Castell Nantcribba*, on a conical rock east of Forden, is the site of another stone castle which had at least two circular towers. It was built by the Corbets around 1260 but destroyed by the prince of Powys in 1263.

Pembrokeshire

The south-west corner of Wales has a notable group of medieval castles. Pembroke Castle was founded in 1093, and Henry I encouraged Norman and Flemish settlers into the southern prong of Pembrokeshire. So solid was their occupation that this area became known as 'Little England beyond Wales'. Their castles were positioned to obtain supplies by sea from Milford Haven. North of this great estuary, a line of castles marks the 'Landscar' – the frontier of colonisation. Beyond it lay Welsh Deheubarth, though further castles denote isolated Marcher baronies along the north coast of Pembrokeshire.

Norman earthwork castles are common. In addition to the usual motte-and-baileys, including Castell Nanhyfer, Pointz and Wiston, there are ringworks such as St David's and Walwyn's Castle. However, stone castle building was slow to take off, with nothing before the late Norman period. The Barris' hall-keep at Manorbier is the best Norman relic (Castell Coch is a later copy). Otherwise there are just the remains of a tower at Haverfordwest and a ruinous shell keep on Wiston's motte.

As elsewhere in Wales, the great age of castle building is the thirteenth century. The palatine earls of Pembroke took the lead, William Marshal erecting the mighty circular keep at Pembroke. His sons continued the work by enclosing Pembroke Castle within a towered curtain – one of the most ambitious in Wales – and building the twin round towers of Cilgerran. Manorbier has a well-preserved curtain of that era. The Edwardian conquest brought a renewed spate of castle building: Queen Eleanor's castle at Haverfordwest, Nicholas de Carew's fine quadrangle at Carew with its spurred towers, and the more ruinous remains at Narberth and Newport. Upton and Benton castles are delightful miniatures, while the U-shaped keep at Roch crowns a rock. Picton Castle – one of the few inhabited castles of Wales – is an elaborate fortified hall house. Tenby preserves an Edwardian town wall with regular flanking towers, although its castle is fragmentary. There are also some remains of Pembroke's town wall.

In this heyday of castle building only the bishops of St David's felt secure enough to erect unfortified palaces, at Lamphey and St David's. The latter stands within a semi-defensive wall surrounding the cathedral close. During the French invasion scare of the 1370s, the bishop turned his manor house at Llawhaden into a castle. Cilgerran was strengthened and Angle received a small castle of enclosure. The vulnerability of the south coast is attested by tower houses at Eastington and Caldy Priory, and a rebuilt castle at Dale.

ANGLE CASTLE overlooks Angle Bay near the entrance to Milford Haven. This great estuary was exposed to French raids during the Hundred Years War, and a French army landed here in 1405 to support Owain Glyndwr. Little wonder that the Shirburn family built themselves a small castle around that time. It occupied a square enclosure beside the parish church. The stone-lined moat is still partly wet at high tide. Otherwise all that survives is the shell of a square corner tower. It contained four low storeys, the lowest vaulted. An angle turret contains a spiral stair linking the upper floors. Projecting corbels at the wall-head show that there was once a machicolated parapet. The tower is generally regarded as one of the rare later medieval tower houses of Wales. However, a similar tower once occupied the opposite corner of the enclosure, so Angle is better regarded as a quadrangular castle in miniature.

Access: Visible from the churchyard.
Reference: Archaeologia Cambrensis (3rd series, XIV).
Relations: Castles on Milford Haven at Dale, Eastington and Pembroke.

BENTON CASTLE   is one of several in Pembrokeshire positioned to obtain supplies from Milford Haven. It stands on a rock above the broad River Cleddau, a mile east of Burton. The castle formed a small enclosure which has disappeared except for the picturesque, whitewashed entrance front. This consists of two round towers, linked by a short piece of curtain containing the gateway. The tower on the left, capped by an octagonal parapet, is the larger and higher of the two. It is nevertheless too small and spartan to be described as a keep, despite the projecting latrine turret. There is not even a spiral stair linking the floors, so they must have been connected by ladders. The castle is traditionally attributed to Thomas Bek, bishop of St David's (1280–93), but it is more likely to have been built by the de la Roche family earlier in the century. The surviving portion was restored from ruins in 1932.

Access: Private.
Reference: Archaeologia Cambrensis (3rd series, XI).
Relations: The de la Roche castle at Roch. Castles on the Cleddau at Carew, Picton and Upton.

CALDY PRIORY   Caldy Island was an early centre of the Celtic church, so it is appropriate that monks have returned here in the twentieth century. A short distance inland from the present abbey is its predecessor, a Benedictine priory which is a remarkably complete example of a small medieval monastery. Its buildings date mainly from the thirteenth century. The rustic church with its little steeple forms one side of a diminutive cloister court. Only the north range has perished. A narrow gate passage pierces the west range, while the little dormitory on the east could only have accommodated a couple of monks. Next to it, the north-east corner of the complex forms a small tower house, its embattled parapet pierced by arrow slits. Just two storeys high in keeping with the rest of the buildings, it contained the prior's bed chamber over a vaulted kitchen. The tower was probably added towards the end of the fourteenth century, at a time of French raids during the Hundred Years War.

Access: Open daily (church and cloister only). Caldy is reached by boat from Tenby in summer.

Reference: GAHW *Dyfed.*
Relations: Compare the ecclesiastical fortifications at St David's and Ewenny.

CAREW CASTLE   is one of the most attractive of the many ruined castles of
Wales. It stands five miles east of Pembroke, on a low ridge overlooking the Carew
River which flows into the Cleddau. The castle is an Edwardian stronghold tem-
pered by Tudor alterations – a transition from fortress to mansion which is quite rare
in Wales. According to tradition the castle was founded soon after 1100 by Gerald
de Windsor, constable of nearby Pembroke Castle and grandfather of Giraldus
Cambrensis. Gerald's descendants adopted the name Carew. There are no Norman
earthworks here, but a small gate tower is embedded in the later east range. This
tower may have been built after the Lord Rhys attacked the castle in 1192. That episode apart, Carew remained secure from Welsh attacks.

The present castle is mainly the work of Sir Nicholas de Carew (d.1311), a
veteran of Edward I's Welsh wars, whose mailed effigy can be seen in the nearby
church of Carew Cheriton. He created a four-sided courtyard with circular towers
rising from square bases at the western corners, and two towers projecting more hap-
hazardly on the east. The whole western side is occupied by the great hall, while the
east range contained Nicholas' personal apartments. This castle suited the needs
of the Carews for the rest of the Middle Ages. Then in 1480 they leased it to Sir
Rhys ap Thomas. Despite assuring Richard III that he would oppose any rebel
landing, Rhys changed sides when Henry Tudor came ashore in Milford Haven,
playing an important part in his victory at Bosworth. Rhys held a tournament
outside the castle in 1507 to celebrate his enrolment in the Order of the Garter. He
modernised the old domestic buildings, so much so that most of the architectural
features are Tudor.

Carew received further additions under another charismatic local magnate. Sir
John Perrot, rumoured to be an illegitimate son of Henry VIII, obtained the castle
from Queen Mary despite his Protestant beliefs. He erected a grand new north
range. This masterpiece of Elizabethan architecture was probably under construction during the 1580s, when Sir John served as lord lieutenant of Ireland. Unfortunately it was still roofless in 1591, when he was arrested on a charge of treason. Sir
John cheated the executioner, dying a natural death while imprisoned in the Tower
of London.

Returning to the Carew family after a legal battle, the castle finally saw action in
the Civil War. After changing hands twice without much resistance, the Royalist
garrison made a stand, enduring a short siege before surrendering to Major-General
Laugharne in 1645. The south curtain was largely destroyed to render the castle
untenable, but the Carews continued to occupy the rest until 1686.

Before approaching the castle the visitor should pause by the roadside to look at
the Carew Cross. This important piece of Dark Age sculpture commemorates a
prince of Deheubarth who fell victim to internal strife in 1035. The V-shaped earthwork guarding the approach is a ravelin of the Civil War period. A low outer wall in
front of the main east curtain is pierced by arrow slits. This concentric defence is an

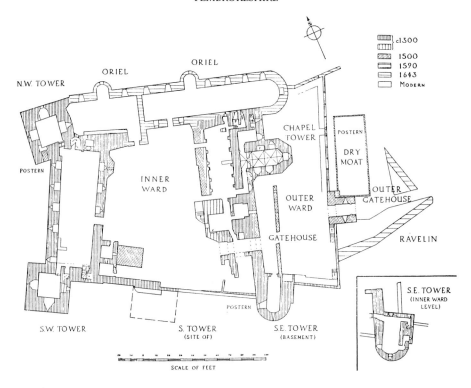

N.W. TOWER

ORIEL

ORIEL

|||||| c1300
|||||| 1500
|||||| 1590
|||||| 1643
|||||| MODERN

POSTERN

CHAPEL TOWER

POSTERN

DRY MOAT

INNER WARD

OUTER WARD

OUTER GATEHOUSE

GATEHOUSE

RAVELIN

POSTERN

S.E. TOWER
(INNER WARD LEVEL)

S.W. TOWER

S. TOWER
(SITE OF)

S.E. TOWER
(BASEMENT)

SCALE OF FEET

CAREW CASTLE

early addition to the castle, but the gate tower was added or rebuilt by Rhys ap Thomas.

The east front of the castle is puzzling, because the towers do not occupy the logical positions one might expect in the Edwardian period. The rounded projection at the north end actually belongs to Sir John Perrot's wing. Close by is the semi-octagonal Chapel Tower, which commands the east front. To the left differences in the masonry betray the late Norman gate tower, its archway walled up when the rest of the east range was built. High up at this point is an ornate oriel window, added by Rhys ap Thomas but now badly mutilated. When the old entrance was blocked a new gateway was inserted alongside. This is just a passage through the curtain. Strangest of all is the U-shaped tower at the south end, its rounded front positioned to flank the south side of the castle but not the more vulnerable east. Its back, closed by a thin wall, faces the outer courtyard rather than the inner. This suggests that the curtain was intended to continue around an outer courtyard which was never built, the concentric wall being added once the more ambitious scheme had been abandoned.

A portcullis groove, murder holes and deep recesses for drawbars show that the inner gateway was adequately defended. To the right a passage leads to the vaulted undercroft of the east range, which is divided into two by a cross-wall. Another passage in the thickness of the curtain connects with a vaulted kitchen in the ground floor of the Chapel Tower. The spiral stair beside it leads to the first floor, the main axis of which formed the Carews' private hall. Rhys ap Thomas remodelled this room, inserting the distinctive Tudor windows. He also created a third storey above, known as the Royal Bedchamber from the ornate fireplace bearing Henry VII's arms. At hall level the Chapel Tower houses a rib-vaulted chapel, while the room above it probably formed the lord's solar. Small chambers for the kitchen steward and the chapel priest are contrived between the Chapel Tower and Sir John Perrot's wing. This is an intricate and ingeniously planned medieval house. In the absence of a keep-gatehouse, its frontal position enabled the Carews to keep watch over the entrance.

Sir John Perrot's north range provides a note of contrast, with its great mullioned and transomed windows which sadly never received any glass. This three-storey shell would have contained splendid rooms on its three storeys, notably a long gallery on the top floor. To obtain extra space the entire building lies outside the line of the medieval curtain, foiling the projection of the north-west flanking tower.

Extending fully across the west side of the courtyard is the great hall. Though built by Nicholas de Carew, it also has round-headed windows of Sir Rhys ap Thomas' time, along with a projecting oriel and a porch. This porch bears the arms of Prince Arthur and Catherine of Aragon, and can therefore be precisely dated to their brief union of 1501–02. A flight of steps led up to it. The undercroft beneath the hall has a row of arrow slits through the curtain.

To fully appreciate its grandeur the castle must be examined from outside. Sir John Perrot's north range is at its most majestic here. There are two rows of windows high up, and twin bay windows projecting like towers. As at Laugharne Castle, which Perrot also remodelled, the castellated appearance was carefully adhered to. Despite the presence of the great hall against the west curtain, this side of the castle is uncompromisingly defensive. The great pyramid spurs rising out of the square bases of the two flanking towers should be noted, though Tudor windows have replaced the original arrow slits. Although most of the south curtain has fallen, the U-shaped South-East Tower survives intact.

Access: Open daily in summer.
Reference: Guidebook by P. R. Davis. *Archaeological Journal* (CXIX).
Relations: For Gerald de Windsor see Cilgerran. Compare the spur towers of Carreg Cennen, Caerphilly, Chepstow and Goodrich (Herefordshire).

CASTELL COCH, one of several 'Red Castles' in Wales, stands behind the farmhouse known as Newhouse. It is one of a handful of Welsh hall-keeps, occupying a square enclosure with a deep surrounding ditch. Its defensive character is evident from the mutilated arrow slits in the undercroft. The hall itself occupied the upper floor and was reached by an outside staircase. No doubt modelled on the hall at Manorbier, it probably dates from sometime in the thirteenth century, though its builder is quite obscure. A later cross-wall with Tudor fireplaces cuts off one end of the building. The decaying shell stands in woods near the Eastern Cleddau, two miles north of Martletwy.

Access: Visible from a public footpath.
Reference: Archaeologia Cambrensis (7th series, II).
Relations: Manorbier and the other hall-keeps at Chepstow, Monmouth and Grosmont. Don't confuse with Castell Coch in Glamorgan.

CASTELL NANHYFER, or Nevern Castle, is an impressive motte-and-bailey earthwork on a hill overlooking Nevern village. It was raised soon after 1100 by Robert Fitz Martin, lord of Cemais. His grandson William married the Lord Rhys' daughter, but this family tie did not prevent Rhys from capturing the castle in 1191. Fitz Martin then raised a new castle at Newport a few miles away. Three years later the ageing Rhys suffered the indignity of being imprisoned in Castell Nanhyfer by his own rebellious sons. Fortunately for him, they soon fell out and he was freed.

Nevern's church is well worth a visit for its Dark Age crosses. A steep road climbs the hill from the village. The castle enclosure is triangular, with a conical motte in the north-west corner. Powerful ramparts and ditches extend south and east from the motte, the latter having a ditch behind the rampart as well. On the south-east the steep slope to the little River Gamman provided a natural defence. However, the site is so well wooded that, in summer, one can barely see the castle for the trees. Taking the path from the entrance, you cross the open space of the bailey. From here, it is possible to mount the rampart, cross the motte and follow the rampart again. The eastern extremity of the bailey is separated from the rest by a rock-cut ditch attributed to the Lord Rhys or his sons. This precipitous corner became the new focus of the castle, despite the threatening proximity of the motte. A square keep stood here but has vanished.

Access: Freely accessible.
Reference: Archaeologia Cambrensis (CI). GAHW *Dyfed.*
Relations: Its successor, Newport. Castles of the Lord Rhys at Cardigan and Dinefwr.

CILGERRAN CASTLE stands three miles south-east of Cardigan, its picturesque ruins dramatically perched on a promontory overlooking the junction of the rivers Teifi and Plysgog. It is probably the castle of Cenarth Bychan raised by Gerald de Windsor, constable of Pembroke Castle, in 1108. Gerald had married Nest, daughter of the Welsh prince Rhys ap Tewdwr. In the following year Owain, son of the prince of Powys, sneaked into the castle with a band of henchmen. Gerald is said to have escaped by jumping down a latrine shaft. Owain abducted Nest, who thus became known as the Helen of Wales. Gerald did not recover his wife until 1112, though he later avenged his honour by killing Owain in battle. If the story of the latrine shaft is true, then stone residential buildings had been erected here remarkably quickly. Fragments of Norman masonry are embedded in the later walls.

Its exposed position on the frontier between Normans and Welsh ensured a stormy early history for Cilgerran. The Lord Rhys captured the castle in 1165 and repulsed two Norman attempts at recovery. It remained Welsh until William Marshal, earl of Pembroke, seized it in 1204. The castle succumbed to Llywelyn the

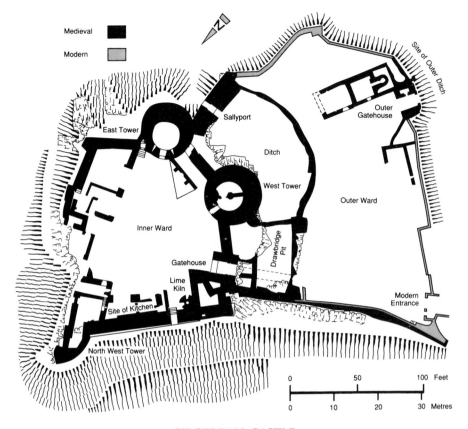

CILGERRAN CASTLE

Great in 1215, only to be recaptured during the younger William Marshal's reconquest of 1223. William immediately began to transform the castle into a strong stone fortress, a process continued by his brother Gilbert in the 1230s. Five Marshal brothers successively held the castle and the earldom of Pembroke.

The castle they created is not large but is nevertheless powerful. An outer bailey closed the only level approach. This is now fragmentary, with little more than the footings of a small gatehouse and an outbuilding. That it was once more substantial is implied by the thick stretch of curtain (pierced by a postern) which crosses the rock-cut ditch dividing the two baileys. This ditch goes back to the original Norman castle, though it was probably widened by the Marshals.

Immediately behind the ditch is the powerful cross-wall which forms the best-preserved part of the castle. Two massive round towers are connected by a short stretch of curtain. Another length of curtain (with a mural passage) leads to a small gate tower, which has largely collapsed except for its inner archway. The two round towers are a matching pair but their unusual proximity is difficult to explain. A joint in the curtain between them demonstrates that they belong to different building

159

campaigns. The East Tower (on the right) is the oldest part. It was built by William Marshal the Younger as a smaller version of his father's keep at Pembroke Castle.

Gilbert Marshal completed the cross-wall and added the West Tower, which occupies a bolder position in the middle. Both towers are uncompromisingly defensive to the outside world, and pierced only by arrow slits. The chambers within are so placed that the walls of the towers are much thicker to the outside than they are to the courtyard. Windows pierce both towers on the courtyard side. The entrance to the West Tower, which was the more comfortable of the two, was originally placed at first-floor level. It therefore appears that the West Tower supplanted the East Tower as the castle's focal point, so Cilgerran has the rare feature of two successive keeps.

On the more secure promontory sides of the inner bailey the curtain was lower, and a long stretch has collapsed down the steep slope into the Teifi. The Marshal line died out in 1245. Twelve years later the castle was strong enough to survive a siege from Llywelyn the Last. A period of decay ended in 1377 with a substantial remodelling, prompted by fears of a French landing in South Wales. This was done by order of the dying Edward III, when the earl of Pembroke was an infant. The main addition was a U-shaped tower at the apex of the promontory. It was as large as the two Marshal towers, but half of it has fallen into the river and the rest is fragmentary. New domestic buildings were provided at this time, though only some foundations can be seen. The refurbished castle suffered damage during Owain Glyndwr's rebellion. Soon afterwards it appears to have been abandoned.

Access: Open daily (Cadw / NT).
Reference: Guidebook by J. B. Hilling.
Relations: Gerald de Windsor also founded Carew. Compare the Marshal brothers' work at Pembroke, Carmarthen, Chepstow and Usk.

DALE CASTLE, on a peninsula at the entrance to Milford Haven, was originally called Vale. When Robert de Vale died in 1303 his estates were divided between his four daughters, Dale passing to the Walters family. The present 'castle' is a Victorian mansion, but its south wing incorporates a row of three vaulted undercrofts from the fourteenth century. They probably underlay the hall. Nothing is left of any defences and it is possible that this was a castle in name only, despite its position on the vulnerable Pembrokeshire coastline. Henry Tudor landed at Dale when he came to claim the throne in 1485. It is said that the local magnate, Rhys ap Thomas, lay beneath Dale Bridge while Henry rode across, in order to fulfil his pledge to Richard III that Henry would only pass 'over his belly'.

Access: Private.
Reference: RCAHMW *Pembrokeshire.*
Relations: Angle guards the other side of the estuary.

EASTINGTON CASTLE lies half a mile north-west of Rhoscrowther, overlooking Angle Bay. Despite the name, this was a medieval manor house which at best can be regarded as semi-fortified. The surviving building, attached to a farmhouse,

160

formed the solar, standing over a vaulted undercroft. It dates from c. 1300 and has an external doorway reached by a flight of steps. On the wall is the gabled imprint of the hall which stood alongside. The solar is capped by an embattled parapet with arrow slits – perhaps this was added during the period of French raids in the late fourteenth century. So the solar block was converted into a tower house, though it remained just two storeys high. A thin-walled annexe contains vaulted chambers. This was the ancestral home of the Perrot family, ancestors of the local Elizabethan magnate Sir John Perrot.

Access: Private.
Reference: Archaeologia Cambrensis (3rd series, XIV).
Relations: Tower houses at Caldy, Candleston and Llandough.

HAVERFORDWEST CASTLE resembles Cilgerran in its position on a promontory, with a compact inner ward at the apex fronted by a fragmentary outer ward on the only level approach. Guarding a crossing of the Western Cleddau river, it stood between the Norman colonies of south Pembrokeshire and the Welsh lands to the north. The castle may have been established by Gilbert de Clare, earl of Pembroke, in the 1120s. Giraldus Cambrensis visited during his tour through Wales in 1188. A small keep embedded in the later curtain must date from around that time. The castle's strategic position attracted the two Llywelyns, and it did well to repel them in 1220 and 1257. All the more so because, apart from the keep, the castle was still an earth-and-timber fortification.

The existing remains date mainly from the Edwardian period. In 1289 the castle was granted to Queen Eleanor as part of her considerable new estate in Wales. In her brief remaining time £807 was spent here, but building cannot have got very far when she died the following year. The castle reverted to William de Valence, lord of Pembroke, so perhaps he should be credited with its completion before his death in 1296.

Although the outer curtain has perished, its line is followed by a low retaining wall on the old foundations, with two tower projections on the north side. The outer ward is dominated by the county gaol of 1818, now housing Haverfordwest Museum.

Ahead lies the ruined inner ward, which forms a roughly pentagonal enclosure. The portion of curtain facing the outer bailey was levelled during the Civil War slighting. Here stands the old gaoler's house, with a semi-circular projection embodying one of the flanking turrets of a small gatehouse. The rest of the high curtain is intact except for its battlements. A plain round tower guards the northern angle. Just beyond, a kink in the circuit is caused by the junction with the older Norman keep. This modest, oblong tower survives on the two sides where it forms the outer wall of the castle. However, the other two sides of the keep were deliberately removed at some point, perhaps when the curtain was built. Haverfordwest thus became a keep-less castle.

Residential buildings – intended as Queen Eleanor's palace – stood against the east and south curtains. These do not survive, although the footings have been exposed. The east range housed the solar at first-floor level, lit by three Gothic windows through the curtain. These were walled up to protect the castle from bombardment during the Civil War. Below them, embrasures for arrow slits strike a more defensive note. A square projection near the south end contained a chapel on the upper floor. Its east window has lost its tracery. The three windows high up in the south curtain mark the site of the hall. Such large windows reflect a new security in the aftermath of Edward I's conquest, although this part of the perimeter was naturally secure owing to the steep drop. Beyond the hall, a semi-circular tower projects from the curtain. It contains a mural stair descending from the hall to a postern.

In 1405 the castle withstood an attack from Owain Glyndwr's French allies. Its military record was tarnished by changing hands five times in the Civil War, as the tide ebbed and flowed between local Royalists and Roundheads. The museum preserves Oliver Cromwell's letter, written in 1648 during the siege of Pembroke, ordering the destruction of the castle. Thankfully, the townsfolk found it too hard a task without explosives so the slighting was a half-hearted one.

The town below the castle (originally called Haverford) has lost its surrounding wall. It was burnt by the Welsh on several occasions – the splendid parish church of St Mary was rebuilt in its present form after Llywelyn the Last's attack. By the river are the ruins of a priory built under the patronage of the earls.

Access: Open daily (LA).
Reference: GAHW *Dyfed. HKW* (II).
Relations: Cilgerran's similar layout. See William de Valence's work at Pembroke and Tenby, and his castle of Goodrich (Herefordshire).

LLAWHADEN CASTLE is a ruinous but attractive pile standing four miles north-west of Narberth. It was one of the extensive possessions of the medieval bishops of St David's. The castle is a surprising contrast to their unfortified palaces at Lamphey and St David's. Most of it dates from the late fourteenth century, which is unusually late for a major Welsh castle. However, the castle originated much earlier as one of the line of fortifications defending the frontier of Norman settlement in south Pembrokeshire. The ringwork underlying the later masonry was raised by one of the Norman bishops of St David's. This castle was captured and destroyed by the Lord Rhys in 1192. In the next century the bishops erected a towered curtain on top of the rampart. This has largely been swept away, although the footings of two towers can be still seen on the destroyed north-west part of the perimeter. One is a circular tower, not large enough to be a keep, while the other is a solid round turret.

Whether this walled enclosure was ever completed is unclear. Towards the end of the thirteenth century a large hall was constructed on the north-east, taking the place of any earlier curtain which might have existed here. Thomas Bek, bishop in 1280–93 and brother of the powerful bishop of Durham, is the likely builder, since he founded a borough at Llawhaden. Not much is left of the hall itself, but the long undercroft retains part of its barrel vault. Cross-wings at each end contained the kitchen and solar. This would have been an impressive residence but it is not particularly defensive in character, reflecting the security of Edward I's final conquest. At this stage the castle must have relied chiefly upon its deep surrounding ditch.

The re-fortification of Llawhaden in the late fourteenth century reflects the general fear of a French invasion, Llawhaden being situated on the Eastern Cleddau river which was navigable to this point. Bishop Adam de Houghton (1362–89) is responsible for the towered curtain which extends around the south side of the castle between the hall and the gatehouse. His master mason, John Fawle, was appointed constable of the castle. The new curtain remains largely intact with two semi-octagonal flanking towers.

Nevertheless, defence was not the only object. A long residential range stood against the curtain. This is now quite ruinous but one section of the courtyard wall stands high, together with a slender porch rising five storeys to command a view over the outer walls. The western part of the range contained two guest apartments for visiting dignitaries, served by a suite of latrines in the tower between them. The eastern part housed a chapel at first-floor level, denoted by the three lancet windows through the curtain. This would have been an unusually grand chapel for a Welsh castle, as befits a bishop's residence. The adjacent Chapel Tower has vaulted chambers, including a sacristy reached from the chapel. A grimmer reminder of episcopal rule is the pit prison in the base of the tower.

Bishop Houghton's curtain ends at the distinctive gatehouse. This was the last part of the castle to be built, perhaps under Bishop Guy de Mone during Owain Glyndwr's revolt. The tall gate arch is flanked by rounded towers. They rise from square bases with pyramid spurs, which are characteristic of South Wales. Traceried windows lit the upper floors, providing a spacious residence for the constable. It is thus a descendant of the Edwardian gatehouses but, like the contemporary gatehouse at Carmarthen Castle, is altogether less massive. The gatehouse is now just a facade because the inner part has collapsed.

The castle met its end at the Reformation, Bishop Barlow selling off the lead and timber to raise funds for his daughter's dowry. Since then the castle has been a ruin.

Access: Always open (Cadw).
Reference: Guidebook by R. Turner (includes Lamphey Palace).
Relations: Carmarthen's similar gatehouse. See the bishops' fortified close at St David's.

MANORBIER CASTLE, midway between Tenby and Pembroke, occupies a narrow ridge overlooking Manorbier Bay. Though not quite as magnificent as nearby Carew Castle, it is an evocative Marcher barons' stronghold. Now an empty shell, the castle is almost intact – even most of the chunky battlements are still in place. It is a monument to the de Barri family, who took part in the Norman invasion of Ireland. The castle was probably founded early in the twelfth century by William de Barri, whose fourth son Gerald was born here around 1146. Better known as Giraldus Cambrensis, his *Itinerary* and *Description* of Wales are remarkable medieval travelogues. He describes his birthplace as the 'most pleasant spot in Wales'.

Giraldus' three elder brothers succeeded to the castle in turn, and one of them must have built the hall which is the oldest part of the castle, dating from the late twelfth century. It stands at the west end of a large, roughly oblong bailey. A curtain surrounds this bailey, quite plain except for the two towers guarding the eastern

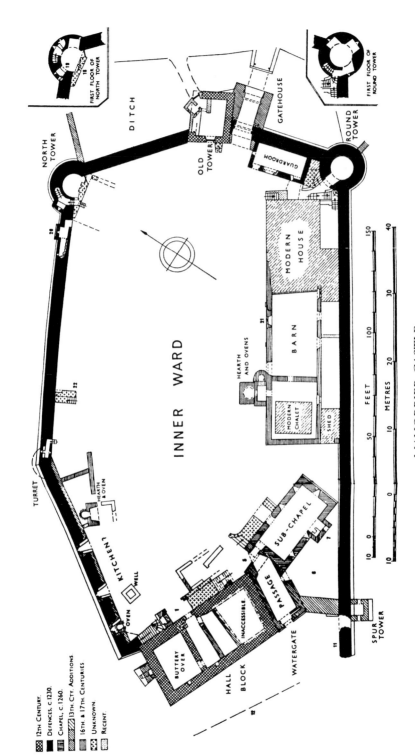

MANORBIER CASTLE

FIRST FLOOR OF NORTH TOWER

FIRST FLOOR OF ROUND TOWER

DITCH

NORTH TOWER

OLD TOWER

GATEHOUSE

GUARDROOM

ROUND TOWER

INNER WARD

MODERN HOUSE

BARN

HEARTH AND OVENS

MODERN CHALET

SHED

TURRET

HEARTH & OVEN

KITCHEN?

WELL

OVEN

SUB-CHAPEL

PASSAGE

INACCESSIBLE

BUTTERY OVER

HALL BLOCK

WATERGATE

SPUR TOWER

12TH CENTURY.
DEFENCES, c.1230.
CHAPEL, c.1260.
13TH. CTY. ADDITIONS.
16TH. & 17TH. CENTURIES.
UNKNOWN.
RECENT.

FEET

METRES

150

100

50

40

30

20

10

10

0

corners. This curtain is attributed to David de Barri (d.1262). It was originally lower, the walled-up battlements being visible in places. A piecemeal heightening of the curtain took place later in the thirteenth century, along with the addition of a gate tower in the middle of the east front. Meanwhile the older hall was augmented with a new solar and chapel, the features of the latter suggesting a date in the 1260s. It seems likely that most or all of these additions took place under the second David de Barri, son of the first. He attained unusual prominence for a member of his family, becoming justiciar of Ireland.

An outer bailey was also added sometime in the thirteenth century. In contrast to the inner enclosure, its remains are now fragmentary. Bits of curtain still stand, along with the footings of a U-shaped tower. The more prominent ruin within the outer bailey belongs to a Tudor barn.

Ahead is the east front of the main castle which, being the most accessible side, was the most strongly defended. A square tower guarded the entrance long before the rest of the circuit was rebuilt in stone. This Norman tower is the most ruined part of the inner defences, two sides having collapsed. Originally there was just a gateway beside it, the projecting gatehouse being a later addition. Though dating from the Edwardian period it is a simple gate tower, with a guard chamber over the entrance passage. Rounded towers flank the vulnerable eastern angles of the curtain. The handsome South-East Tower is cylindrical and rises well above the curtain. The lower North-Eastern Tower is semi-circular, and was originally open-backed. Both towers have stairways curving up through the thickness of the wall. Evidently the east curtain was heightened in two different building campaigns. Along the stretch south of the gatehouse the original wall-walk was covered over to form a mural passage, but to the north the new parapet is carried on a series of arches.

On the long side walls of the inner bailey the heightening was also carried out in different ways. The north curtain is solid throughout, a slight angle being marked externally by a projecting round turret at parapet level. By contrast, the straight southern curtain was heightened by raising the parapet to create a thin screen wall. This economy was justified in view of the ravine on this side. The arrow slits which pierce the merlons of the original parapet remained open for archers. Against the south curtain is the shell of another Tudor barn, one end of which has been converted into a house.

At the back of the courtyard is the Norman hall. Although the first-floor entrance is quite normal for a medieval hall standing over an undercroft, the building is substantial enough to be regarded as a hall-keep on the model of Chepstow. The original windows are little more than slits and the embattled parapet appears to be original. They are probably the oldest battlements in Wales. The hall itself formed a lofty though dimly-lit room. Its northern end was once partitioned off from the rest and divided into two storeys – a buttery below and the original solar above. Two round chimneys are early additions.

The second David de Barri added his new solar at the opposite end of the hall. Again there is an upper chamber, covered by a pointed vault. David's chapel stands at an angle to the main block to obtain the correct orientation. The chapel is a vaulted structure with considerable architectural refinement in its Gothic windows and priest's seat. Like the hall, it stands over an undercroft and is reached by a stair from the courtyard.

David's solar overlies a gate passage leading to the bay. Evidently the curtain was intended to enclose a small yard at the back of the hall, but this extension may never have been completed. To close the short gap between the new solar and the south curtain, the second David de Barri built a thick spur wall. It contains a passage leading from the solar to a latrine turret. Hence the waste could drop harmlessly down the steep slope instead of accumulating outside the back gate – an unusually thoughtful example of medieval sanitation!

Secure in the southern prong of Pembrokeshire, there are no recorded Welsh attacks upon Manorbier. Its medieval tranquillity was disturbed once, Richard de Barri taking advantage of the general unrest during Edward II's overthrow to seize the castle from his nephew. The Barri line died out in 1392, after which the castle suffered the common fate of absentee ownership with tenant farmers in occupation. The only siege took place in 1645, when General Laugharne captured the castle for parliament.

Access: Open daily in summer.
Reference: Archaeologia Cambrensis (CXIX). Guidebook.
Relations: Nearby Carew. Compare the hall-keeps of Castell Coch, Chepstow, Grosmont and Monmouth. Barry Castle also belonged to the de Barris.

NARBERTH CASTLE is a forlorn ruin on the edge of the little town. The palace of the legendary Pwyll, prince of Dyfed, is said to have occupied the site. However, the Castell-yn-Arberth of Norman times lay two miles south. The present castle may not have been founded until Andrew de Perrot came here in 1246. This castle was destroyed by Llywelyn the Last's supporters in 1257. In 1282 Narberth was granted to Roger Mortimer, the king's justiciar, and he probably built the Edwardian castle. In 1405 it resisted Owain Glyndwr's French allies. Narberth was one of the castles modernised by the local magnate Sir Rhys ap Thomas in Tudor times. Its subsequent decay may have been hastened by a Civil War slighting.

Today the castle is fragmentary. The only part standing reasonably complete is the south-west corner tower, a typical Edwardian cylinder still rising complete. Its twin at the south-east corner has been reduced to a tall fragment, and the short stretch of curtain between them has fallen. Behind stood the hall, its courtyard wall standing precariously with undercroft windows inserted by Sir Rhys. At right-angles to the hall is the vaulted undercroft of the solar. Virtually nothing survives from the northern half of the castle. A chunk of masonry formed part of the circumference of a circular keep at the north-east corner. This may be part of Andrew de Perrot's original castle. A twin-towered gatehouse occupied the north-west corner, but nothing remains.

Access: On private land, but visible from the road.
Reference: Archaeological Journal (CXIX).
Relations: Roger Mortimer's castle at Chirk. For Rhys ap Thomas see Carew, Kidwelly, Laugharne and St Donat's.

NEWPORT CASTLE was founded by William Fitz Martin, lord of Cemais, after he had lost Castell Nanhyfer to the Lord Rhys in 1191. The site is a powerful ring-work, overlooking a coastal village which was once a flourishing port. Fitz Martin no doubt intended that his new castle could be relieved from the sea in the event of fur-ther attacks by the Welsh. However, the castle fell to Llywelyn the Great when he invaded in 1215, and again to Llywelyn the Last in 1257. Between them they destroyed whatever stone defences the first castle possessed, and the present remains date from a rebuilding in the last decades of the thirteenth century. The castle passed to the Audley family in 1326. They seldom came here and the castle gradually sank into ruins. The gatehouse was restored and converted into a house in 1859.

This was a strong Edwardian castle, its thick curtain built on the edge of the cir-cular ringwork. Today the remains amount to no more than three of the four towers which projected deeply from the circuit. One of these towers formed the gatehouse. Although not large, it was a gatehouse of the Edwardian type with twin flanking turrets. Only the rounded turret on the right now survives, its polygonal top added later. The gate passage was blocked during the conversion of 1859. To the right a Victorian garden wall on the site of the curtain connects with a large, U-shaped tower known as Hunter's Hall, of which only one side stands high.

Another U-shaped tower at the back of the courtyard is better preserved, though it is now only half its original height. This tower rises from a square base – its pyramid spurs are typical of Edwardian towers of South Wales. Attached to it is the last surviving portion of the courtyard buildings: a small undercroft with a ribbed vault supported on a central column. It may have formed the undercroft of a chapel.

Access: Private, but visible from the village.
Reference: Newport Castle by D. M. Browne and D. Percival.
Relations: Its predecessor, Castell Nanhyfer. Not to be confused with the other Newport Castle in Monmouthshire.

PEMBROKE CASTLE AND TOWN WALL Pembroke has one of the most majestic castles in Wales. Arnulf de Montgomery, son of the earl of Shrewsbury, chose this strong position on one of the inlets to Milford Haven after sweeping through Deheubarth in 1093. When the Welsh rose up against the new invaders three years later Pembroke narrowly withstood their onslaught. Its desperate consta-ble, Gerald de Windsor, sent a letter to his overlord boasting (quite falsely) of the castle's ample provisions, knowing the information would be 'leaked' to the besiegers by the bishop of St David's. Gerald's grandson, Giraldus Cambrensis, relates that the Welsh fell for the trick and abandoned the siege. Gilbert de Clare was created earl of Pembroke in 1138, the first of a distinguished line of palatine earls. It was from here that his son Richard, the notorious 'Strongbow', sailed to conquer Ireland. So Pembroke is a symbol not just of the Norman invasion of Wales but of Ireland too.

No masonry can be attributed to the de Clares, and the castle probably remained entirely of earth and timber throughout the Norman period. Its transformation into a mighty stone fortress took place under the celebrated Marshal family. In 1189

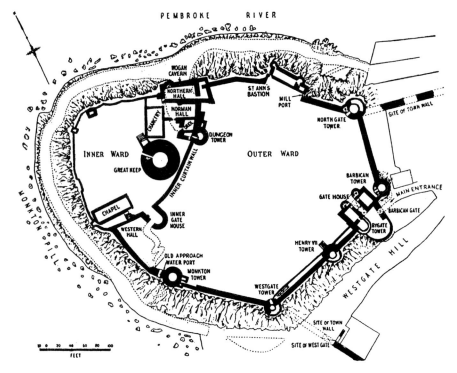

PEMBROKE RIVER

PEMBROKE CASTLE

Richard I granted the earldom to a poor knight, William Marshal, paradoxically in recognition of his loyalty to Henry II while Richard himself was in revolt. William Marshal was one of the most capable of the Marcher barons. He began to rebuild the castle in an up-to-date form not hitherto seen in Wales. Llywelyn the Great chipped away at the earldom while William was defending England against the Dauphin Louis' invasion, though Pembroke remained secure from attack.

To William Marshal are ascribed the inner ward at the tip of the promontory and the mighty round keep. After his death in 1219 his sons continued the work, building the great towered curtain around the outer ward. Five brothers held the castle and earldom in turn. First there was William Marshal the Younger, who drove back Llywelyn in 1223. Then came the rebellious Richard, who joined forces with Llywelyn against Henry III, fleeing to Ireland where he was murdered in 1234. There was probably a pause in building during this crisis, but work continued under Gilbert Marshal before his accidental death in a tournament in 1241. Walter Marshal was followed by the youngest brother, Anselm, who held the earldom for just eleven days in 1245. All died childless, fulfilling the curse of a dispossessed Irish bishop.

William de Valence then acquired Pembroke by marriage, though he was never officially given the title of earl. He added a new great hall to the castle, but his chief contribution lay in walling the town which had grown up outside. Few alterations have taken place since then. In 1324 the earldom passed (again by marriage) to the

168

Hastings family, but they seldom visited. Jasper Tudor was more often in residence. He had a rather chequered career as earl, losing the title twice during the Wars of the Roses as the pendulum swung between Lancaster and York. His nephew Henry Tudor was born in the castle in 1457, but they were forced into exile when the Yorkists besieged Pembroke in 1471. They finally returned in 1485, landing at Milford Haven and recovering Pembroke en route to Henry's victory over Richard III at Bosworth.

Pembroke was one of the few places in Wales to remain staunchly parliamentarian throughout the Civil War, due to the energies of its mayor, John Poyer. In 1644 the town was besieged until a parliamentary fleet came to its relief. Afterwards the Royalist commander, Lord Carberry, was dismissed for incompetence. However, during the Royalist uprising of 1648 Poyer went over to the rebels. He was joined by the disillusioned General Rowland Laugharne, who had contributed so much to the Roundhead victory in South Wales. Together they held Pembroke against Oliver Cromwell, now rising to the top of the army. At one point Cromwell's troops managed to storm the town and reach the castle gatehouse, only to be repulsed. The resolve of the castle had been weakened by cutting off its piped water supply. However, it was the failure of the promised relief and the arrival of heavy guns which finally drove the garrison to surrender in July after a siege of seven weeks. Cromwell supervised the slighting of the castle and town wall, while John Poyer drew the short straw and was shot as a traitor in London.

The castle occupies a splendid promontory site between the Pembroke River and the Monkton Pill. It is naturally protected by low cliffs which drop down to the water. Although the castle is complete enough for its towers to be ascended and its wall passages explored, its intact appearance is the result of an extensive restoration undertaken by Sir Ivor Philipps in 1929–34. Before that the castle, while still impressive, was very much a ruin. The towers on the outer curtain had suffered the greatest damage, most of them having been blown up by Cromwell. Their missing outer fronts were rebuilt in quite a scholarly manner, though the concrete floors inserted at that time strike a jarring note. All the battlements are restorations, only the keep retaining the jagged parapet of a ruin.

Approaching the castle from the town we first encounter the mighty outer curtain built by the Marshal brothers. It is unusually ambitious, with five circular towers, the curious St Ann's Bastion and a large gatehouse along its line. The towers were not just defensive flankers but self-contained units housing residential chambers. With their stair turrets rising a little above the main parapet they anticipate the towers of the Edwardian period. They stand astride the curtain, blocking off each section of wall-walk, which would be advantageous if one stretch of curtain had been scaled. Four of the towers, as well as the gatehouse, are concentrated on the south-east front facing the walled town, which was the only easy approach. A barbican stands in front of the outer gatehouse. The restored gateway to this small, semi-circular enclosure is placed at right-angles to the gatehouse, forcing attackers to expose their shield-less right sides while under fire from the adjacent Barbican Tower.

The outer gatehouse is an oblong structure, its central gate passage once defended by two portcullises, three murder hole slots and several arrow slits from the flanking guard chambers. Although the twin-towered gatehouse was making its debut at this time, the gatehouse at Pembroke possesses a semi-circular flanking tower on the left side of the gateway only (this too has been rebuilt from the old foundations). A second tower was unnecessary because this side is closely flanked by the Barbican Tower at an angle of the enclosure. Connecting wall passages make this tower an integral part of the gatehouse. The upper part of the gatehouse contains two floors which no doubt formed the constable's residence. Twin stair turrets project at the back, connected by an embattled fighting gallery above the inner gateway. So this was a prototype keep-gatehouse, defensible from the courtyard as well as outside.

When Cromwell blew up the Barbican Tower the explosive charge backfired. Hence, unlike the other towers facing the town, its outer front is original but the courtyard side is a reconstruction. At the Northgate Tower the curtain turns to crown the rock overlooking the Pembroke River. Midway along is an oblong projection with corner turrets, known as St Ann's Bastion. This is similar to the Traitors' Gate in the Tower of London, so it may be an addition by William de Valence during the Edwardian period. A postern is concealed in one of the side walls.

Another advanced feature of the castle is the archers' mural gallery extending westwards from the gatehouse, leading to the Henry VII Tower and onwards to the Westgate Tower. Small windows and fireplaces show the residential role of these towers. A Tudor fireplace in the Henry VII Tower may mark the room where the future Henry VII was born in 1457. The long stretch of curtain between the gatehouse and the Westgate Tower has been doubled in thickness, probably during the Civil War to withstand cannon bombardment. Beyond the Westgate Tower the parapet is too high for the wall-walk. Evidently the mural passage was intended to continue along this stretch, with the wall-walk above, but building was left incomplete. Next comes the Monkton Tower, which is larger than its neighbours and more authentic, since this is the only one of the outer ward towers which Cromwell did not blow up. All the mural towers could have acted as independent defence points if the outer ward was penetrated, and the Monkton Tower commands the approach to the inner gatehouse. Beside the tower a postern leads onto the rock.

No doubt the large outer ward was once filled with ancillary buildings, but it is now an open space. Ahead, the inner ward occupies the apex of the promontory. We now go back a generation to the elder William Marshal. His lofty keep dominates the castle, standing just inside the curving cross-wall which divided the inner and outer wards. The middle portion of this wall was demolished during the Civil War to provide material for the reinforced outer curtain, so only the foundations survive. Also reduced to its base is the U-shaped inner gatehouse, which resembled the barbican in front of the outer gatehouse.

The northern part of the cross-wall survives because it backs onto the main residential buildings. Here is the circular Dungeon Tower – aptly named because its basement is a grim prison. Just beyond is the protruding front of William de Valence's hall block. The west end of the cross-wall also remains owing to the narrow vaulted chamber behind it. From here the inner curtain continues around the tip of the promontory. Such is the steep drop that it forms a retaining wall, its parapet scarcely above courtyard level.

William Marshal's magnificent keep is eighty feet high. Although there are earlier examples in England, this keep is the oldest and greatest of the round keeps which became popular in thirteenth-century Wales. Its bulk is impressive, but it is a simple cylinder without any weakening projections. The keep rises from a broad plinth, where the walls are nineteen feet thick. Its narrow ground-floor doorway is a later insertion. The original entrance is higher up, reached by a later flight of stone steps which have taken the place of a wooden stair. Internally, the keep contained four storeys connected by a spiral staircase. However, the floors have not been restored here, so the interior forms a vast, dimly-lit cylinder rising to its crowning dome. All the windows are narrow slits except for a two-light window on the secure top floor. A doorway at second-floor level connected via a drawbridge to the destroyed parapet of the cross-wall. The dome is not unique in Welsh castles but is much the largest. Externally it forms an inner turret rising a little above the main parapet.

Despite its grand scale the keep was primarily a military structure, offering little comfort – there are not even any built-in latrines. Like most other Welsh keeps it was intended for occupation only during emergencies. Hence the roofless residential buildings at the east corner of the inner ward are centred upon a hall, which was also built by William Marshal. William de Valence converted the original hall into a solar and added a new great hall alongside. Projecting beyond the curtain, the large Gothic windows show a relaxation of security, though the cliff makes the castle virtually unassailable at this point. Both halls stood at first-floor level over cellars. Across the tiny yard in front is a more ruinous third hall, built as a court house for the earldom.

A spiral stair descends from William de Valence's hall undercroft to a deep natural cave (the Wogan Cavern) in the limestone rock. The earls walled up the cave entrance but left an arched gateway. One theory is that the cave served as a boat-house. It may also have contained the castle's only natural water supply. It is a curious weakness of this great stronghold that water had to be piped in, a circumstance which contributed to its fall in 1648.

The old town occupies a narrow ridge between the broad Pembroke River and its former tributary, the Monkton Pill, which is now dry. Medieval Pembroke consisted chiefly of one long street stretching between two churches, though the town's most interesting church (Monkton Priory) lies outside the walled area. The town wall enclosed an unusually elongated area, extending for over a mile. William de Valence is said to have built the wall in the late thirteenth century, though no doubt the townsfolk had to contribute.

In contrast to the castle, the remains of the town wall are not extensive but Barnard's Tower is worth seeking out. The wall left the castle at the Westgate Tower, and on Westgate Hill is a fragment of the West Gate. Car parks occupy the dried-up Monkton Pill, overlooked by a retaining wall on the foundations of the town wall. The original wall survives near the east end of this long southern stretch. Two semi-circular towers project here, one of them capped by a nineteenth-century summer house. The short east side of the circuit offered the only easy approach. It was destroyed by Cromwell, along with the East Gate. This was another U-shaped tower. Barnard's Tower survives at the north-east corner of the circuit – a remarkably large tower for a town wall, comparable with those in the castle. Like them, it is circular and crowned by a domed vault. A portcullis barred the entrance. Apart from a solid bastion a little further west, virtually all the long northern stretch overlooking the Pembroke River has vanished. There is just a fragment near the junction with the castle's Northgate Tower.

> *Access:* The castle is open daily (Pembroke Castle Trust), while the town wall can be followed (LA).
>
> *Reference:* Castle guidebook by R. Innes-Smith, *Archaeologia Cambrensis* (CXXVII for the castle and CXXXI for the town wall).
>
> *Relations:* Castles of the Marshals at Cilgerran, Carmarthen, Chepstow and Usk. Smaller round keeps such as Dinefwr, Bronllys, Tretower and Dolbadarn. Compare the better preserved town wall at Tenby.

PICTON CASTLE overlooks the River Cleddau where it branches into two, four miles south-east of Haverfordwest. This positioning for supply by boat is typical of many Pembrokeshire castles. An unusual fortified hall-house, Picton is one of the few castles in Wales to have become a stately home. It is the only one in the south-west.

A Norman castle existed here – its motte rises to the east. At that time it was dependent on the barony of Wiston, but Sir John Wogan made Picton his chief seat and built the present castle. He was justiciar of Ireland in 1295–1313. Inspired by fortified halls in Ireland, his castle is more elaborate than the hall-keeps of Norman times. Semi-circular towers project at the four corners, while the entrance at the east end is built like an Edwardian gatehouse, with rounded flanking turrets. A fifth tower once projected at the back. This remarkable hall formed the main defence of the castle. Although there was once a walled courtyard in front, the surrounding curtain was quite plain and there was never an accompanying ditch. Admittedly the whole complex might really be called a fortified manor house – a sign of growing security in the decades after the Edwardian conquest.

Sir John Wogan's hall-keep is still complete. Three of the four projecting towers rise from polygonal bases. The hall itself stands at first-floor level, over an undercroft. No doubt the far end was partitioned off to form a solar, and the embattled towers provided ample private accommodation. Owain Glyndwr's French allies are said to have damaged the castle during their march through Pembrokeshire in 1405. Having been stormed by the Royalists in a surprise night attack, the castle was recaptured by parliament after a three-week siege in 1645.

Although no slighting was attempted, successive generations of the Philipps family have transformed the castle. As early as the fifteenth century the defensive character of the hall was muted by the insertion of traceried windows. These have been replaced by sash windows. The squat towers show the original height of the hall, but they are now lower than the main block because an upper storey was added in 1697. Within, the hall and the other rooms are now entirely Georgian. The tower at the back was taken down about 1800 to make way for the large, keep-like block which doubled the living space. Half a century later the character of the gatehouse was irrevocably changed. Originally the entrance passage led into the undercroft, but the outer gateway was buried when the forecourt was raised. A new entrance was created at hall level, fronted by an incongruous mock-Norman porch.

Access: Limited opening times in summer.
Reference: Guidebook. *Archaeologia Cambrensis* (7th series, II).
Relations: The earlier castle at Wiston. There is a similar hall with projecting towers at Woodsford (Dorset).

POINTZ CASTLE   is an impressive motte surrounded by a ditch. The depression on the summit is evidence that a stone keep of some kind stood here. There is now no trace of a bailey. The castle is named after Pons, a tenant of the bishop of St David's who was here in the 1180s, so presumably the motte was raised by him. Later the castle was occupied by the bishops. It lies on a farm, two miles east of Solva.

Access: On private land.
Reference: GAHW *Dyfed.*
Relations: The mottes of Castell Nanhyfer and Wiston.

ROCH CASTLE   is an arresting sight on the main road midway between Haverfordwest and St David's. This solitary tower stands on an outcrop of volcanic rock – a natural motte – which has given the castle its name. According to tradition it was raised about 1200 by Adam de la Roche. The story goes that it was not so much the defensive advantages but Adam's phobia of snakes which drove him to build on this site. Inevitably, Adam was killed by the bite of a viper inadvertently brought in with a basket of firewood.

The tower is a U-shaped keep reminiscent of those built by Llywelyn the Last in North Wales. Above a cellar partly hewn out of the rock are two main floors, plus a top one later contrived at the level of the corbelled parapet. A square turret projects from the apse. This contains several vaulted chambers, one of them perhaps a tiny chapel. The tower is later than Adam de la Roche's time but probably of the thirteenth century. Closer dating is not possible owing to the lack of original features. The last of the de la Roche family died in 1420 and the castle was then jointly held by two absentee families. However, it remained occupied by tenants and was even modernised, all the small mullioned windows being Tudor insertions. The castle changed hands three times during the Civil War. Restoration took place around 1900, when the lower building was added. A bailey lay below the rock but there is no evidence of any stone curtain.

Access: Closely visible from the road (the castle is available as a holiday let).
Reference: *Archaeologia Cambrensis* (3rd series, XI).
Relations: U-shaped keeps at Castell-y-Bere, Ewloe and Montgomery. Compare the de la Roche castle at Benton.

ST DAVID'S CASTLE AND CLOSE   Half a mile west of the cathedral is a strong ringwork known as Parc-y-Castell, its overgrown rampart covering a semi-circular area. There is no bank and ditch on the east, where the steep drop to the River Alun was considered adequate protection. This ringwork castle may have been raised by Bishop Bernard, who was appointed in 1115. As the first Norman to occupy this ancient Welsh see he may well have felt in need of a refuge.

By 1200 the earthwork castle had been superseded by the present Bishop's Palace beside the cathedral. As rebuilt by Bishop Henry de Gower (1328–47) this is the grandest medieval mansion in Wales, with its two large halls and a distinctive arcaded parapet. Even in ruins it is a worthy companion to the finest church in Wales. The palace was quite unfortified but was afforded some protection by the defensive wall which Bishop Gower built to surround the cathedral close. This wall only enclosed the cathedral, the palace and the canons' houses – the tiny borough of St David's lay outside. Admittedly the plain wall cannot have been a very formidable obstacle. Its circumference (three quarters of a mile) exceeded some Welsh town walls! A few English cathedrals also had semi-fortified close walls, illustrating the grandiosity of the Church in the later Middle Ages.

The highlight of the circuit is the Porth-y-Twr, an oblong gatehouse overlooking the east end of the cathedral. Its severity contrasts sharply with Bishop Gower's sumptuous palace. The octagonal tower flanking the gateway is actually an older bell tower. Three other gates into the close have perished. Much of the actual wall survives but is very ruinous, and there is a long gap on the north-west side of the circuit. Its defensive limitations are clear from the lack of flanking towers. A ruined circular tower projects at the vulnerable west corner, behind the Bishop's Palace. Apart from that there is just the base of a square tower on the south-west, where the wall crossed the River Alun.

> *Access:* Much of the close wall can be followed. The castle is visible from the road.
> *Reference: Archaeologia Cambrensis* (CIII).
> *Relations:* The bishops' castle at Llawhaden. Compare the fortified priory at Ewenny.

TENBY CASTLE AND TOWN WALL   Despite its popularity as a seaside resort, Tenby remains an idyllic and unspoilt harbour town. Its narrow streets cluster around St Mary's Church, one of the largest old parish churches in Wales, while an evocative example of the medieval town's domestic architecture can be seen in the Tudor Merchant's House. Tenby retains most of its defensive wall, as well as the sparse remains of a castle positioned on the headland.

Tenby is first mentioned in 1153 when the castle was captured by the young Rhys ap Gruffudd (the Lord Rhys) and his brother Maredudd. Rhys' son Maelgwn sacked the town in 1187, and Llywelyn the Last burnt it again in 1260. The town wall is contemporary with Edward I's town walls in North Wales. William de Valence, lord of Pembroke, is credited with its construction, though no doubt the townsfolk bore much of the cost. Further building took place from 1328, when permission to levy the tax known as murage was granted. Tenby resisted a siege by Owain Glyndwr's French allies in 1405. In 1457 Jasper Tudor and the townsfolk jointly paid for

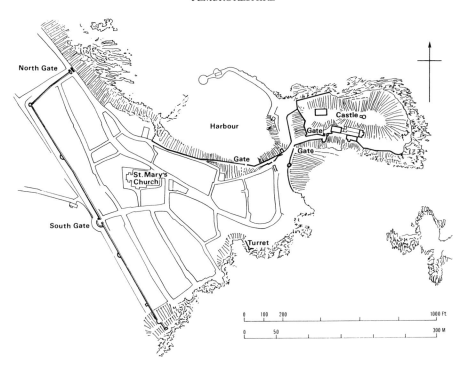

TENBY TOWN WALL

repairs. Jasper and his young nephew Henry Tudor escaped by boat from here to Brittany on the approach of the Yorkists in 1471, enduring fourteen years of exile before their triumphant return. Tenby changed hands twice in the main Civil War. It declared for the king during the Royalist uprising of 1648, only to be stormed by Oliver Cromwell. The preservation of so much of the town wall is largely due to the efforts of a Doctor Chater. In 1873 he obtained an injunction to prevent the corporation from demolishing it.

The old town occupies a promontory which culminates in the castle headland. Guarding the landward approaches from the north and west, the town wall is nearly complete. Only the eastern end of the north wall has vanished. That stretch was pulled down before Doctor Chater's time, along with the North Gate which spanned the High Street. The wall now appears just beyond, turning south at the circular north-west corner tower. It then runs in a straight line along South Parade until it reaches the south cliff. It has flanking towers at regular intervals. In places walled-up battlements can be seen a little below the present parapet. The heightening of the wall probably accounts for the renewed activity from 1328. Even at its present height the wall does not appear a great obstacle, but it would have been more formidable when the ditch lay in front. Arrow slits pierce the wall and the merlons of the battlements.

A passage has been cut through the first tower beyond the north-west corner. We

175

then reach the U-shaped West Gate, better known as the Gate of the Five Arches. Of the four openings in the curved outer wall only that facing north is original. It is set at right-angles to the inner gateway – an arrangement also seen in the U-shaped gatehouses at Pembroke. Steps lead from the town wall parapet to a loop-holed mural passage, from which the portcullis of the outer gateway was operated. The other arches were cut through the wall in the nineteenth century to ease the flow of traffic. South of this gatehouse are two more semi-circular towers. Between them is the only square tower on the circuit. Because of its shape it is traditionally attributed to Jasper Tudor. However, the tower is bonded with the town wall, so Jasper's contribution is limited to the early gun ports (rare in Wales) which have been inserted here. Beyond a Victorian archway the town wall terminates in a square turret on the edge of the cliff.

Steep falls protect the seaward sides of the promontory, but even here lengths of wall were constructed to protect the town from attack by sea. Part of a retaining wall survives on the south cliff, and there is the base of a tower near the harbour. A destroyed gateway led onto the harbour.

William de Valence may also have reconstructed the castle in stone. It soon fell into ruins. The situation of the castle is a strong one, but the remains are now fragmentary. It was only a modest fortification taking advantage of the natural defences. From the harbour a path ascends to the castle headland, overlooked by a stretch of curtain. Ahead is the stump of a small gate tower with a rebuilt archway. It is fronted by a semi-circular barbican, its entrance placed in a side wall like the Gate of the Five Arches. Just beyond is Tenby Museum, incorporating masonry from the castle hall. An embattled length of curtain overlooks the bay, low down near the water's edge. These are just fragments of a wall which once surrounded the headland.

Best preserved is the circular tower occupying the highest point. One would expect a keep to be so centrally placed but this tower is much too small. Its diminutive size is emphasised by the attached square turret containing a spiral stair, which is nearly as big as the tower itself. This tower was merely a watch tower, positioned to dominate the rest of the castle. It may also have served as a lighthouse. The adjacent St Catherine's Island is crowned by a strongpoint of a different era – a Victorian fort built to defend the approach to the naval dockyard in Milford Haven.

> *Access:* The town wall can be followed externally and the castle is freely accessible (both LA).
>
> *Reference: Archaeologia Cambrensis* (CXLII). *Town Defences in England and Wales* by H. L. Turner.
>
> *Relations:* The semi-circular gateways of Pembroke Castle. Compare the town walls of Caernarfon, Conwy, Denbigh and Chepstow.

UPTON CASTLE occupies splendid woodland on the west bank of the Carew River before it flows into the Cleddau, two miles north-west of Carew Cheriton. Overlooking the grounds is a nineteenth-century house incorporating part of a medieval castle at the back. Its north front is still intact, comprising an embattled curtain flanked by three rounded towers. Two of the towers are closely spaced to form a gatehouse. The gateway between them has an external portcullis groove and a machicolation archway. A short length of curtain connects this gatehouse to the round north-east corner tower. The hall was probably in the west range, which has been transformed as part of the later house. If the castle was ever completed, there can only have been a tiny yard in the middle.

What is most striking is the small scale of the whole edifice. This is a castle in miniature, built by a minor lord who was attempting to emulate the great barons around him. Dating from the Edwardian period, it belonged to the Malefants, who held the manor until the Tudor era. Two medieval effigies of the family can be seen in the adjacent chapel.

> *Access:* The grounds are open regularly in summer, but the castle is out of view at the back of the house.
>
> *Reference: Castles* by C. Oman.
>
> *Relations:* The smaller inhabited castles of Picton, Fonmon and Penhow.

WALWYN'S CASTLE probably takes its name from one of the Flemish settlers who colonised south Pembrokeshire in Norman times, but nothing is known about him. The castle stands on a spur beside the parish church, in the village of the same name. It is a ringwork, with a powerful bank and ditch surrounding a roughly circular summit. The enclosure is divided into two by a cross-ditch. A large outer bailey incorporates the defences of an Iron Age fort.

> *Access:* Visible from the churchyard.
>
> *Reference: Archaeologia Cambrensis* (7th series, II).
>
> *Relations:* Ringworks at St David's, Aberrheidol and Caer Penrhos.

WISTON CASTLE Like its neighbours, Haverfordwest and Llawhaden, Wiston is one of the castles which guarded the frontier of Norman colonisation in south Pembrokeshire. Many of the settlers were Flemish, and one of their leaders was Wizo, from whom Wiston takes its name. His castle existed by 1112. It is a good example of a motte-and-bailey castle, with a ditched motte and a rampart surrounding the unusually large bailey. Wizo moved on to try his fortunes in Scotland. The Welsh captured Wiston in 1147 and 1193, but on both occasions it was quickly recovered. Then in 1220 Llywelyn the Great destroyed the castle. Henry III ordered William Marshal the Younger, earl of Pembroke, to restore it.

Perhaps the ruined keep on the motte dates only from that time. It is a shell keep, comprising a low polygonal wall around the summit. Such keeps are more typical of the Norman period and it seems antiquated in comparison with William's work elsewhere, but Wiston was a relatively minor stronghold. The wall has suffered one breach. Its gate arch was only defended by a stout door which could be kept shut by a drawbar. No stone wall was ever built on the bailey rampart. Wiston ceased to be the centre of the barony when Sir John Wogan built Picton Castle, and the castle was abandoned soon after.

> *Access:* Freely accessible (Cadw).

Reference: Archaeologia Cambrensis (CXLIV). Guide by R. Turner.
Relations: Its successor, Picton. Compare the shell keeps at Cardiff, Brecon and Tretower.

OTHER SITES　Pembrokeshire has the usual group of Norman motte-and-bailey castles:

Camrose Motte	*Hayscastle*
Castell Crychydd (near Star)	*Henry's Moat*
Castell Dyffryn Mawr (near Crymmych)	*Llanfyrnach Castle*
Castlebythe	*New Moat*
Dingstopple Motte (near Llawhaden)	*St Ishmael's Tump*
Green Castle (near Crinow)	*Wolf's Castle*

Castell Cynen (near Lampeter Velfrey), *Castell Moel* (Puncheston) and *Castell Pen-yr-Allt* (near Cilgerran) are ringworks. Another occupies the Iron Age hillfort of *Rudbaxton Rath* (near Haverfordwest). Moving into Tudor times, two circular gun towers guarded the entrance to Milford Haven. They formed the only Welsh links in Henry VIII's chain of coastal forts, erected from 1539 to counter the threat of invasion from the Catholic powers of Europe. Both have vanished. Victorian fortifications near Dale occupy the site of the *West Blockhouse*, while the *East Blockhouse* crowned a cliff on the Angle side of the estuary.

Radnorshire

This county corresponds with the Marcher lordship of Maelienydd, carved out in Norman times by the de Braose lords of Brecon but then acquired by the Mortimers. They built several stone castles, notably Castell Tinboeth, New Radnor and the two on the ridge of Cefnllys. Only earthworks and some rubble are left at these sites, though their elevated positions repay a visit. At Painscastle too, the Norman motte-and-bailey is still impressive but Henry III's masonry has vanished. Thus Radnorshire, though possessing many earthworks – including the commanding ringwork of Castell-y-Blaidd – is the only Welsh county now lacking substantial stone castles. It is odd that so much should have perished at such remote sites – the poor quality of the local mortar is to blame.

CASTELL TINBOETH,　or Castell Dinbaud, rises two miles north-west of Llanbister. It occupies a commanding hill overlooking the River Ithon and the A483. The summit (1,275 feet) forms an oval ringwork surrounded by a rock-cut ditch. Some footings of a curtain are buried in the rampart and one precarious stone fragment marks the site of the gatehouse. This was one of the Norman castles of the de Braose family. Llywelyn the Last seized it from the Mortimers in 1262. Rebuilding in stone probably began on their return five years later, though a rare Welsh licence to crenellate (fortify) was granted in 1316. The Mortimers forfeited the castle six years later owing to their part in an abortive revolt against Edward II. Although they soon recovered their inheritance, this castle seems to have been abandoned.

Access: Freely accessible (uphill walk).
Reference: GAHW *Clwyd and Powys.*
Relations: Mortimer castles at Cefnllys, New Radnor and Chirk.

CASTELL-Y-BLAIDD is another of the spectacular hilltop castles of central Wales. This oval ringwork rises two miles north-east of Llanbadarn Fynydd. Historically there is no mention of the castle. No doubt it was raised by the de Braose lords or one of their feudal sub-tenants. There is no trace of an outer bailey, and the gap in the surrounding bank and ditch suggests that the castle was left unfinished.

Access: Freely accessible (uphill walk).
Reference: GAHW *Clwyd and Powys.*
Relations: Ringworks such as Castell Tinboeth, Aberrheidol and Caer Penrhos.

CEFNLLYS CASTLES The magnificent ridge known as Castle Bank, two miles east of Llandrindod Wells, is further protected by the River Ithon which winds around it. Despite the fragmentary remains, this is one of several hilltop castles in central Wales where the effort of reaching the summit is amply rewarded by the view. It is likely that the site was first fortified in the Iron Age. The steep ascent begins at Cefnllys Church. Successive castle sites can be found at either end of the ridge, the open space between them marking the position of a vanished medieval borough. The hummocky motte-and-bailey castle at the northern end of the ridge was raised in Norman times. Nothing remains of its stone rebuilding by Ralph Mortimer in the 1240s. The Mortimers were driven out of Maelienydd by Llywelyn the Last in 1262.

Llywelyn allowed them to return after the Treaty of Montgomery (1267), but protested when Roger Mortimer began a new and stronger castle at the narrow south end of the ridge in 1273. (The historical record is confused by several Roger Mortimers in this period: this one was the uncle of Edward I's justiciar and grandfather of Edward II's nemesis.) Roger created a square enclosure with corner towers, closely surrounding an octagonal keep. It was in good condition when the last Mortimer died in 1425, but was in ruins just a century later. Now only the rock-cut ditch separating this end of the ridge survives, together with the stump of the keep, buried in the turf. Excavations would no doubt reveal a lot, but the site is a sorry reminder of how time and stone-robbing can destroy a castle even in so remote a place as this.

Access: Freely accessible (uphill walk).
Reference: RCAHMW *Radnorshire.*
Relations: The Mortimer castles of Castell Tinboeth, New Radnor, Chirk and Narberth. Compare the hilltop settings of Castell Dinas and Castell Dinas Bran.

NEW RADNOR CASTLE AND TOWN DEFENCES   Philip de Braose established a castle at Radnor in 1096. This was probably the modest earthwork at Old Radnor (Castle Nimble), but it is possible that 'New' Radnor owes its origin to that event. Authorities are divided on the issue, and dates up to 1233 have been suggested. Radnor passed to the powerful Mortimers. Llywelyn the Great dismantled the castle twice, and Llywelyn the Last temporarily expelled the Mortimers in 1262. It was probably after their return in 1267 that Edward Mortimer rebuilt the castle in stone. Owain Glyndwr stormed it in 1402 and massacred the defenders – many decapitated skeletons were unearthed here in 1845. However, a new English garrison was quickly installed. By Tudor times the castle was very ruinous except for the gatehouse, which was kept in repair as a prison. Everything was swept away after parliamentary troops captured New Radnor during the Civil War. Little is known about the stone castle and no masonry survives. Nevertheless the earthworks are prodigious, based on a natural hill which was scarped into an enormous motte. There is an oblong bailey in front, separated from the motte by a deep ditch.

The castle lay within the town defences. Permission to levy the tax known as murage was granted in 1257 and renewed in the 1280s. This suggests at least an intention of walling the town in stone, but only the earth rampart and ditch can be seen. The grid of streets within the enclosure is evidence of thirteenth-century town planning, but the mile-long circuit proved too ambitious and New Radnor is still not large enough to fill it. The tree-lined rampart runs south from the castle bailey, then turns eastwards to meet the Summergil Brook. Beyond that it continued north to rejoin the castle, but this eastern stretch has largely disappeared.

Access: The castle is freely accessible. Much of the town rampart can be followed.
Reference: RCAHMW *Radnorshire*. GAHW *Clwyd and Powys*.
Relations: Philip de Braose also founded Builth Castle. Castell Tinboeth, Cefnllys and Chirk were other Mortimer castles.

PAINSCASTLE   This impressive motte-and-bailey earthwork dominates the village of the same name. Unusually the rampart is placed in front of the ditch, and surrounds the entire site. The castle takes its name from Payn Fitz John, Henry I's chamberlain, who raised it early in the twelfth century. There was an accompanying Norman borough, on a road (now the B4594) which was then one of the main routes into central Wales. The castle passed to the de Braose lords of Brecon, who frequently lost and regained it in their struggles with the Welsh. In one of these sieges (1198) Maud de Braose defended the castle so staunchly against the prince of Powys that it became known as Maud's Castle. She was later starved to death by King John following the failure of her husband's revolt.

The last William de Braose was hanged by Llywelyn the Great for conducting an affair with his wife. This event prompted Henry III to invade in 1231. For two months his army camped here. Over the next two years a stone castle was built over the earthworks, with a towered curtain and a round keep on top of the motte. We do not know the cost owing to a gap in the Pipe Rolls. Henry soon granted the castle to Ralph de Tony, thus charging him with the responsibility for defence. The castle was last garrisoned against Owain Glyndwr. It fell into ruins after that and the disappearance of the royal masonry is a great misfortune, though many stones still peep through the turf.

> *Access:* Obtain permission to visit at the adjacent farm.
> *Reference: HKW* (II). RCAHMW *Radnorshire.*
> *Relations:* Compare Henry III's work at Montgomery and Deganwy. For Maud de Braose see Hay Castle.

OTHER SITES *Rhayader's* castle was raised by the Lord Rhys, prince of Deheubarth, in 1177. It occupied a bend in the River Wye, remains of a rock-cut ditch cutting off the landward side. Ringworks include The Warden at *Presteigne* and *Colwyn Castle* (near Hundred House). Two square castles of the thirteenth century have all but disappeared. *Knucklas*, a seat of the Mortimers, preserves some footings of the curtain on its hilltop. *Aberedw Castle*, subject of a rare Welsh licence to crenellate in 1285, is a ditched site with a fragment of one round corner tower. Three years earlier Llywelyn the Last visited the nearby motte of *Hen Castell* before his death in the skirmish at Cilmeri. This is just one of the typical Welsh concentration of Norman motte-and-bailey castles. Others worth mentioning are:

Barland Motte (near Evenjobb)	*Clyro Castle*
Bleddfa Castle	*Dolybedwyn Motte* (near Newchurch)
Boughrood Castle	*Knighton Castles* (two)
Brynllwyd Mount (Hundred House)	*Llanbedr Motte* (near Painscastle)
Burfa Mound (near Walton)	*Norton Castle*
Castell Crugerydd (near New Radnor)	*Penarth Mount* (near Hundred House)
Castell Cymaron (near Llandegley)	*Tomen Beddugre* (near Llanddewi)
Castle Kinsey (near Clyro)	*Womaston Motte* (near Walton)
Castle Nimble (Old Radnor)	

Over the Border

The present boundary of Wales was defined by the Act of Union in 1536. Some portions of Marcher territory, which might be regarded as Welsh in character, were incorporated into the border counties of England, and it was from these counties that the Norman invasions of Wales began. The castles on the English side of the border should therefore be included in any survey of Wales, though fuller details are to be found in my *English Castles.*

Of the three semi-independent or 'palatine' earldoms established by William I, the Cheshire palatinate lasted by far the longest. Although the earldom of Chester was taken over by the Crown in 1237, its prerogatives were only abolished with the Act of Union. From the time of Hugh d'Avranches to Edward I, *Chester* was the emporium from which campaigns into North Wales were organised. Its important castle is reduced to a couple of modest towers amid later assize buildings, but the two-mile circuit of the city wall can still be walked. Extensively repaired as a promenade after Civil War damage, the city wall has lost its original gates and many of its towers. Consequently, it suffers from comparison with the shorter but intact town walls of Conwy and Caernarfon. Earl Ranulf de Blundeville's dramatic, hilltop castle of *Beeston* has a twin-towered gatehouse which is almost contemporary with Montgomery.

Shropshire equates with Roger de Montgomery's palatine earldom of Shrewsbury, which came to an end in 1102 with the rebellion of his son, Robert de Belleme. There are numerous castles near the Welsh border, the western districts once forming the Marcher lordships of Oswestry, Caus and Clun. *Ludlow Castle* is the most impressive in the county. Its towered curtain is remarkably early, probably being the work of Roger de Lacy before 1095. Within are domestic buildings erected by that Roger Mortimer who overthrew Edward II, as well as a rare, circular Norman chapel. Nearby *Stokesay* is an evocative fortified manor house of the 1280s, with an unspoilt hall preserving its original timber roof. *Shrewsbury* was naturally defended by a loop of the River Severn, its small and much restored royal castle guarding the neck of the loop. The strong castle site at *Clun* is dominated by the ruins of an oblong Norman keep. Smaller keeps at *Alberbury*, *Hopton* and *Wattlesborough* reflect border insecurities. *Caus Castle* is reduced to formidable motte-and-bailey earthworks. *Oswestry's* important castle is attested by its motte, while nearby *Whittington Castle* is a fragmentary ruin with a twin-towered gatehouse.

Herefordshire had the briefest of the three Norman palatinates, being abolished after William Fitz Osbern's son took part in a revolt against William I. *Hereford* has lost its royal castle – 'one of the largest, fairest and strongest' according to John Leland – and its city wall is reduced to a stretch beside a by-pass. Ruined *Wigmore* was the chief seat of the Mortimers, while masonry fragments still cling to the motte-and-bailey earthworks of *Huntington* and *Richard's Castle*. *Brampton Bryan* preserves its twin-towered barbican, and *Lyonshall* has the shattered remnant of a round keep. *Croft Castle*, though much altered by subsequent occupation, is an example of the later medieval, quadrangular type of castle so rare in Wales.

The part of Herefordshire beyond the River Wye was Welsh before the Normans came and contains a high concentration of castles. First and foremost is *Goodrich Castle*, its spurred Edwardian towers and gatehouse erected around a square Norman keep by William de Valence, lord of Pembroke. His son Aymer added a concentric wall on the two sides not protected by the rock-cut ditch. *Longtown* has a well-preserved circular keep resembling nearby Skenfrith. *Pembridge Castle* is an evocative but much restored little stronghold, while there are sorry fragments of other round-towered enclosures at *Clifford* and *Wilton*. *Ewyas Harold* is the best of numerous motte-and-bailey castles in the district. Others with masonry fragments can be seen at *Kilpeck* and *Snodhill*. *Kentchurch Court* preserves a medieval tower house in which Owain Glyndwr is said to have found refuge.

With its short frontier marked by the deep valley of the River Wye, Gloucestershire hardly counts as a border county and it was never a palatinate. Nevertheless *St Briavels*, near the border, has a twin-towered gatehouse built by Edward I. It strengthened a castle which housed the royal arsenal of crossbow bolts. The towns of *Gloucester* and *Bristol* supplied the castles of South Wales, but their own royal castles – both centred on large Norman keeps – have sadly disappeared. *Berkeley Castle*, with its shell keep and splendid domestic buildings, was originally founded by William Fitz Osbern to complement his castle of Chepstow on the Welsh side of the Severn estuary.

GLOSSARY

Apse   A semi-circular projection, sometimes found at the sanctuary end of a chapel. Apsidal towers are round-fronted or U-shaped. They were common in the thirteenth century, as in the keeps of *Ewloe* and *Roch*.

Arrow slits   enabled archers defending a castle to fire upon besiegers with little risk to themselves. The opening through the wall was tall and narrow (no more than a few inches wide), but the sides splayed outwards to give the bowman greater latitude; the recess or embrasure behind the slit had to be large enough to accommodate him. Flanking towers are well provided with arrow slits, commanding the adjacent stretches of curtain and the ground in front. Slits sometimes pierce curtains as well, and there are smaller versions in the merlons of many battlements. At *Beaumaris*, *Caernarfon* and *Pembroke* archers' galleries are contained within the great thickness of the walls, enabling bowmen to fire from more than one level. Cross-slits, with a horizontal slot designed to increase the range of fire, appear from Edwardian times. *Caernarfon* shows some experimental arrow slits with triple openings. Many arrow slits have been reduced by later stone-robbing to gaping holes. Owing to the restricted space, the crossbow rather than the longbow was usually employed. Its greater power compensated for the time it took to reload.

Ashlar   masonry is made from smooth, finely-cut blocks of stone. It is rare in the functional castles of Wales, but it appears in the ornate late Norman gateway of *Newcastle* (Glamorgan). Ashlar is used for several keeps and gatehouses, while the handsome late castle of *Raglan* is built of ashlar throughout.

Bailey   The bailey, ward or courtyard of a castle is the area enclosed by the earth rampart or stone curtain. Although baileys are often empty now, there would have been little open space when they were filled by halls and kitchens, workshops and stables. This is still evident at *Conwy* and *Oystermouth*. The compact nature of many Welsh castles was dictated by defensive positioning on hilltops and ridges. However, this very compactness gave further defensive advantages, since the high curtains surrounding these small enclosures could be effectively defended by a small garrison of archers. Normally there was an outer bailey, and this too was often walled in stone. The outer bailey is usually positioned in front of the inner, so that attackers were faced with a sequence of obstacles. This is taken to extremes at *Chepstow*, where four baileys occupy the narrow ridge on which the castle stands. In concentric castles, the outer bailey forms a narrow space between the two lines of walls.

Many Welsh castles are laid out irregularly to take advantage of the terrain. Even *Caernarfon* has little sense of symmetry. However, some Edwardian castle builders recognised the advantages of a simple, rectangular layout. The curtain could be effectively flanked by a minimal number of towers (generally one at each corner), with the gatehouse positioned in the middle of one side. *Caerphilly*, a castle which set new standards in several ways, was the first of this type. It influenced the symmetrical layouts of Edward I's concentric castles at *Rhuddlan*, *Harlech* and *Beaumaris*.

Barbican   A barbican is a small enclosure or passage placed in front of a gatehouse. It protected the main entrance from direct assault and increased the number of barriers which a besieger had to force his way through. Attackers caught inside could be showered with arrows from above. England has some classic examples, but most Welsh barbicans have been reduced to fragments. *Pembroke* and the town wall at *Tenby* retain semi-circular examples, involving besiegers in an awkward turn while under fire. *Carreg Cennen's* barbican takes the form of a long stone ramp commanded by the main curtain, while *Conwy* has turreted barbican enclosures at each end of the castle. A barbican was not always deemed necessary in the Edwardian period, when the many obstacles of the gate passage were considered sufficient defence. However, the South Gatehouse of *Beaumaris* was given a barbican when the gate passage was left at half its intended length. *Caerphilly* has the most dramatic barbican of any Welsh castle – a long screen wall which also acts as a dam for the artificial lake surrounding the castle.

Bastion   A flanking tower of purely defensive purpose, such as those on the town walls of *Caernarfon, Conwy* and *Tenby.*

Battlements   In a medieval fortification defence was conducted primarily from the wall-walk, so embattled parapets were a feature of even the earliest stone castles. The oldest to survive is that crowning the Norman hall-keep at *Manorbier.* Battlements, or crenellations, are divided into two parts: the solid bits (merlons) shielding the defenders and the narrow gaps (crenels) from which they could fire at the enemy. Since they are inherently the most vulnerable part of the wall, battlements have often succumbed to decay. Embattled towers and lengths of curtain still survive in many places, such as *Conwy, Chepstow, Kidwelly, Manorbier* and *Penhow.* However, the complete sets of battlements at *Caernarfon* and *Pembroke* are the result of restoration. Where a curtain was later heightened the original walled-up battlements can still be detected.

Berm   This is a narrow ledge between the curtain and the edge of the ditch. Besiegers who had reached the berm and had begun scaling or battering the walls could be counter-attacked by defenders emerging from a postern.

Bridges   leading into towns were often fortified with a gate tower built astride one of the piers. Europe preserves some splendid examples but the only Welsh survivor is the gate spanning the Monnow Bridge at *Monmouth.*

Buttery   The room in which beer and wine were stored, usually located between the hall and the kitchen.

Castle   Deriving from the Latin *castellum,* meaning 'little fort', this term is popularly applied to many fortifications and residences. The Welsh word *castell* is equally elastic. A more precise definition, embraced by most authorities and followed in this book, restricts it to the feudal strongholds of the Middle Ages, which had a dual role as fortress and residence. The term is broad enough to include Norman earthworks in addition to the more familiar stone castles. Often the residential buildings have suffered more than the surrounding walls, so the domestic nature of many castles is now less apparent. Great barons holding land in different areas would only be in residence periodically, and the royal castles of Wales were seldom visited by the monarch or prince. Nevertheless, the Pipe Rolls record many repairs to the king's halls and chambers in these castles, and Edward I's mighty castles were intended to house the royal retinue. A third and equally important role – often outlasting the defensive and residential aspects – was administrative, castles being centres of local tax collection and justice.

Chapels   formed an integral part of a great medieval lord's household. There would usually be a private chapel in the castle, even if a parish church existed nearby. However, comparatively few Welsh castle chapels survive. Sometimes the chapel stood among the buildings of the bailey, as seen in the well-preserved examples at *Chirk*, *Manorbier* and *Oystermouth*. In Edwardian castles the chapel was often located in one of the mural towers. Those of *Beaumaris*, *Carew* and *Kidwelly* are fine architecturally without much loss of security, as the windows were restricted to narrow lancets. In keep-gatehouses the room over the gate passage was a convenient location, as at *Caernarfon* and *Harlech*, despite the disruption which must have been caused when the portcullises were raised. Other small chapels occupied mural chambers in keeps and residential towers. Artistically the chapel would have been the finest of the castle buildings. They are now bereft of their paintings and fittings, and often the delicate carvings have been mutilated. Look out for the holy water basin, or *piscina*.

Concentric castles have two parallel lines of defence, the outer wall closely surrounding the inner. In addition to providing a double obstacle against attackers, the inner curtain rises higher than the outer so that defenders could fire upon the enemy from two levels simultaneously. Furthermore, besiegers who had forced their way into the outer courtyard would find themselves trapped in a narrow space while under fire from the inner curtain. Concentric fortifications existed in late antiquity, and can still be seen in the magnificent Theodosian Walls of Constantinople. Crusaders built concentric castles such as Krak des Chevaliers in the Holy Land. The filtering through of these ideas to Wales is evident by the mid-thirteenth century. At *Tretower* the building of a round keep within an earlier shell keep created a small concentric layout, and Llywelyn the Last followed suit in surrounding *Ewloe*'s keep with a concentric wall. Another concentric keep was built in the fifteenth century at *Raglan*.

Nevertheless the major concentric castles all date from the Edwardian period. They form a small but formidable group. Gilbert de Clare began the trend with *Caerphilly* (1268–71), its double line of walls further protected by an artificial lake. Edward I, having built a concentric outer wall around the Tower of London, chose concentric plans for four of his eight new Welsh castles: *Aberystwyth*, *Rhuddlan*, *Harlech* and *Beaumaris*. The latter, begun in 1295, is the most sophisticated, its outer wall not just a screen for the main curtain but a formidable defence in its own right, with projecting towers. In South Wales, two of the baronial castles – *Kidwelly* and *St Donat's* – were strengthened by the addition of concentric outer walls.

Constable The constable, or castellan, was the official in charge of a castle during the owner's absence. Many castles, particularly the royal ones, were left in the charge of the constable and a small caretaker household for long periods. He occupied quarters which were distinct from the lord's, often in the keep or keep-gatehouse. The constableship of some of the royal castles was a prestigious post granted to men of high rank. They were usually elsewhere, leaving the day-to-day administration in the hands of a deputy or lieutenant. The master mason James of St George became constable of his newly-built castle of *Harlech*. In the later Middle Ages trusted Welshmen were often constables, such as Hywel ap Gruffudd of *Criccieth* and Dafydd ap Ievan of *Harlech*.

Corbel A stone bracket projecting from a wall, supporting a roof or machicolations.

Courtyard *see* Bailey.

Crenellations *see* Battlements. In England kings gave their approval for private castle building by means of a *licence to crenellate*. This was a charter permitting a subject to crenellate or fortify his manor house. However, Marcher barons were not obliged to obtain permission, so Welsh licences are few.

Crenels are the narrow gaps in an embattled parapet. They were sometimes closed by hinged shutters for greater protection, as seen in the reconstructed examples at *Castell Coch* (Glamorgan).

Curtain The curtain is the wall surrounding a bailey. Its chief characteristic was the embattled parapet on top. A few stone English curtains (Ludlow, Richmond) were built in the generation after the Norman Conquest, and part of an early Norman curtain survives at *Chepstow*. Otherwise, in Wales it was only in the late twelfth century that stone walls began to replace the timber palisades of earthwork castles. These first curtains were plain except for a square tower guarding the simple entrance, as at *Coity, St Donat's* and *White* castles.

About 1200 William Marshal strengthened *Chepstow* with a cross-wall flanked by circular towers. From then on, round-towered curtains became the norm in Wales, and many examples survive. Often there is a second curtain beyond the inner bailey, whether placed sequentially or concentrically. Curtains became thicker to withstand the pounding of siege engines, and higher to frustrate attempts at scaling them. In some cases the curtain was later heightened. Owing to the threat of undermining the curtain was most vulnerable at its base. Consequently the wall is thickest here, often rising from a sloping plinth. The medieval curtain reached its greatest strength in the Edwardian period. Those at *Caernarfon* and *Beaumaris* are fifteen feet thick, although they contain mural passages for archers. Edwardian curtains are sometimes pierced by arrow slits. However, from this time onwards windows began to pierce stretches of curtain, providing better lighting for the residential buildings which stood against them. This was generally done where steep falls made a stretch less vulnerable to attack, as at *Chepstow* and *Haverfordwest*.

Ditch *see* Moat.

Donjon *see* Keep.

Drawbridge The medieval drawbridge was an ingenious device, alternating as bridge and barrier. In the thirteenth century the most common variety was the turning bridge, which pivoted half in and half out of the gate passage. When the outer part was raised, the inner part sank into a deep pit which would present a further obstacle to assailants if they succeeded in smashing their way through. In many ruins a modern bridge crosses the ditch and the drawbridge pit, but the only operable turning bridge is the reconstructed example at *Castell Coch* (Glamorgan). The drawbridge was raised by means of a windlass within the gatehouse. A later method involved a pair of wooden beams above the gateway, which raised the drawbridge when their inner halves were lowered. Recesses for these beams are still visible on *Raglan's* keep. A drawbridge was never long enough to span the full width of the moat, so its outer end would have connected with a fixed bridge projecting from the far side.

Drum towers are rounded or D-shaped, characteristic of the thirteenth century.

Ecclesiastical fortifications Despite the wars which sometimes resulted in abbeys and cathedrals being pillaged, Wales has few fortified churches or monasteries. *Ewenny Priory* is the best example, its precinct wall becoming a towered curtain in the Edwardian period. The priory cloister on *Caldy* Island has a tower house in one corner. Henry de Gower, bishop of St David's, erected a semi-fortified wall around *St David's* Cathedral on the model of some English cathedral closes. Episcopal castles such as *Llandaff* and *Llawhaden* are indistinguishable from those of secular lords.

Edwardian   castles represent the high point of medieval military architecture. They are distinguished by their high, thick curtains, round flanking towers and twin-towered gatehouses. It should be noted that the term is something of a misnomer. Although Edward I is associated with some of the best examples, all the elements had already appeared before his accession. Welsh castles had been maturing towards the 'Edwardian' layout throughout the first half of the thirteenth century. Hence *Chepstow* has round flanking towers dating from around 1200, while the twin-towered gatehouse made its debut in Britain at *Montgomery* in the 1220s. However, the first distinctly Edwardian castle is Gilbert de Clare's magnificent stronghold of *Caerphilly* (1268–71). As well as being the earliest British example of a fully concentric castle, it is also the first to have a keep-gatehouse.

Caerphilly provided the blueprint for Edward I's famous castles of North Wales, which were erected to consolidate his conquest of the Welsh principalities. *Aberystwyth*, *Flint* and *Rhuddlan* were commenced during Edward's first Welsh campaign of 1277, and were largely complete by the time war broke out again in 1282. The even more formidable castles of *Caernarfon*, *Conwy* and *Harlech* rose from 1283, after Gwynedd had been conquered, while *Beaumaris* was begun in 1295 following the last Welsh uprising. James of St George was the architect of *Rhuddlan* and the later castles. Most of them are characterised by a striking symmetry, but they are nevertheless quite individual in design. *Aberystwyth*, *Harlech* and *Beaumaris* are concentric and dominated by keep-gatehouses. *Rhuddlan* is also concentric but its twin gatehouses are less developed. *Flint* was given the more traditional feature of a circular keep, while *Conwy* has neither keep nor gatehouse. *Caernarfon* is the most impressive and the least regular of the group. The layout of destroyed *Builth*, Edward's one new castle in the south, was determined by the older motte-and-bailey earthworks on which it stood. *Haverfordwest Castle* was built (or at least begun) by Edward's queen.

James of St George may also have designed the castles erected by the new Marcher lords of north-east Wales. Hence *Denbigh* has polygonal towers and a complex gatehouse modelled on *Caernarfon*, *Hawarden*'s keep was inspired by *Flint*, while *Chirk* is a simplified version of the inner curtain at *Beaumaris*. In the Marcher baronies of the south, the Edwardian era has bequeathed mighty towered enclosures such as *Carew* and *Carreg Cennen*, and the concentric castles of *Kidwelly* and *St Donat's*. Edward I had strengthened the Norman curtain of *White Castle* with round towers and a gatehouse before he became king. This was also the age of town walls, which survive remarkably intact at *Caernarfon*, *Conwy*, *Denbigh*, *Chepstow* and *Tenby*.

Embrasure   The recess behind an arrow slit or window.

Fireplaces   are a common feature in domestic buildings and residential towers. The oldest is in the early Norman hall at Chepstow, though halls sometimes retained the traditional central hearth for all-round heating. Many fireplaces have been damaged by stone-robbing, so often only the back can be seen. Hoods where they remain are usually plain, though carved examples can be seen at *Beaupre* and *Carew*. St Donat's has the finest old fireplaces in any Welsh castle, but these have been brought in from elsewhere. Medieval chimneys occasionally survive, notably the fine example at *Grosmont*.

Garderobe   *see* Latrines.

Garrison   It is a misconception to imagine castles as permanently filled with armed retainers. In times of peace a large garrison would be an unnecessary and costly conceit. Even in wartime too large a garrison could be a liability, consuming provisions without contributing effectively to defence. A castle required enough men – mostly archers – to maintain a healthy

189

resistance from the wall-head and arrow slits. Our only records relate to the royal castles of Wales. *Caernarfon's* normal garrison in the years following Edward I's conquest was forty men, with thirty each at *Conwy* and *Harlech. Caernarfon* had no more defenders when it held out against Owain Glyndwr, and the garrisons of other castles which successfully resisted him were often smaller. No doubt in the long decades of peace before and after Glyndwr's revolt, garrisons were minimal. Nevertheless fighting men formed just part of a castle's complement. We should remember the stewards, blacksmiths, administrators, stablers, carpenters and watchmen who were permanent members of the establishment under the constable. Their numbers would be swelled when the lord or king was in residence.

Gatehouse The entrances are the most vulnerable parts of a fortification, and much attention was paid to this problem by medieval builders. Hence the simple gateway of Norman times evolved within a century into the mighty Edwardian keep-gatehouse. There are four stages in the development.

Late Norman stone curtains were pierced by plain archways closed by wooden gates. The single towers or keeps of these castles, as at *Coity, Ogmore* and *Hay*, stand beside the gateway and thereby offer it some protection. *Newcastle* (Glamorgan) preserves a surprisingly ornate Norman gate arch. Despite the subsequent development of the gatehouse, the simple archway remained a viable option, particularly where the approach was difficult or there were further defences in front. Even the Edwardian castles of *Conwy, Chirk* and *Kidwelly* (in its first form) had no proper gatehouse, although their entrances are closely flanked by mural towers.

Nevertheless the gateway was considerably strengthened if it was placed through a mural tower. Gates could then close each end of the passage, increasing the number of barriers confronting attackers, while the drawbridge and portcullis could be operated from the chamber above. *Carew* has the earliest Welsh example of a stone gate tower, followed by the well-preserved inner gatehouse of *Llansteffan*. Despite the development of the twin-towered gatehouse, the square gate tower remained an economical alternative. There are several Edwardian examples, such as *Laugharne, Manorbier* and *St Donat's*. They appear later as back gates at *Coity, Raglan* and *Powis*, and on town walls at *Chepstow* and *Kidwelly*.

Single gate towers were vulnerable to close-up assault because the gateway was out of sight to the defender stationed on the battlements, unless he leant so far forward that he became an easy target for enemy archers. If the outer archway was flanked by towers, however, this hidden ground could be covered by arrow slits. The twin-towered gateway originated in Roman times, and was revived in the West as a result of the Crusades. Since this development coincided with the arrival of round mural towers, the characteristic B-plan emerged, with a long, tunnel-like gate passage between the round-fronted towers. *Montgomery Castle*, begun by Henry III in 1223, probably has the earliest example in Britain. The Marshals built similar gatehouses at *Chepstow* and *Pembroke*, while Llywelyn the Great provided *Criccieth* with a native example.

In the Edwardian period the twin-towered gatehouse became the norm in major castles. They also feature on the Edwardian town walls of *Caernarfon* and *Conwy*. Gilbert de Clare's revolutionary castle at *Caerphilly* has no less than seven. It also possesses the first of the really big ones, a keep-gatehouse dominating the rest of the castle. It was a logical step to make the gatehouse the strongest part of the castle, occupied by the constable who could personally control the main entrance. *Caerphilly's* keep-gatehouse, as much as its concentric design, influenced Edward I's own castle-building programme. Hence keep-gatehouses are a feature of *Aberystwyth* and *Caernarfon. Harlech* is the best preserved, while the incomplete pair at *Beaumaris* would have been the largest keep-gatehouses of all. Baronial builders also took up the theme at *Kidwelly* and *Denbigh*, the latter an elaborate complex of three towers around a central gate hall. These are the big Welsh examples, but smaller gatehouses at *Llansteffan*, *Powis*, *Neath* and *St Quintin's* may also have served as self-contained residences.

In some of these Edwardian gatehouses the inner end of the gate passage was closed against the courtyard, suggesting that the gatehouse could be held as an independent unit like the tower keeps of the previous generation. However, the courtyard facades of these gatehouses are seldom as formidable as their outer fronts. Windows here provided light for the constable's hall and other apartments. The presence of the constable's hall on the courtyard front of the gatehouse made the gate passage still longer, though the raising of the portcullises would have disturbed his domestic peace.

The Edwardian gatehouse was a formidable obstacle. Even if there was no barbican requiring a preliminary assault, it would be necessary to cross the moat and batter down the drawbridge while under fire from the flanking towers. Behind the drawbridge there would be a portcullis and a heavy pair of gates, as well as the pit which received the inner half of the turning bridge. Portcullises and gates would repeat further along the gate passage, while murder holes in the vault and arrow slits in the side walls turned the passage into a death trap.

Later medieval gatehouses were not quite as formidable. At *Carmarthen* and *Llawhaden* the flanking towers are rather slender by Edwardian standards, while the main gatehouse at *Caldicot* eschews flanking towers altogether. Nevertheless *Raglan's* gate passage was still stoutly defended by the traditional obstacles, while *Newport* (Monmouthshire) has a water gate leading directly into the castle from the river.

Gun ports   In quelling Owain Glyndwr's revolt Prince Henry brought cannon to Wales for the first time, and used them – to little effect – during his long sieges of *Harlech* and *Aberystwyth* castles. *Raglan*, the one great castle of fifteenth-century Wales, has simple gun ports, while others were inserted into an older tower on *Tenby* town wall. These early gun ports are simple, circular openings. Firearms had no further impact in Wales, and there are no examples of the squatter castles which appeared in Europe. Henry VIII's two blockhouses guarding the entrance to Milford Haven, part of a chain of English coastal forts designed for defence by cannon, have disappeared.

Hall   The hall formed the centre of medieval domestic life. It was the centre of administration and justice as well as the dining area. The lord and his personal household sat on a platform or *dais* at one end of the hall, while the rank and file sat on benches lower down. Most of the retainers actually slept here, at least in Norman times. Heating was increasingly provided by means of fireplaces, though the traditional hearth in the middle of the floor was sometimes preferred, smoke escaping through a hole or *louvre* in the roof. Many halls stand over an undercroft and are reached by a flight of steps. In medieval houses the hall was flanked on one side by the lord's private apartments, notably his great chamber or solar, and on the other side by the kitchen and other service buildings. This standard plan had to be adjusted to fit in with the irregular layout of many castles.

William Fitz Osbern built a stone hall – the first in Britain – at *Chepstow* within a few years of the Norman Conquest. Strong enough to serve as a fortified hall-keep, it provided the model for the later Norman halls of *Monmouth*, *Grosmont* and *Manorbier*. Although tower keeps also contained residential chambers which might be described as halls, these small and ill-lit rooms would only have been occupied by their lords in times of danger. They were generally accompanied by more comfortable accommodation in the bailey. Hence William Marshal built a stone hall to complement his mighty keep at *Pembroke* soon after

1200. The keep-gatehouses of Edwardian times contained spacious halls, as at *Harlech* and *Beaumaris*, but even these supplemented larger courtyard halls.

The hall and its adjuncts were usually placed against the curtain. Where the terrain permitted they occupied the least accessible side, allowing windows to be cut through the outer wall without much loss of security. At *Chepstow* and *Pembroke* the halls overlook cliffs. Such positioning led to some awkward domestic planning. *Conwy's* great hall, for example, bends to keep parallel with the curtain. Apart from the chief or great hall, there are sometimes lesser halls for the constable and other officials. *Conwy* and *Carew* have public halls for the garrison and private halls for the lord. *Chepstow* preserves three halls in all, while the two keep-gatehouses of *Beaumaris* (had they been completed) would have contained four in addition to a great hall in the courtyard.

Many halls, less robust than the outer walls, have perished leaving only foundations or fragments. Although the examples already mentioned are now substantial ruins, few Welsh castle halls survive in their original state. *St Donat's* and the two in *Tretower Court* are late medieval exceptions with original timber roofs, while *Caerphilly's* hall was re-roofed in Victorian times.

Hall-keep   The first stone keeps of northern France were fortified hall houses rather than towers. William Fitz Osbern followed this design when he built *Chepstow's* splendid hall-keep soon after his arrival in 1067. It formed the model for later Norman hall-keeps at *Monmouth*, *Grosmont* and *Manorbier*. These elongated structures contained the hall and solar, positioned side by side over an undercroft. *Picton Castle* is a curious Edwardian version of the theme, its hall defended by semi-circular flanking towers and entered through a twin-towered gateway.

Hoarding   In a medieval castle there was a certain amount of 'blind' ground at the foot of the wall, which defenders on the battlements could not control without exposing themselves to enemy fire. Consequently, covered wooden galleries were placed above the gateway and other vulnerable points. Assailants could then be fired upon through holes in the floor. The sockets for the beams which supported these hoardings can sometimes be seen in the masonry below the parapet. There is a reconstructed example above the gateway of *Castell Coch* (Glamorgan). Hoardings were vulnerable to fire, and in the later Middle Ages they were translated into stone with the appearance of machicolations.

Keep   Many castles have one tower which dominates the rest. Depending on the size of the castle it may be the only tower, or the chief tower of many. This is the keep, donjon or great tower. In Wales the story begins remarkably early with the imposing hall-keep at *Chepstow*, built c.1067–71. In England the most impressive monuments of Norman castle building are the lofty tower keeps of London, Rochester and Dover, but Wales has nothing comparable. A group of Norman towers in South Wales can be called keeps, but they are quite modest. *Ogmore* and *Penllyn* date from the early twelfth century. The rest, such as *Coity, Fonmon, Usk* and *Hay*, belong to the last quarter of the century. Most of them are boldly placed beside the castle gateway. This was a departure from the passive defence exhibited by most of the Norman keeps of England, and anticipates the frontal position of the Edwardian keep-gatehouse.

These Norman keeps were square or oblong in shape. The Welsh princes continued to build oblong keeps, such as *Dolwyddelan* and *Dolforwyn*. However, most keeps of the thirteenth century followed the new trend for rounded defensive forms, with no vulnerable corners to undermine. Since many mural towers of this period are round-fronted or U-shaped, we encounter U-shaped keeps at *Castell-y-Bere, Ewloe* and *Roch*. Nevertheless the pure cylinder became the most popular kind, and again the first of the genre proved to be the greatest. William Marshal's circular keep at *Pembroke* (c.1200) is a magnificent structure, once excelled only by the destroyed French keep of Coucy-le-Chateau. It spawned a number of smaller imitations, mostly in South Wales. Round keeps were built on Norman mottes at *Bronllys, Caldicot* and – just over the Herefordshire side of the border – Longtown. At *Skenfrith* the appearance of a motte was deliberately contrived by piling up earth against the base, probably to keep siege engines at bay. *Tretower's* round keep was built within an earlier shell keep to create a concentric defence. *Dinefwr* and *Dolbadarn* have native Welsh examples.

These keeps – whether square, U-shaped or circular – were entered at first-floor level for greater security. The doorway was reached by a flight of steps, though the forebuildings which housed these steps in many English keeps are usually absent in Wales. The walls of the keep rose higher than its two or three storeys to shield the roof from blazing projectiles, but later this roof space was often converted into another storey. Welsh keeps were never as palatial as the greater Norman keeps of England. They provided rather spartan accommodation, for use only in times of emergency, so there were more comfortable residential buildings in the bailey. This was even the case at *Pembroke*.

Round keeps were still being built in the Edwardian period. Edward I's castle of *Flint* is dominated by a circular keep, though here the remarkably thick walls contain a mural gallery and the long entrance passage is placed on the ground floor. *Hawarden*, another round keep on a motte, was modelled on *Flint*. However, a significant feature of some Edwardian castles is the fusion of the keep with the gatehouse. Some of these keep-gatehouses (*Caerphilly, Harlech, Beaumaris*) could perhaps be held independently of the rest of the castle.

It has been argued that reliance on a keep as a last resort proved to be a flawed strategy, since defenders held on to the outer walls with less tenacity! For this reason, some castles of the thirteenth century do not appear to have a keep at all. They are castles of enclosure, relying wholly upon the curtain and a number of flanking towers for defence. Many mural towers, round towards the courtyard as well as the outside, were capable of independent resistance. However, while it is true that the castles of Wales are rarely as keep-dominated as the Norman castles of England, few of them are entirely keep-less. *Caernarfon*, despite its uniform mass of towers, has an unfinished keep-gatehouse and one tower which is singled out for special prominence by its three surmounting turrets. Even the twin round towers of *Cilgerran* appear to be successive keeps. *Conwy, Chirk* and *Carew* are rare examples of truly egalitarian castles, where the towers are all of equal status and there is no great gatehouse. Only at *Haverfordwest* and *White* castles do earlier keeps appear to have been deliberately demolished to create a keep-less enclosure.

From the later Middle Ages Wales preserves a group of small 'tower houses', resembling the more numerous pele towers of northern England. These simple, square towers were built by minor gentry – native Welsh in the case of *Broncoed*. They usually formed the solar blocks of otherwise unfortified manor houses, as at *Beaupre, Candleston, Llandough* and *Scethrog*. Only *Raglan* has something on a far grander scale. William ap Thomas' moated, hexagonal keep dominates the last great castle of Wales. It ranks alongside Ashby-de-la-Zouche and Tattershall in England as an example of the ambitious tower houses built by fifteenth-century magnates.

Keep-gatehouse The large gatehouse with keep-like functions which formed the dominant part of some Edwardian castles (*see* Gatehouse).

Kitchens were an essential feature in a castle, but few Welsh examples are well preserved. In a number of instances only foundations are visible, though their massive fireplaces can be seen embedded in the curtain. Preferably located in a detached building owing to the risk of fire, lack of space forced the kitchen into the hall undercroft at *Weobley* and the chapel undercroft at *Oystermouth*. The kitchens of *Caerphilly*, *Denbigh* and *Raglan* occupy mural towers.

Lancet   A narrow, pointed window.

Latrines   Castles are surprisingly well equipped with latrines (often known as garderobes). Sometimes the seat has disappeared, but any wall passage coming to a dead end is likely to have been one. If possible the chute was positioned to discharge directly into a river, but cesspits – which would need cleaning out – are common. Sometimes whole towers served as latrine blocks, as at *Brecon*, *Coity* and *Llawhaden*. A row of twelve latrine chutes forms a curious sight on *Conwy* town wall.

Machicolations   are stone versions of the wooden hoardings which overlooked gateways and other vulnerable spots. The embattled parapet projects from the wall face on corbels, and in the gap between each corbel is a hole through which heavy objects could be dropped onto besiegers at the foot of the wall. The earliest machicolations cover the gateways of *Conwy* (1283–87). Better preserved examples can be seen on castle gatehouses at *Beaumaris*, *Carmarthen* and *Kidwelly*, as well as the bridge gate at *Monmouth*. Some gatehouses have a wide machicolation slot overhanging the outer archway. Machicolations are more liberally applied in some later English castles, whole towers being crowned by them. In Wales only *Raglan* was machicolated in this lavish manner.

Master mason   The medieval architect was called a master mason. History has consigned most of them to oblivion, and in Wales our knowledge is largely confined to those in royal service. Edward I's architect, James of St George, is the best known. A native of Savoy, where he built castles for the count, he came to Wales at Edward's invitation in 1278 and supervised the construction of *Rhuddlan Castle*. As Master of the King's Works in Wales he went on to design the four great Edwardian castles of Gwynedd: *Conwy*, *Caernarfon*, *Harlech* and *Beaumaris*. It must be said that James was indebted to the unknown designer of *Caerphilly*, using themes such as the keep-gatehouse and the concentric layout introduced there, but he did bring the Edwardian castle to full maturity.

Merlons   are the solid parts of an embattled parapet. They are often pierced by arrow slits.

Moat   The moat or ditch surrounding a castle or town was as vital for defence as the curtain or rampart bank. Indeed, it is the combination of the two which made defence credible, because without a moat there would be nothing to prevent attackers and their siege engines from reaching the walls. Welsh terrain only allowed a minority of castles to have the luxury of a wet moat. *Beaumaris* and *White* castles are still enclosed by water-filled moats, and so are the keeps at *Cardiff* and *Raglan*. By far the most ambitious water defence is the artificial lake around *Caerphilly Castle*, which is held in place by a massive dam. The vast majority of Welsh castles, on their elevated sites, had to make do with dry ditches, though a ditch with steep sides is just as effective a barrier. Often (as at *Harlech* and *Carreg Cennen*) the ditch was hewn from solid rock, which must have involved a tremendous effort by hoards of labourers with picks.

Motte   The artificial mound forming the strongpoint of many Norman earthwork castles is called a motte (*tomen* in Welsh). Mottes were formed by piling up soil from a surrounding ditch, though sometimes a natural hillock could be scarped into the required shape. These conical, flat-topped mounds can be an imposing sight, even if none of the Welsh mottes are as grand as the biggest examples in England. *Cardiff* is the largest, rising some forty feet, but the vast majority are less than half that height. Some in fact are very small and clearly the homesteads of minor knights claiming a piece of land. Mottes are usually accompanied by one or more baileys, although isolated examples exist. Excavations at *Hen Domen* have given us a detailed picture of the timber palisades and internal buildings.

The first Norman invaders of the late eleventh century left a trail of impressive motte-and-baileys across Wales. *Abergwyngregyn, Castell Aberlleiniog* and *Tomen-y-Mur* are relics of the short-lived occupation of Gwynedd by Hugh d'Avranches, while *Gro Tump, Hen Domen* and *Rhos Ddiarbed* recall Roger de Montgomery's push up the Severn valley. *Brecon, Builth, Caerleon* and *Cardiff* formed the centres of new Norman lordships in the south. Mottes proliferated in Wales as the Normans continued to advance. Nearly two hundred remain, mainly in the border counties and the south. *Castell Nanhyfer, Trecastle* and *Twmbarlwm* are among the better preserved examples. However, not all mottes are Norman, because the Welsh responded by raising their own. The Welsh *Chronicle of the Princes* records the erection of the first native motte in 1116. *Mathrafal, Tomen-y-Rhodwydd* and *Tomen-y-Faerdre* are good examples, while *Castell Prysor* is uniquely formed out of a pile of rocks.

Wales had few stone castles in the Norman period, and as a comparatively quick type of fortification mottes probably continued to be raised into the thirteenth century. The motte was the earthwork equivalent of the keep. Its summit carried a wooden tower, or a palisade surrounding the lord's hall. The palisade was sometimes rebuilt in stone, creating a shell keep as at *Cardiff*. Circular keeps were later built on the motte-tops of *Bronllys, Caldicot* and *Hawarden*, and other motte-and-bailey castles were given stone defences. However, sometimes the earthworks have outlasted the masonry, as at *Builth* and *Painscastle*.

Murage   was the tax levied by boroughs to pay for the building of town walls.

Murder holes   are openings or slots in the vault of a gate passage, through which stones could be dropped on the heads of assailants.

Native castles   Influenced by the Norman invaders, the Welsh princes adopted the alien practice of castle building and erected some interesting castles of their own. Norman motte-and-baileys such as *Tomen-y-Mur* and *Rhos Ddiarbed* fell into Welsh hands, and native princes raised impressive earthworks such as *Tomen-y-Rhodwydd* and *Caer Penrhos*. It is a pity that nothing is known of the Lord Rhys' castle at *Cardigan*, which was the first native stone castle of Wales (1171). *Castell Garn Fadrun* is a rude drystone effort built by one of Owain Gwynedd's sons. Its elevated site (inherited from the older hillfort which it occupies) would become typical of native castles.

In the thirteenth century the princes of all four Welsh principalities erected stone castles. Gwynedd took the lead, Llywelyn the Great building several castles on rugged hilltops in Snowdonia. He copied the latest developments in English castle architecture. Thus his castles evolve from a Norman-style oblong keep at *Dolwyddelan* to a round keep at *Dolbadarn*, a towered curtain at *Castell-y-Bere* and a twin-towered gatehouse at *Criccieth*. Llywelyn the Last strengthened his grandfather's castles and built others on conquered territory. His signature is the U-shaped keep, a feature of *Ewloe* and *Castell-y-Bere*. However, *Dolforwyn* has the rather archaic motif of an oblong keep, and the towers on his outer curtain at *Criccieth* are oblong too. The last castle of the princes of Gwynedd was *Caergwrle*, built by Llywelyn's brother Dafydd before his revolt in 1282.

Powys was slow to embrace stone castles. *Castell Dinas Bran* was erected by the lord of Ial, who was a supporter of Llywelyn the Last. The prince of Powys probably did not begin *Powis Castle* until his return from exile in 1277; even then it began rather modestly. Only in the next generation were an Edwardian-style gatehouse and outer curtain added, but by that time the prince of Powys had become a Marcher lord.

In Deheubarth the Lord Rhys' squabbling descendants also built stone castles. *Dinefwr* is the best preserved of all the native castles, its tall curtain dominated by a circular keep. *Dryslwyn*, which also had a round keep, is much more ruinous, while *Newcastle Emlyn* was rebuilt after the Edwardian conquest. Senghenydd has some fragmentary stone castles. The one ambitious castle of the princes of Senghenydd is *Castell Morgraig*. It is the only native castle to be built in the Edwardian idiom, its pentagonal curtain flanked by mighty U-shaped towers. However, the castle was left unfinished in 1266 when Gilbert de Clare annexed Senghenydd and began *Caerphilly Castle* nearby.

The native Welsh castles are sometimes compared unfavourably with English work of the period. On the whole they are small and economically built, with flanking towers sparingly applied and no gatehouses (except at *Criccieth*). However, their precipitous locations amply compensated for these defects. Although Llywelyn the Last surprisingly made no attempt to match the Edwardian castles of the Marcher barons, *Castell Morgraig* shows what the Welsh princes might have built had they survived. Edward I's conquest brought many of the native castles into royal hands. Edward initially repaired and strengthened them, but those in the wilds of Snowdonia proved untenable during the revolt of 1294 and were abandoned. *Criccieth*, *Dinefwr* and *Dryslwyn* continued as English garrisons. One final native fortification is the tower house of *Broncoed*, built by a Welsh lord during the Wars of the Roses.

Parapet   The embattled wall shielding defenders on the wall-walk.

Plinth   A plinth is a sloping projection at the base of a wall. This is a common architectural feature giving greater stability, all the more necessary in fortifications where the base is vulnerable to undermining or battering.

Portcullis   One of the standard defensive features of a medieval gateway, the portcullis was a grille which could be lowered to block the entrance passage. It was made of wood reinforced with iron strips. Raising and lowering were accomplished by means of a windlass located in the chamber above the gate passage. The grooves into which the portcullis slotted are often visible, and modern portcullises can be seen at *Caldicot* and *St Donat's*. Two or three portcullises closed the long gate passages of the Edwardian period.

Postern   In addition to the gatehouses, castles are often provided with subsidiary entrances. Such posterns or sallyports take the form of doorways cut through the curtain or flanking towers. Convenience of access was no doubt a factor but they could also serve as exits for counter-attacking besiegers.

Prisons   Although castles were intended to keep attackers out, it followed that their strong walls should often be used to keep prisoners in. There is a tendency to misrepresent any dimly-lit undercroft as a dungeon when it was really a store room, but prisons do exist in many Welsh castles. They are grim chambers in the basements of towers, ventilated by narrow slits and once entered only through trap-doors in the ceiling. This at least was the inhospitable environment for the common malefactor – distinguished prisoners enjoyed better conditions. Llywelyn the Last imprisoned his brother for twenty-two years in *Dolbadarn*'s keep, while the regicide Henry Marten was confined for nearly as long in the tower named after him at *Chepstow*. It would seem that keeps or donjons often served as prisons in their declining years – hence the term dungeon. *Carmarthen* and *Haverfordwest* castles housed county gaols long after their other functions had ceased.

Putlog holes are often visible in the masonry. They received the ends of wooden beams which supported the scaffolding during construction. Similar holes just below the parapet were the sockets for hoardings.

Rampart An earth wall, created by piling up the spoil from the surrounding ditch. Norman ringworks and baileys are defended by ramparts. They were once crowned by timber palisades.

Ringwork Some Norman earthwork castles have no motte, leaving the inner bailey as the last line of defence. Such enclosures, generally round or oval in shape, are called ringworks. Ringworks are less common than mottes except in Glamorgan. With their strong ramparts and ditches, ringworks such as *Aberrheidol*, *Dinas Powys* and *Walwyn's Castle* were formidable strongholds. *Caer Penrhos* is a native Welsh example. Some were later given stone curtains, as at *Coity* and *Kidwelly*. Excavations have shown that *Loughor's* ringwork was later built up into a motte, and this was probably not the only example.

Royal castles The Norman conquest of Wales began as a private enterprise under three palatine earls. Much of Wales would remain divided into semi-independent Marcher lordships until 1536, so the great majority of Welsh castles were baronial strongholds. However, as Welsh resistance grew, English kings were increasingly drawn in to support the beleaguered Marcher barons. Most kings from William the Conqueror onwards led campaigns into Wales until Edward I's final conquest, and royal castles were an inevitable consequence of their involvement. *Cardiff's* great motte may have been raised by William I during his expedition of 1081, though Henry I founded the first permanent royal castle at *Carmarthen*. We can follow the construction of some of the royal castles owing to the royal accounts known as the Pipe Rolls, which begin under Henry II. They record Henry's expenditure on *Carmarthen* and *White* castles in the 1180s, though the sums are trifling compared with his prolific castle-building programme in England.

Henry III, another great castle builder in England, erected the first major royal castles of Wales. Under Llywelyn the Great Gwynedd had become a force to be reckoned with, and Henry built several castles to contain him. *Montgomery*, a castle which cost over £2,000 in 1223–28, probably had the first twin-towered gatehouse in Britain. Unfortunately Henry's castles have suffered badly, those at *Deganwy* and *Dyserth* having been destroyed by Llywelyn the Last. *Montgomery* is now very ruinous, his keep at *Cardigan* has vanished, while his masonry on the older earthworks at *Painscastle* has completely disappeared.

Henry's son made by far the greatest royal contribution to the castles of Wales, and some of them survive in all their glory. To consolidate the conquest of North Wales Edward I embarked upon an unprecedented building campaign. Seven great new castles rose: *Aberystwyth*, *Flint* and *Rhuddlan* from 1277, *Caernarfon*, *Conwy* and *Harlech* from 1283, and *Beaumaris* from 1295. *Caernarfon* and *Conwy* have accompanying town walls which are major fortifications in their own right. Edward also rebuilt the Marcher castle at *Builth* and strengthened some of the native castles of Gwynedd and Deheubarth. The Pipe Rolls record a total expenditure during his reign of £81,178. This seemingly modest sum in fact equates to billions after seven centuries of inflation. Edward II continued building at *Caernarfon* and *Beaumaris*, which together account for most of the £11,000 spent on Welsh castles during his reign.

The Edwardian royal castles, intended as the palatial fortresses of a resident prince, mouldered as neglected garrison outposts for the rest of the fourteenth century. One last royal building campaign took place in the aftermath of Owain Glyndwr's revolt. Even then it was confined to the south-west, where it was prompted by fears of another French landing. Here, several castles had become royal when the duchy of Lancaster merged with the Crown upon Henry IV's usurpation. However, the sums expended by the Lancastrian kings on *Carmarthen*, *Carreg Cennen* and *Kidwelly* ran to hundreds rather than thousands of pounds.

Sallyport *see* Postern.

Shell keep An alternative to the tower form of keep was the shell keep, so called because it is a polygonal enclosure surrounded by a wall. The shell keep was a direct replacement of the wooden palisade on top of a Norman motte. They are common in the Norman castles of England but only a handful of Welsh examples survive. *Cardiff* has the best, with a later gate tower guarding the entrance. At *Tretower* the shell keep has two straight walls which formed the outer sides of the hall and solar. *Wiston* and *Brecon* are more ruinous examples, while *Llandovery* has an Edwardian version of the theme. The shell keep at *Carmarthen* encases the motte instead of standing on its summit.

Sieges Most Welsh castles and towns were besieged at one time or another. Some are known to have been attacked frequently, and no doubt many sieges have gone unrecorded. The first major siege in Wales was at *Pembroke* in 1096, the new Norman castle just managing to survive the Welsh onslaught. Both Owain Gwynedd and the Lord Rhys attacked and captured Norman earthwork castles as Welsh resistance became better organised in the twelfth century. At that time siege techniques were relatively primitive, involving a lot of hand-to-hand fighting. Not all sieges were Anglo-Welsh duels. The Welsh princes often attacked each other, while baronial feuds were not uncommon.

In the thirteenth century castles developed their defences in response to increasingly powerful weapons of assault. No fortifications – not even the great Edwardian castles – were truly impregnable because, without any prospect of outside relief, it was only a matter of time before provisions ran out. The medieval besieger had two options – direct assault or a slow containment. Starving out the garrison would inevitably be successful if the besieger was strong enough to enforce an effective blockade, but the coastal positions of many of the invaders' castles enabled them to be supplied by sea even when they had been cut off by land. Hence most of Edward I's new castles held out during Madog ap Llywelyn's revolt of 1294. *Aberystwyth* and *Harlech* only surrendered to Owain Glyndwr when a French fleet blockaded the Irish Sea.

With the Welsh usually geared to lightning raids conducted by temporary levies, direct assaults were more common. The besieger's aim was to penetrate a castle's defences, whether by climbing over, breaking through or undermining. As the gatehouse developed into a major fortification in its own right, it was easier to attack a vulnerable stretch of curtain. Most methods of attack could not begin until the assailants had reached the base of the wall. This meant that the ditch or moat must first be crossed by erecting a causeway of earth or rocks – a difficult enterprise while being showered with arrows from the battlements and flanking towers.

It was then possible to reach the parapet by means of scaling ladders or siege towers. Scaling ladders are recorded at the siege of *Llansteffan* in 1146. Siege towers were more formidable, though there is no record of their use in Wales. Once a section of ditch had been filled they were wheeled up to the curtain, a drawbridge being lowered onto the parapet so that attackers could cross *en masse*.

Before the appearance of firearms castle walls could only be battered by rams and catapults. The battering ram, suspended from its protective 'cat', was an effective weapon if it could be sustained for long enough. Catapults or *mangonels* had the advantage of being operable from a distance. The arm was pulled back by means of a windlass, then suddenly released to dispatch a boulder with force. *Cardigan Castle* was breached by Welsh catapults in 1231, and the English captured *Dryslwyn* with the aid of one in 1287. Catapults were sometimes mounted on castle towers to flatten besiegers, as at *Criccieth*.

If other methods failed the besieger was left with the option of undermining. This entailed digging a tunnel towards the castle walls and excavating a wide hollow beneath the foundations. Tunnel and hollow were supported by wooden props which were then set alight, resulting in the collapse of the wall above. Undermining offered a high chance of success but it was a difficult process demanding skilled personnel. At *Dryslwyn* in 1287 the mining tunnel collapsed prematurely, killing some of the diggers. The mine was still an effective weapon during the Civil War as at *Monmouth*.

Sometimes besiegers would be fortunate enough to succeed without serious fighting. At *Conwy* in 1401 the Welsh tricked their way into the castle while the garrison was at church. Alternatively the garrison might simply realise the futility of resistance. It was manifestly better to surrender at once than risk the fortunes of war. Although the starving defenders of *Harlech* managed to negotiate good terms during the Wars of the Roses, Owain Glyndwr massacred the English garrison of *New Radnor*.

When the English finally recovered *Harlech* and *Aberystwyth* from Owain Glyndwr they brought cannon into Wales for the first time. These primitive weapons may not have been very effective – one of them exploded – but no doubt their enormous din had a psychological impact. Cannon were more widely used in the Civil War. Old castles were dragged into the conflict as garrison posts, mainly by the Royalists who were predominant in Wales. Most of the castles pressed into service were ill-prepared for hostilities. Nevertheless where there was a will to resist some castles held out remarkably well in long sieges at *Denbigh*, *Flint*, *Holt* and – the last to fall – *Harlech*. It must be admitted that sometimes the outmoded defences were strengthened against the more powerful cannon of the time. *Pembroke*, which suffered sieges by both sides, had its curtain reinforced, while *Raglan* and *Newcastle Emlyn* were supplemented by artillery-proof earthworks.

Slighting The process of dismantling a fortification to prevent its future use. This was achieved by breaching walls and undermining towers, or later by blowing them up with gunpowder. Llywelyn the Last destroyed the English castles of *Builth* and *Deganwy*. Owain Glyndwr also slighted some of the castles he managed to capture, while *Carreg Cennen* was dismantled during the Wars of the Roses. However, most slightings took place after the Civil War, parliament reducing such castles as *Caerphilly*, *Pembroke*, *Raglan* and *Rhuddlan* to ruins to prevent their future use by the Royalists.

Solar The solar, or great chamber, was the lord's private apartment. In tower keeps the solar occupied the floor above the hall. Courtyard solars are located beyond the *dais* or high table end of the hall, usually standing at first-floor level over an undercroft. *Manorbier*, *Swansea* and *Weobley* preserve good examples. Sometimes the solar occupied a mural tower, as at *Abergavenny*, *Caldicot* and *Carew*. In the later medieval manor houses of *Candleston* and *Eastington* the solar wing is built up into a tower house. *Conwy* and *Oystermouth* preserve further private apartments beyond the solar, while *Raglan* had a whole suite of state apartments around its inner courtyard.

Stairs were provided in keeps and many mural towers. Straight staircases are sometimes found in the thickness of the wall, but the spiral stair is more common. It occupies a hollow cylinder, generally placed on the courtyard side to prevent any weakening of the external wall. Often the stair occupies a projecting turret. Each step radiates from a central post or *newel*.

The majority of newel stairs spiral up to the right. There is a colourful theory that this was a defensive ploy, since attackers fighting their way up the stair would find their sword arms impeded by the newel.

Towers often flank the curtains of masonry castles. Pierced by arrow slits, they commanded the approach and protected the adjacent stretches of curtain. Besiegers attempting to scale or batter down the walls would find themselves under arrow fire. Mural towers, like many other defensive features, were not an invention of the medieval period. Although their revival was largely due to the experience of crusaders in the Holy Land, older examples were much closer to hand. The Roman fortifications of *Cardiff* and *Caerwent* both demonstrate the use of flanking towers in antiquity.

In Wales the first stone castles of the Norman era had a single tower or keep guarding the gateway to a walled bailey. *Newcastle* (Glamorgan) is the first Welsh castle to exhibit two mural towers projecting forwards to flank the curtain. Although the flanking towers of later castles would sometimes be deployed economically at vulnerable points, the greater castles of the thirteenth century were comprehensively flanked by towers. *Grosmont*, *Skenfrith* and *Usk* are early examples. The layout of the castle became more regular to minimise the number of towers required. Hence some of the strongest Edwardian castles, such as *Caerphilly* and *Harlech*, are simple oblongs with corner towers.

Norman towers were square or oblong in plan, but another development associated with the Crusades was the introduction of round towers. These were less vulnerable to undermining, because the angles of square towers were more likely to collapse. Circular towers are the hallmark of the thirteenth-century Welsh castle, first appearing in William Marshal's castles of *Chepstow* and *Pembroke*. Some mid-wall towers are semi-circular or U-shaped, their curved fronts facing the outside world. *Caernarfon* is distinguished by its polygonal towers, deliberately employed to render it unique. However, polygonal towers were soon copied at *Denbigh*, and later at *Raglan*. Paradoxically, some of the Edwardian round towers of South Wales rise from massive square bases, which sink back into the main body of the tower as pyramid-shaped spurs. Examples can be seen at *Carew*, *Chepstow*, the two *Newport* castles and – across the Herefordshire border – Goodrich. They represent an attempt to make the foundations so massive that a mining tunnel would have little effect.

The mural towers on town walls and some outer curtains are purely open-backed fighting platforms. However, the towers of the main curtain were usually complete units which could be held independently against besiegers. The move towards self-contained mural towers coincided with a need for more private accommodation within castles. Most Edwardian towers are residential as well as defensive, containing three or four storeys of apartments served by fireplaces and latrines. This meant that windows had to pierce the walls, at least high up. Circular rooms were always rather inconvenient from a domestic point of view. Hence square towers did not die out completely even in the thirteenth century, and in the later Middle Ages they were sometimes preferred, as at *Coity*.

In the majority of castles mural towers interrupted the wall walk, so that attackers who managed to overwhelm one section could not overrun the entire circuit. However, Edward I's castles – with the exception of *Caernarfon* – have continuous wall walks which by-pass the towers. This arrangement gave the defenders greater mobility, allowing them to concentrate rapidly at points of attack.

Tower house The fortified solar block attached to some later medieval manor houses (*see* Keep).

Town walls Towns were an alien phenomenon to the native Welsh. Only two Roman towns are known to have existed in Wales, but the powerful Roman wall with flanking bastions at *Caerwent* demonstrates that town defences were nothing new. *Carmarthen*, the other Roman town, rebuilt its defensive circuit from 1233 and thus became the first walled town of medieval Wales (the wall has vanished). Elsewhere, towns had been founded in conjunction with Norman castles. Most Welsh towns grew up outside a castle, which was invariably located on the perimeter where it could play its part in the overall defence of the town. The thirteenth century was the heyday of stone town defences throughout western Europe, and most Welsh town walls date from the Edwardian period.

Edward I established boroughs outside his new castles. *Caernarfon* and *Conwy*, founded in 1283, are surrounded by impressive stone circuits with twin-towered gatehouses and semicircular flanking bastions. The town wall of *Conwy*, one of the finest in Europe, rose simultaneously with the castle. *Caernarfon*'s shorter town wall was completed in just two years. Henry de Lacy went further at *Denbigh*, building the town wall before the castle was started. The Edwardian town walls of North Wales were unusual in being erected at royal or baronial expense to encourage English settlers. Elsewhere town walls were also built under baronial patronage, but here the existing burgesses no doubt had to contribute. Murage grants sometimes help to date these works. *Chepstow* and *Tenby* preserve substantial town walls in South Wales, well protected by flanking bastions like their counterparts in the north. However, the gates are simpler, and both are partial circuits relying upon river and sea for their complete protection.

As well as these five splendid examples, portions remain at *Brecon*, *Cowbridge*, *Kidwelly* and *Pembroke*. *Monmouth*'s unique bridge gate should also be mentioned. At least ten more Welsh boroughs possessed stone defences, but they were pulled down as the towns expanded beyond their old limits. Many other medieval towns had only earth-and-timber defences. These have suffered a low survival rate, but long stretches of rampart and ditch can be seen at *Montgomery* and *New Radnor*.

Undercroft The domestic buildings of a medieval house often stand at first-floor level over plain rooms called undercrofts, which were generally used for storing the many provisions which a medieval castle required. They are sometimes vaulted.

Vault An arched roof of stone. Vaults served to prevent the spread of fire, but Welsh castles are generally economical in their provision. A few towers, notably the keep at Pembroke, are covered by stone domes which protected the roof from blazing objects hurled from catapults. The commonest type of vault is the barrel or tunnel vault, of one continuous section. More elaborate vaults with stone ribs are rare in Welsh domestic architecture, though they do appear in the chapels at *Beaumaris* and *Carew*, and in the East Gate of *Powis Castle*.

Ward *see* Bailey.

Water gate A gate leading directly to water – either a river or the sea. Welsh coastal castles were supplied by sea, and the Edwardian royal castles show provision for docking. However, *Newport* (Monmouthshire) has the best example of a water gate, leading to the River Usk.

Wells Every castle needed a reliable supply of drinking water. Wells can be major achievements in their own right, since in many elevated Welsh castles it was necessary to dig a long way through the underlying rock to reach the water table. Sometimes the depth proved too great, so the 'wells' at *Castell-y-Bere* and *Morlais* are actually cisterns. The majority of wells survive as deep shafts in the courtyard, though they are sometimes housed in the security of a mural tower. *Denbigh*'s town wall was extended to contain a vital spring.

BIBLIOGRAPHY

The references at the end of each entry are intended to provide the most accessible or up-to-date sources of further information. For a comprehensive list of references to castles up to 1982, D. J. C. King's *Castellarium Anglicanum* (see list below) should be consulted. Individual guidebooks can be obtained at many castles, ranging from scholarly but increasingly glossy Cadw handbooks to less informative souvenir brochures.

Most Welsh counties are covered in the volumes of *The Royal Commission on Ancient and Historical Monuments in Wales and Monmouthshire* (RCAHMW in the text). Although they vary in quality and comprehensiveness, they are available for Anglesey, Caernarvonshire (three volumes), Carmarthenshire, Denbighshire, Flintshire, Merioneth, Montgomeryshire, Pembrokeshire and Radnorshire. *Glamorgan: The Early Castles* is an RCAHMW study of the castles of Glamorgan founded before 1217. A second volume for the later castles is awaited.

Historical and archaeological journals contain much vital information. Specifically for Wales there are *Archaeologia Cambrensis* and various county periodicals (*Brycheiniog, Carmarthenshire Antiquary, Ceredigion, Morgannwg, Montgomery Collections*).

Cadw has produced a series of regional *Guides to Ancient and Historic Wales* (GAHW). Castles naturally loom large in the four volumes (*Clwyd and Powys, Dyfed, Glamorgan and Gwent, Gwynedd*). The *Buildings of Wales* (BOW) series is so far confined to *Clwyd, Glamorgan* and *Powys*.

The first two volumes of *The History of the King's Works* (HKW) are a valuable source for royal buildings, especially the Edwardian castles in volume one. This part has been reprinted as A. J. Taylor's *The Welsh Castles of Edward I*.

There follows a list of classic works of reference, important articles and some valuable regional guides:

Armitage E. S., *Early Norman Castles of the British Isles* (London, 1912)
Avent R., *Castles of the Princes of Gwynedd* (Cardiff, 1983)
Avent R. and Kenyon J. R. (ed.), *Castles in Wales and the Marches* (Cardiff, 1987)
Brown R. A., *English Castles*, 3rd edn (London, 1976)
———— *The Architecture of Castles* (London, 1984)
Clark G. T., *Mediaeval Military Architecture in England* (London, 1884) 2 vols
Davies J., *A History of Wales* (London, 1993)
Davies R. R., *The Age of Conquest: Wales 1063–1415* (Oxford, 1991)
———— *The Revolt of Owain Glyn Dwr* (Oxford, 1995)
Davis P. R., *Castles of Dyfed* (Swansea, 1987)
———— *Castles of Glamorgan* (Swansea, 1983)
———— *Castles of the Welsh Princes* (Swansea, 1988)
Edwards E. H., *Castles and Strongholds of Pembrokeshire* (Tenby, 1909)
Edwards J. G., 'Edward I's Castle-Building in Wales', *Proceedings of the British Academy* (XXXII, 1946)

Evans L., *The Castles of Wales* (London, 1998)

Fry P. S., *Castles of Britain and Ireland* (Newton Abbot, 1996)

Gaunt P., *A Nation under Siege: The Civil War in Wales* (London, 1991)

Hague D. B., 'The Castles of Glamorgan and Gower', *Glamorgan County History* (III)

Higham R. A. and Barker P. A., *Timber Castles* (London, 1992)

King D. J. C., *Castellarium Anglicanum* (New York, 1983) 2 vols

———— *The Castle in England and Wales* (London, 1988)

King D. J. C. and Hogg A. H., 'Early Castles in Wales and the Marches', *Archaeologia Cambrensis* (CXII, 1963)

———— 'Masonry Castles in Wales and the Marches', *Archaeologia Cambrensis* (CXVI, 1967)

Lloyd J. E., *A History of Wales from the Earliest Times to the Edwardian Conquest*, 3rd edn (London, 1939)

———— *Owen Glendower* (Oxford, 1931)

Miles D., *Castles of Pembrokeshire* (1988)

Morris B. and Grenfell H., *The Castles of Gower* (Swansea, 1970)

Morris J. E., *The Welsh Wars of Edward I* (Oxford, 1901)

Neaverson E., *Mediaeval Castles in North Wales* (Liverpool, 1947)

Nelson L. H., *The Normans in South Wales* (London, 1966)

Oman C., *Castles* (London, 1926)

Prestwich M., *Edward I* (London, 1988)

Reid A., *The Castles of Wales* (London, 1973)

Renn D. F., *Norman Castles in Britain*, 2nd edn (London, 1973)

———— 'The Round Keeps of the Brecon Region', *Archaeologia Cambrensis* (CX, 1961)

Salter M., *The Castles of Gwent, Glamorgan and Gower* (Malvern, 1991)

———— *The Castles of Mid Wales* (Malvern, 1991)

———— *The Castles of North Wales* (Malvern, 1997)

———— *The Castles of South-West Wales* (Malvern, 1996)

Simpson W. D., *Castles in England and Wales* (London, 1969)

Sorrell A., *British Castles* (London, 1973)

Soulsby I., *The Towns of Medieval Wales* (Chichester, 1983)

Spurgeon C. J. (ed.), *Glamorgan: The Early Castles from the Norman Conquest to 1217* (London, 1991)

———— 'The Castles of Montgomeryshire', *Montgomeryshire Collections* (LIX, 1965)

Taylor A. J., 'Castle Building in Thirteenth-Century Wales and Savoy', *Proceedings of the British Academy* (LXIII, 1977)

———— *Four Great Castles* (Newtown, 1983)

———— 'Master James of St George', *English Historical Review* (LXV, 1950)

———— 'Military Architecture', *Medieval England*, ed. A. L. Poole (Oxford, 1958)

———— *Studies in Castles and Castle-Building* (London, 1985)

———— *The Welsh Castles of Edward I* (London, 1986)

Thomas R. (ed.), *Castles in Wales* (Cardiff, 1988)

Toy S., *The Castles of Great Britain*, 4th edn (London, 1966)

Turner H. L., *Town Defences in England and Wales* (London, 1971)

Turvey R., 'The Defences of Twelfth-Century Deheubarth and the Castle Strategy of the Lord Rhys', *Archaeologia Cambrensis* (CXLIV, 1995)

Williams J. G., 'The Castles of Wales during the Civil War', *Archaeologia Cambrensis* (CXXXVII, 1988)

INDEX OF SITES

Main entries are highlighted by an asterisk. Ordnance Survey grid references are given. Where the current administrative county is different, it is shown in brackets:-